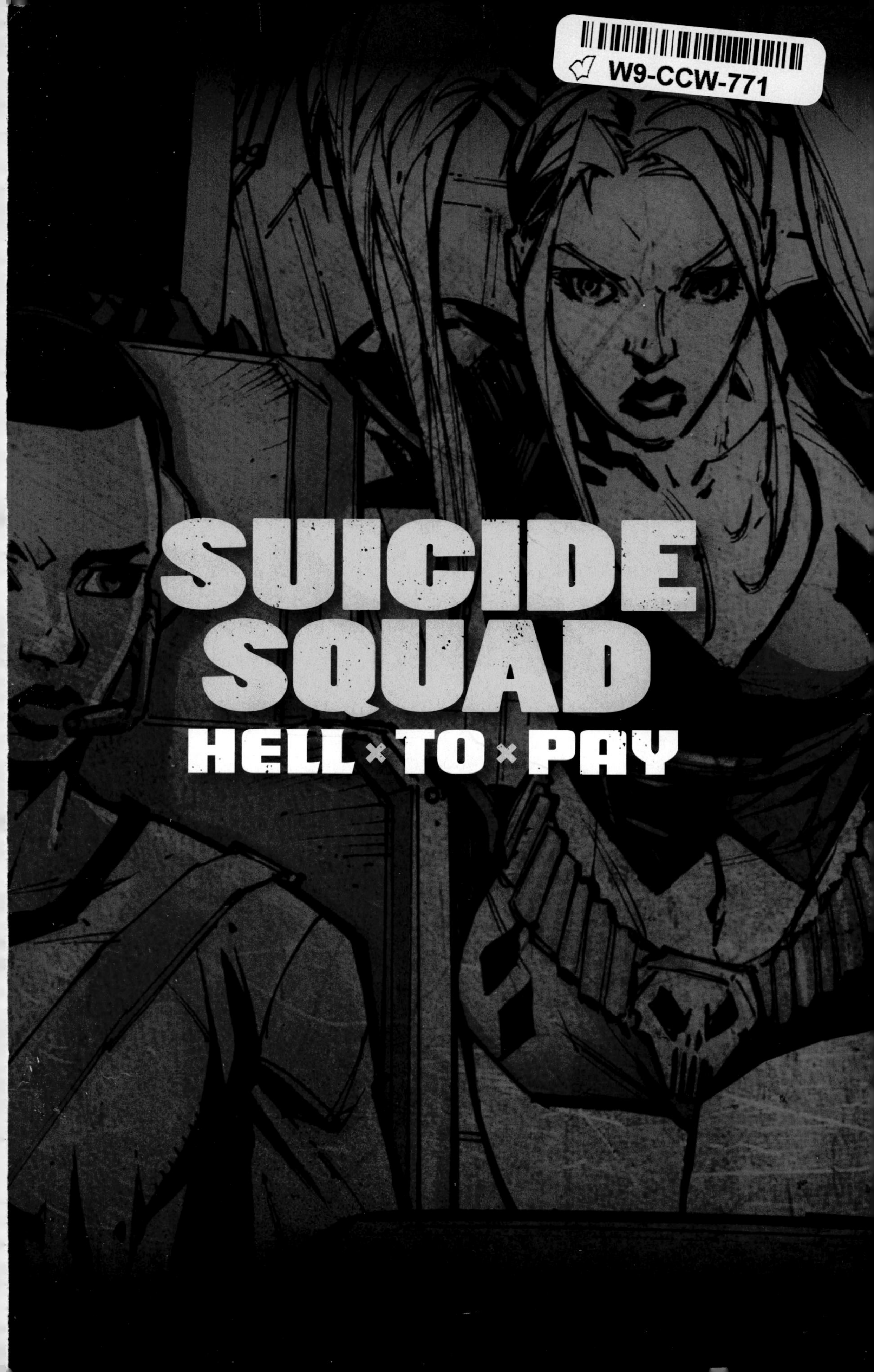
SUICIDE SQUAD
HELL × TO × PAY

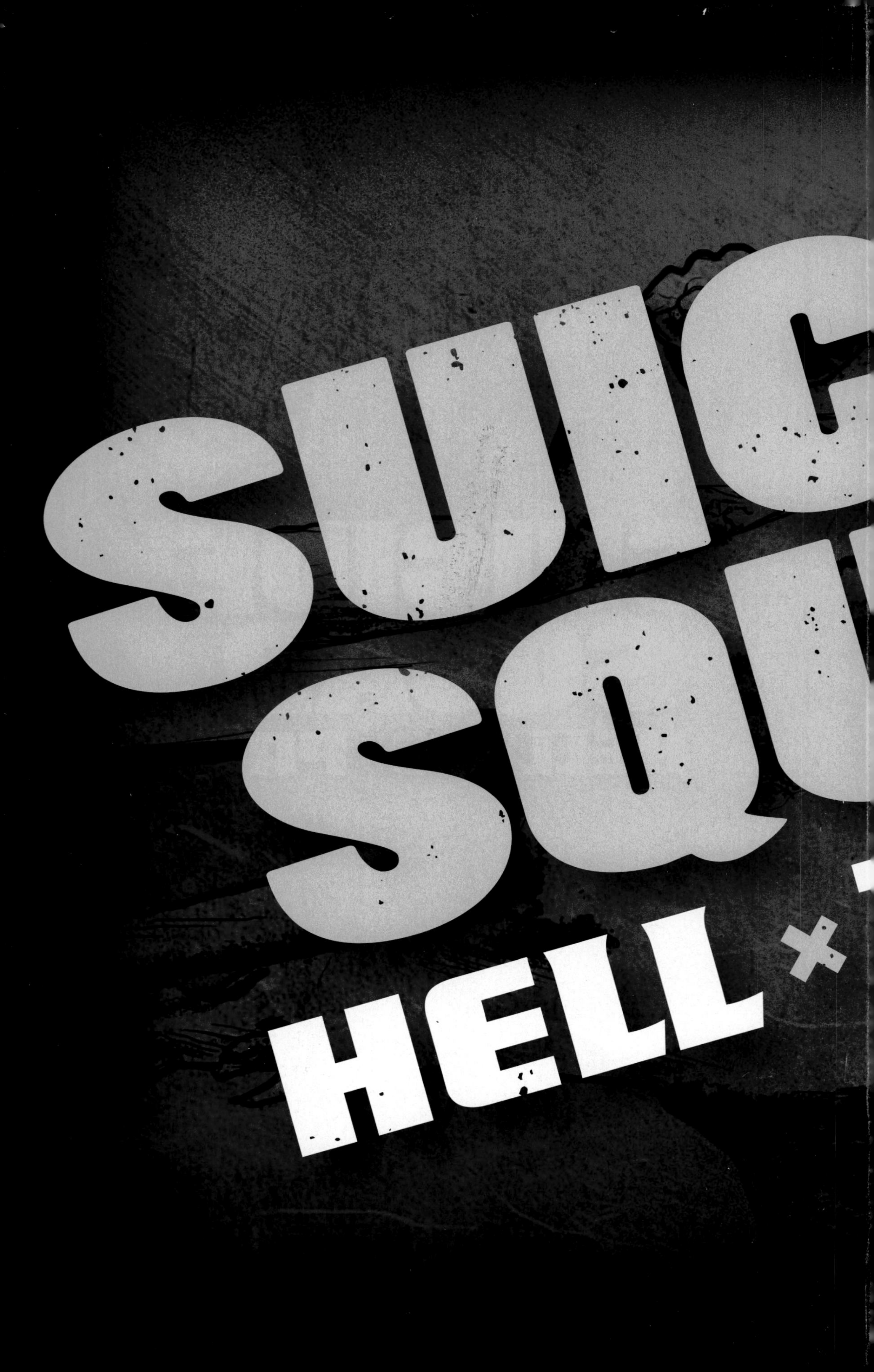
SUIC
SQU
HELL

CIDE
UAD
TO + PAY

JEFF PARKER writer

MATTHEW DOW SMITH

AGUSTIN PADILLA STEFANO RAFFAELE CAT STAGGS artists

TONY AVIÑA colorist DERON BENNETT letterer

RYAN BENJAMIN collection cover artist

KRISTY QUINN Editor - Original Series
JEB WOODARD Group Editor - Collected Editions
TYLER-MARIE EVANS Editor - Collected Edition
STEVE COOK Design Director - Books

BOB HARRAS Senior VP - Editor-in-Chief, DC Comics
PAT McCALLUM Executive Editor, DC Comics

DAN DiDIO Publisher
JIM LEE Publisher & Chief Creative Officer
AMIT DESAI Executive VP - Business & Marketing Strategy, Direct to Consumer & Global Franchise Management
BOBBIE CHASE VP & Executive Editor, Young Reader & Talent Development
MARK CHIARELLO Senior VP - Art, Design & Collected Editions
JOHN CUNNINGHAM Senior VP - Sales & Trade Marketing
BRIAR DARDEN VP - Business Affairs
ANNE DePIES Senior VP - Business Strategy, Finance & Administration
DON FALLETTI VP - Manufacturing Operations
LAWRENCE GANEM VP - Editorial Administration & Talent Relations
ALISON GILL Senior VP - Manufacturing & Operations
JASON GREENBERG VP - Business Strategy & Finance
HANK KANALZ Senior VP - Editorial Strategy & Administration
JAY KOGAN Senior VP - Legal Affairs
NICK J. NAPOLITANO VP - Manufacturing Administration
LISETTE OSTERLOH VP - Digital Marketing & Events
EDDIE SCANNELL VP - Consumer Marketing
COURTNEY SIMMONS Senior VP - Publicity & Communications
JIM (SKI) SOKOLOWSKI VP - Comic Book Specialty Sales & Trade Marketing
NANCY SPEARS VP - Mass, Book, Digital Sales & Trade Marketing
MICHELE R. WELLS VP - Content Strategy

SUICIDE SQUAD: HELL TO PAY

DC Comics, 2900 West Alameda Ave., Burbank, CA 91505
Printed by LSC Communications, Kendallville, IN, USA. 1/11/19. First Printing.
ISBN: 978-1-4012-8778-8

Library of Congress Cataloging-in-Publication Data is available.

PEFC Certified
This product is from
sustainably managed
forests and controlled
sources
PEFC/29-31-337   www.pefc.org

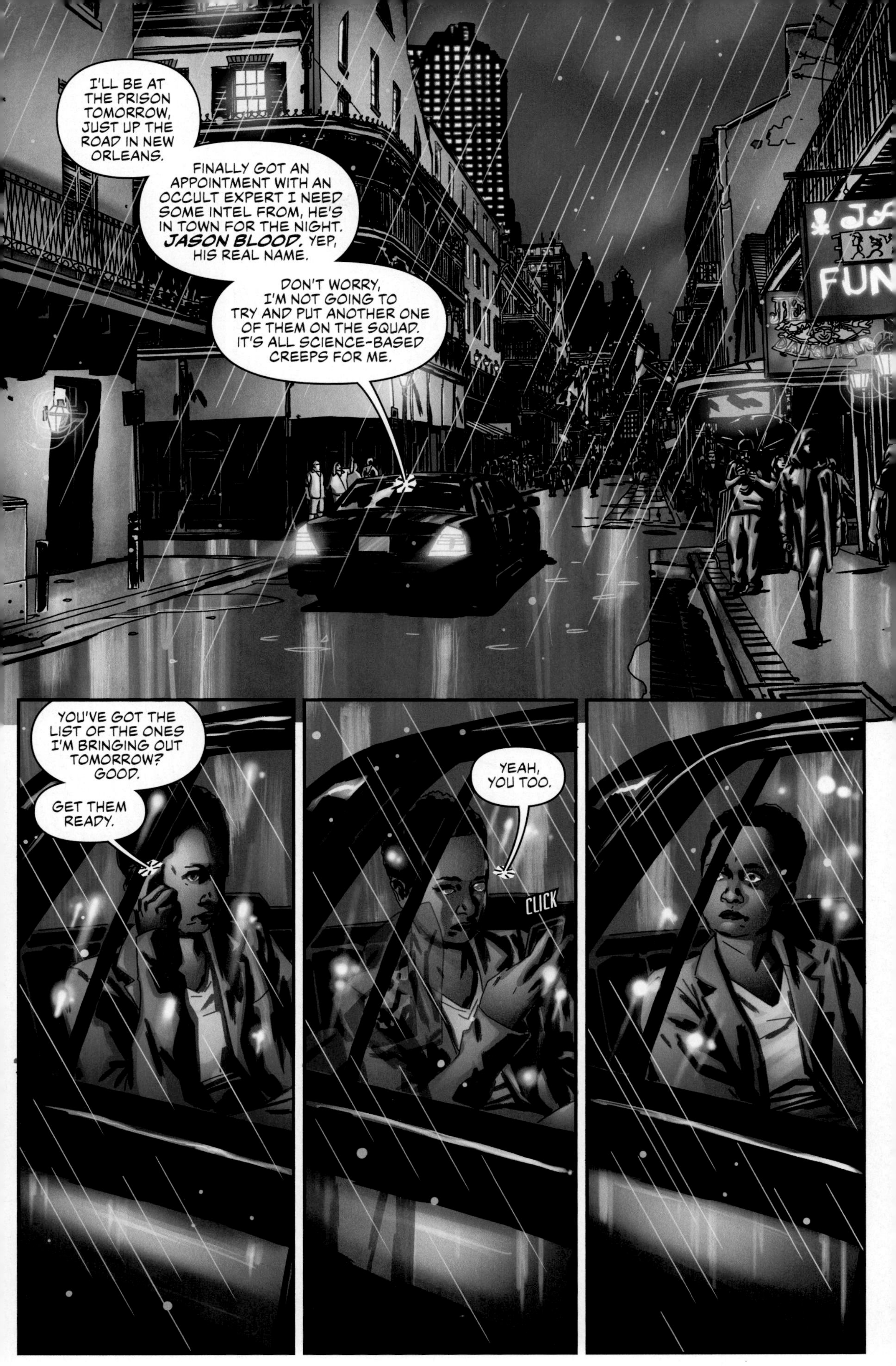

I'LL BE AT THE PRISON TOMORROW, JUST UP THE ROAD IN NEW ORLEANS.
FINALLY GOT AN APPOINTMENT WITH AN OCCULT EXPERT I NEED SOME INTEL FROM, HE'S IN TOWN FOR THE NIGHT. JASON BLOOD. YEP, HIS REAL NAME.
DON'T WORRY, I'M NOT GOING TO TRY AND PUT ANOTHER ONE OF THEM ON THE SQUAD. IT'S ALL SCIENCE-BASED CREEPS FOR ME.
YOU'VE GOT THE LIST OF THE ONES I'M BRINGING OUT TOMORROW? GOOD.
GET THEM READY.
YEAH, YOU TOO.
CLICK

IT'S INTERESTING, YES.

AND VERY REAL--I VOUCH THAT IT IS INFERNAL.

GOOD. NEXT.

WHY DOES IT LOOK LIKE THAT, AND DOES IT DO WHAT IT SAYS?

IT APPEARS IN A FORM THAT FITS THIS AGE.

GET OUT OF HELL FREE

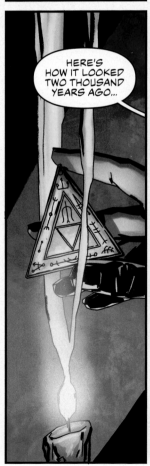

HERE'S HOW IT LOOKED TWO THOUSAND YEARS AGO...

...AND FIVE THOUSAND YEARS AGO.

NOW FOR THE TEST.

HEY...

GET OUT OF HELL FREE

HM.

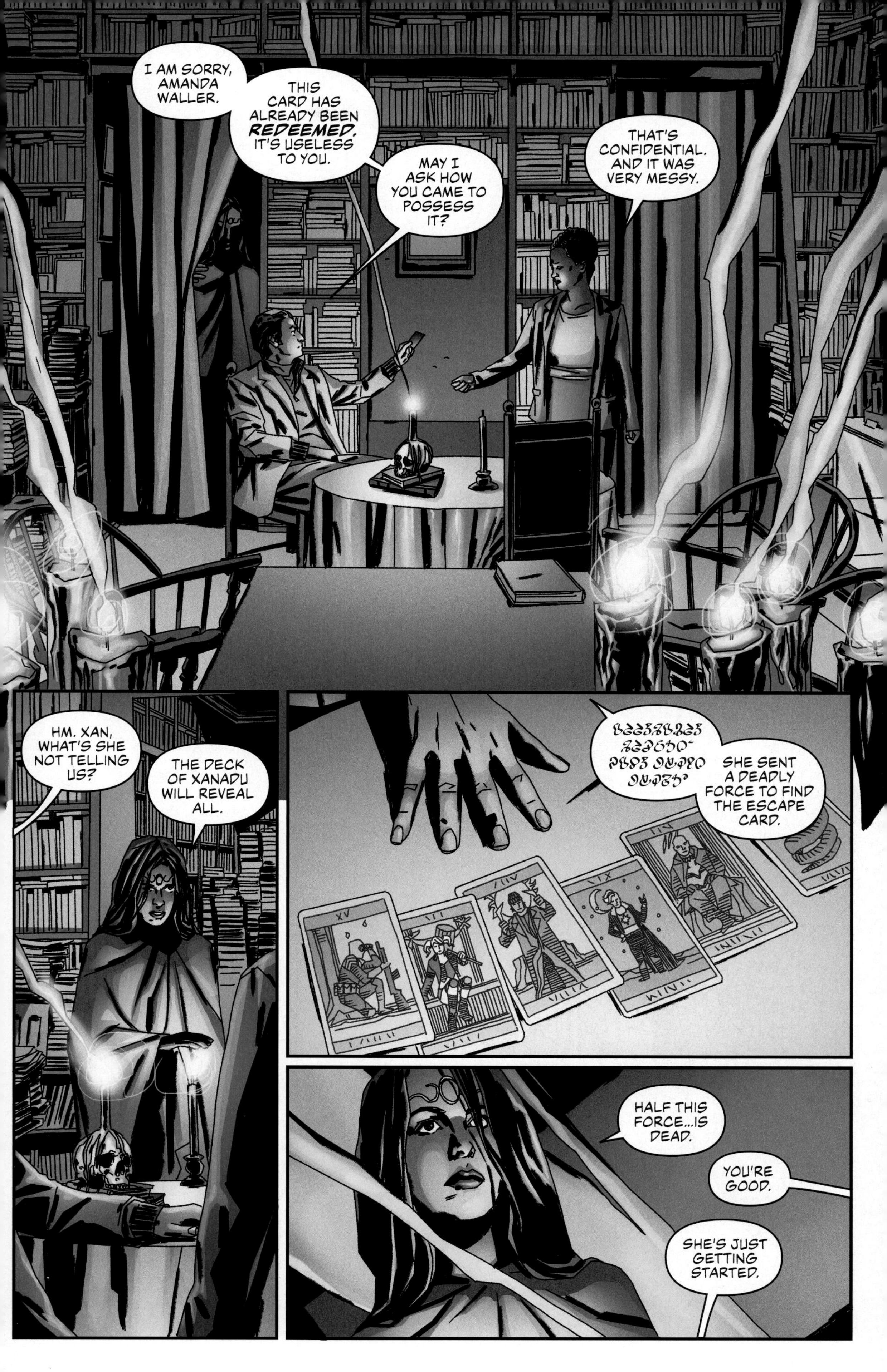
I AM SORRY, AMANDA WALLER.
THIS CARD HAS ALREADY BEEN **REDEEMED.** IT'S USELESS TO YOU.
MAY I ASK HOW YOU CAME TO POSSESS IT?
THAT'S CONFIDENTIAL. AND IT WAS VERY MESSY.
HM. XAN, WHAT'S SHE NOT TELLING US?
THE DECK OF XANADU WILL REVEAL ALL.
SHE SENT A DEADLY FORCE TO FIND THE ESCAPE CARD.
HALF THIS FORCE...IS DEAD.
YOU'RE GOOD.
SHE'S JUST GETTING STARTED.

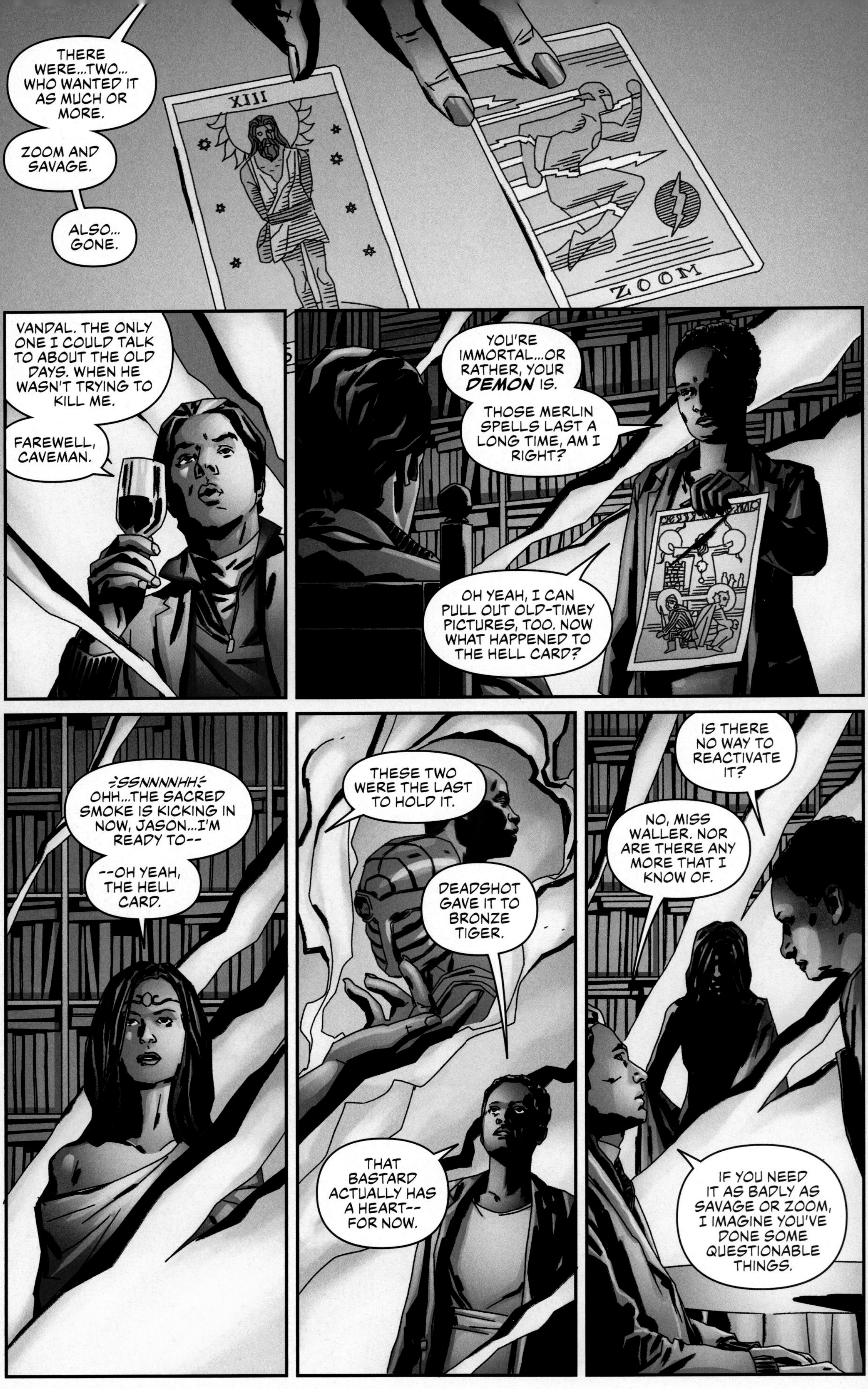
THERE WERE...TWO... WHO WANTED IT AS MUCH OR MORE.
ZOOM AND SAVAGE.
ALSO... GONE.
XIII
ZOOM
VANDAL. THE ONLY ONE I COULD TALK TO ABOUT THE OLD DAYS. WHEN HE WASN'T TRYING TO KILL ME.
FAREWELL, CAVEMAN.
YOU'RE IMMORTAL...OR RATHER, YOUR ***DEMON*** IS.
THOSE MERLIN SPELLS LAST A LONG TIME, AM I RIGHT?
OH YEAH, I CAN PULL OUT OLD-TIMEY PICTURES, TOO. NOW WHAT HAPPENED TO THE HELL CARD?
≈SSNNNNHH≈ OHH...THE SACRED SMOKE IS KICKING IN NOW, JASON...I'M READY TO--
--OH YEAH, THE HELL CARD.
THESE TWO WERE THE LAST TO HOLD IT.
DEADSHOT GAVE IT TO BRONZE TIGER.
THAT BASTARD ACTUALLY HAS A HEART-- FOR NOW.
IS THERE NO WAY TO REACTIVATE IT?
NO, MISS WALLER. NOR ARE THERE ANY MORE THAT I KNOW OF.
IF YOU NEED IT AS BADLY AS SAVAGE OR ZOOM, I IMAGINE YOU'VE DONE SOME QUESTIONABLE THINGS.

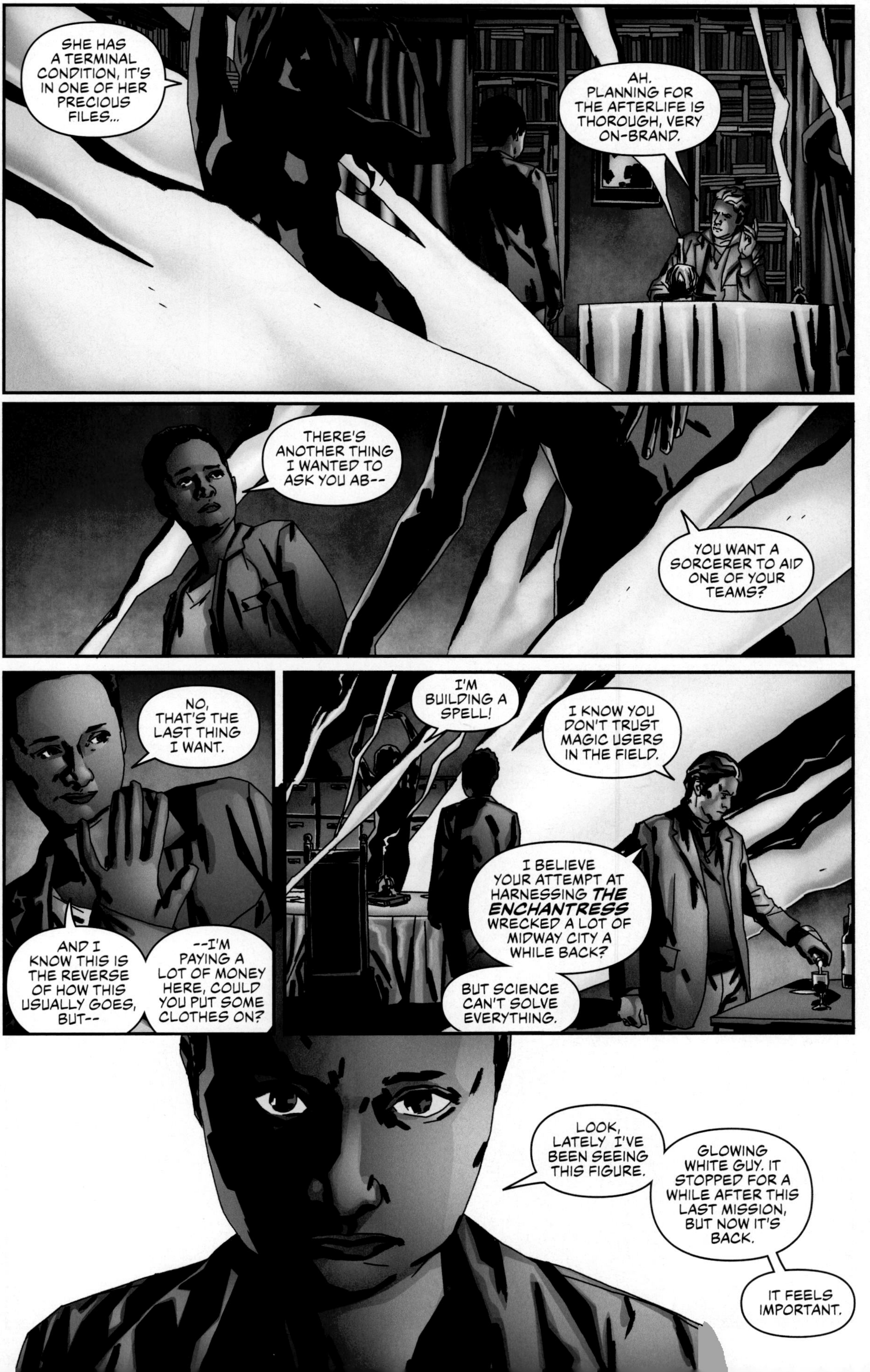
SHE HAS A TERMINAL CONDITION, IT'S IN ONE OF HER PRECIOUS FILES...
AH. PLANNING FOR THE AFTERLIFE IS THOROUGH, VERY ON-BRAND.
THERE'S ANOTHER THING I WANTED TO ASK YOU AB--
YOU WANT A SORCERER TO AID ONE OF YOUR TEAMS?
NO, THAT'S THE LAST THING I WANT.
AND I KNOW THIS IS THE REVERSE OF HOW THIS USUALLY GOES, BUT--
--I'M PAYING A LOT OF MONEY HERE, COULD YOU PUT SOME CLOTHES ON?
I'M BUILDING A SPELL!
I KNOW YOU DON'T TRUST MAGIC USERS IN THE FIELD.
I BELIEVE YOUR ATTEMPT AT HARNESSING THE ENCHANTRESS WRECKED A LOT OF MIDWAY CITY A WHILE BACK?
BUT SCIENCE CAN'T SOLVE EVERYTHING.
LOOK, LATELY I'VE BEEN SEEING THIS FIGURE.
GLOWING WHITE GUY. IT STOPPED FOR A WHILE AFTER THIS LAST MISSION, BUT NOW IT'S BACK.
IT FEELS IMPORTANT.

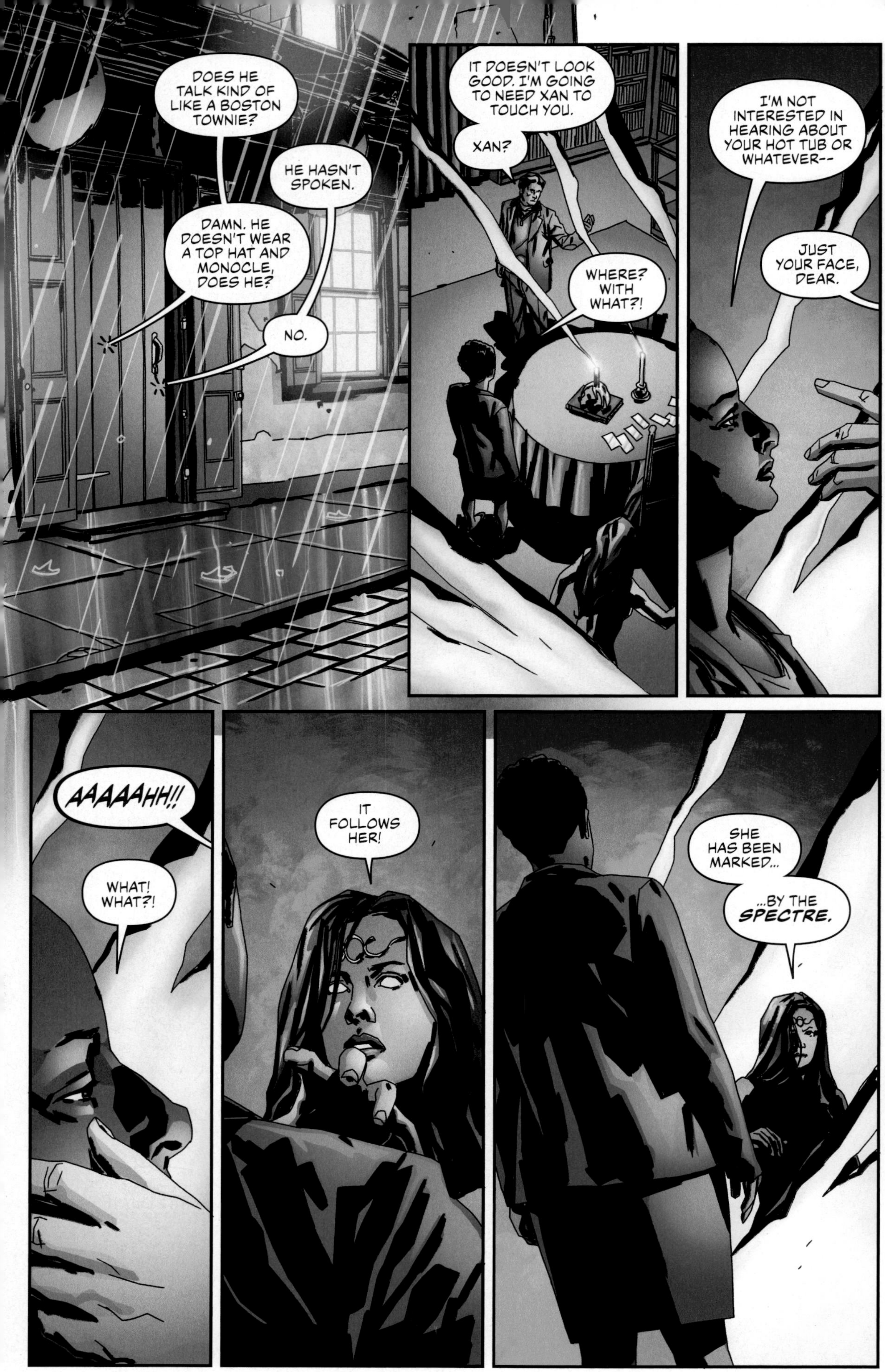
DOES HE TALK KIND OF LIKE A BOSTON TOWNIE?
HE HASN'T SPOKEN.
DAMN. HE DOESN'T WEAR A TOP HAT AND MONOCLE, DOES HE?
NO.
IT DOESN'T LOOK GOOD. I'M GOING TO NEED XAN TO TOUCH YOU.
XAN?
WHERE? WITH WHAT?!
I'M NOT INTERESTED IN HEARING ABOUT YOUR HOT TUB OR WHATEVER--
JUST YOUR FACE, DEAR.
AAAAAHH!!
WHAT! WHAT?!
IT FOLLOWS HER!
SHE HAS BEEN MARKED...
...BY THE SPECTRE.

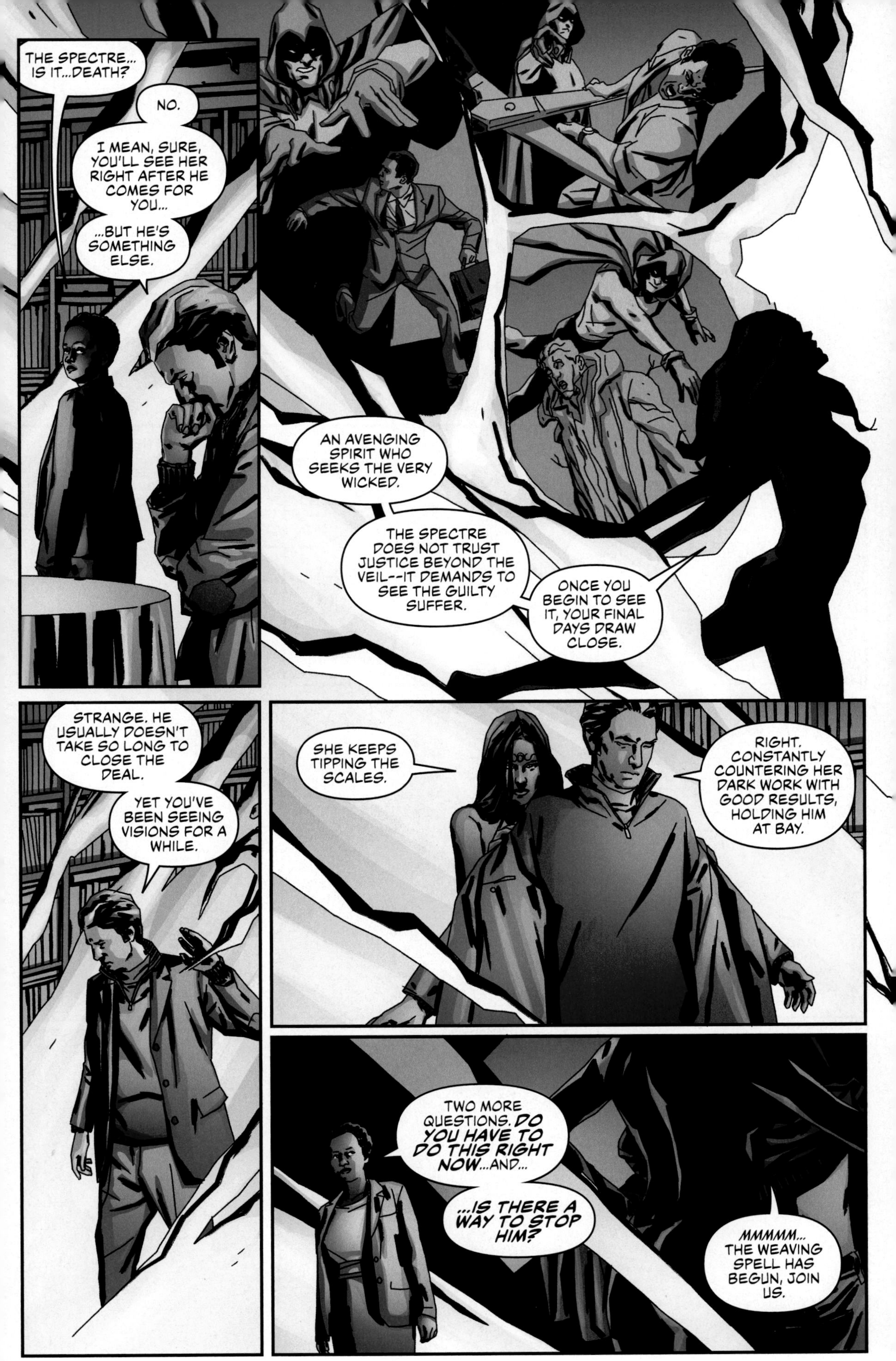
THE SPECTRE... IS IT...DEATH?
NO.
I MEAN, SURE, YOU'LL SEE HER RIGHT AFTER HE COMES FOR YOU...
...BUT HE'S SOMETHING ELSE.
AN AVENGING SPIRIT WHO SEEKS THE VERY WICKED.
THE SPECTRE DOES NOT TRUST JUSTICE BEYOND THE VEIL--IT DEMANDS TO SEE THE GUILTY SUFFER.
ONCE YOU BEGIN TO SEE IT, YOUR FINAL DAYS DRAW CLOSE.
STRANGE. HE USUALLY DOESN'T TAKE SO LONG TO CLOSE THE DEAL.
YET YOU'VE BEEN SEEING VISIONS FOR A WHILE.
SHE KEEPS TIPPING THE SCALES.
RIGHT. CONSTANTLY COUNTERING HER DARK WORK WITH GOOD RESULTS, HOLDING HIM AT BAY.
TWO MORE QUESTIONS. *DO YOU HAVE TO DO THIS RIGHT NOW*...AND...
...IS THERE A WAY TO STOP HIM?
MMMMM... THE WEAVING SPELL HAS BEGUN, JOIN US.

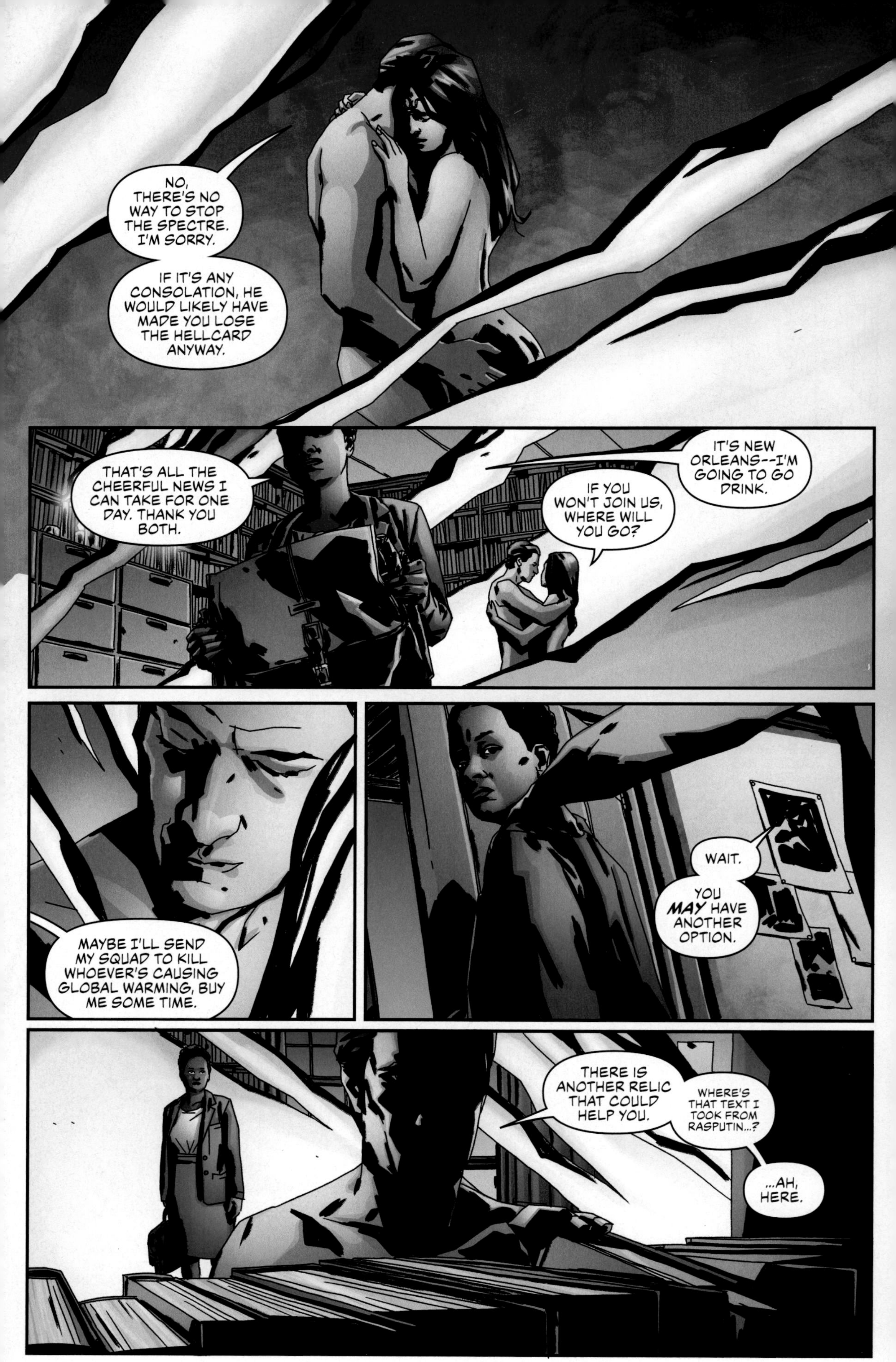
NO, THERE'S NO WAY TO STOP THE SPECTRE. I'M SORRY.
IF IT'S ANY CONSOLATION, HE WOULD LIKELY HAVE MADE YOU LOSE THE HELLCARD ANYWAY.
THAT'S ALL THE CHEERFUL NEWS I CAN TAKE FOR ONE DAY. THANK YOU BOTH.
IF YOU WON'T JOIN US, WHERE WILL YOU GO?
IT'S NEW ORLEANS--I'M GOING TO GO DRINK.
MAYBE I'LL SEND MY SQUAD TO KILL WHOEVER'S CAUSING GLOBAL WARMING, BUY ME SOME TIME.
WAIT.
YOU MAY HAVE ANOTHER OPTION.
THERE IS ANOTHER RELIC THAT COULD HELP YOU.
WHERE'S THAT TEXT I TOOK FROM RASPUTIN...?
...AH, HERE.

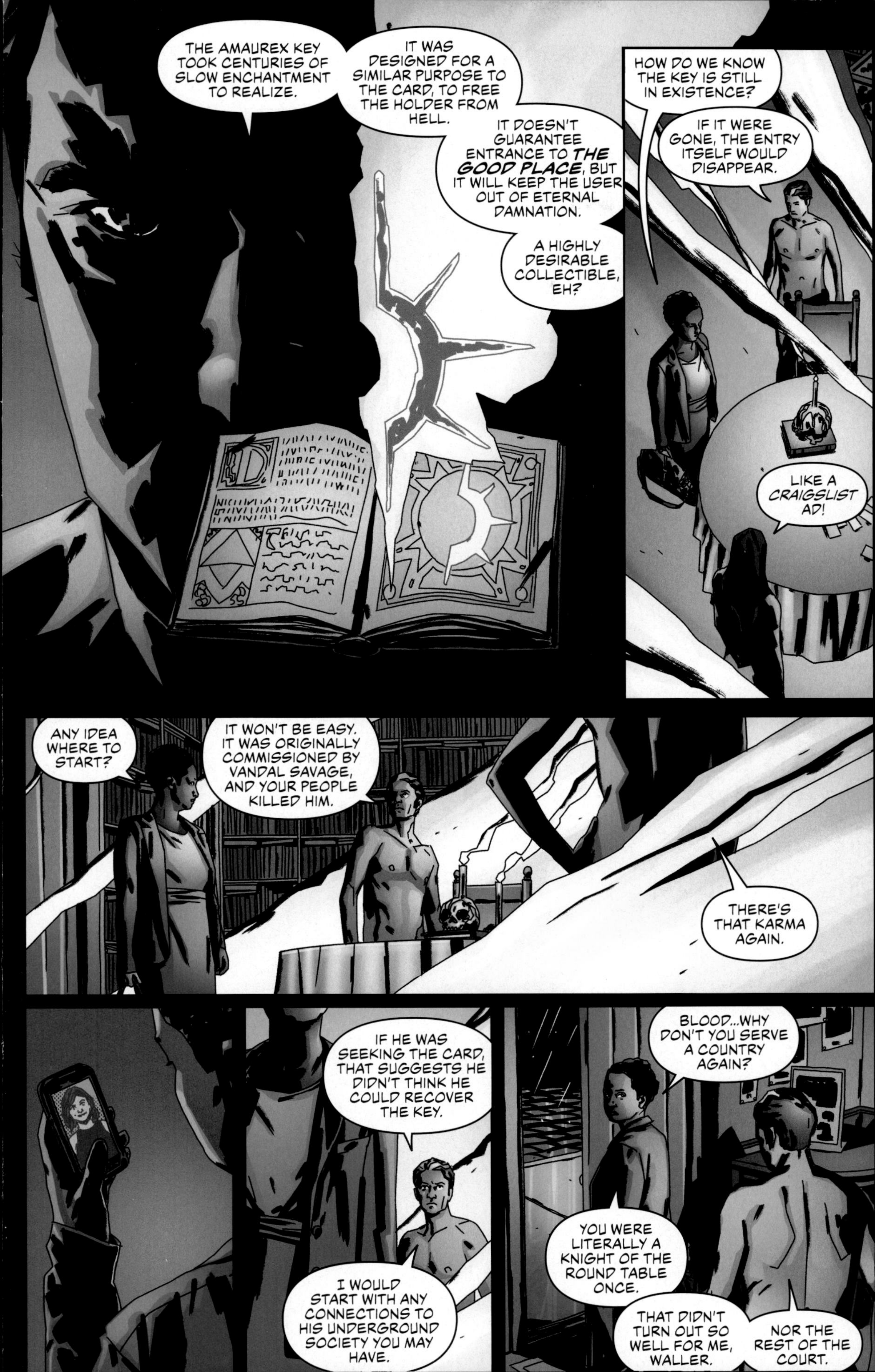
THE AMAUREX KEY TOOK CENTURIES OF SLOW ENCHANTMENT TO REALIZE.
IT WAS DESIGNED FOR A SIMILAR PURPOSE TO THE CARD, TO FREE THE HOLDER FROM HELL.
IT DOESN'T GUARANTEE ENTRANCE TO THE GOOD PLACE, BUT IT WILL KEEP THE USER OUT OF ETERNAL DAMNATION.
A HIGHLY DESIRABLE COLLECTIBLE, EH?
HOW DO WE KNOW THE KEY IS STILL IN EXISTENCE?
IF IT WERE GONE, THE ENTRY ITSELF WOULD DISAPPEAR.
LIKE A CRAIGSLIST AD!
ANY IDEA WHERE TO START?
IT WON'T BE EASY. IT WAS ORIGINALLY COMMISSIONED BY VANDAL SAVAGE, AND YOUR PEOPLE KILLED HIM.
THERE'S THAT KARMA AGAIN.
IF HE WAS SEEKING THE CARD, THAT SUGGESTS HE DIDN'T THINK HE COULD RECOVER THE KEY.
I WOULD START WITH ANY CONNECTIONS TO HIS UNDERGROUND SOCIETY YOU MAY HAVE.
BLOOD...WHY DON'T YOU SERVE A COUNTRY AGAIN?
YOU WERE LITERALLY A KNIGHT OF THE ROUND TABLE ONCE.
THAT DIDN'T TURN OUT SO WELL FOR ME, WALLER.
NOR THE REST OF THE COURT.

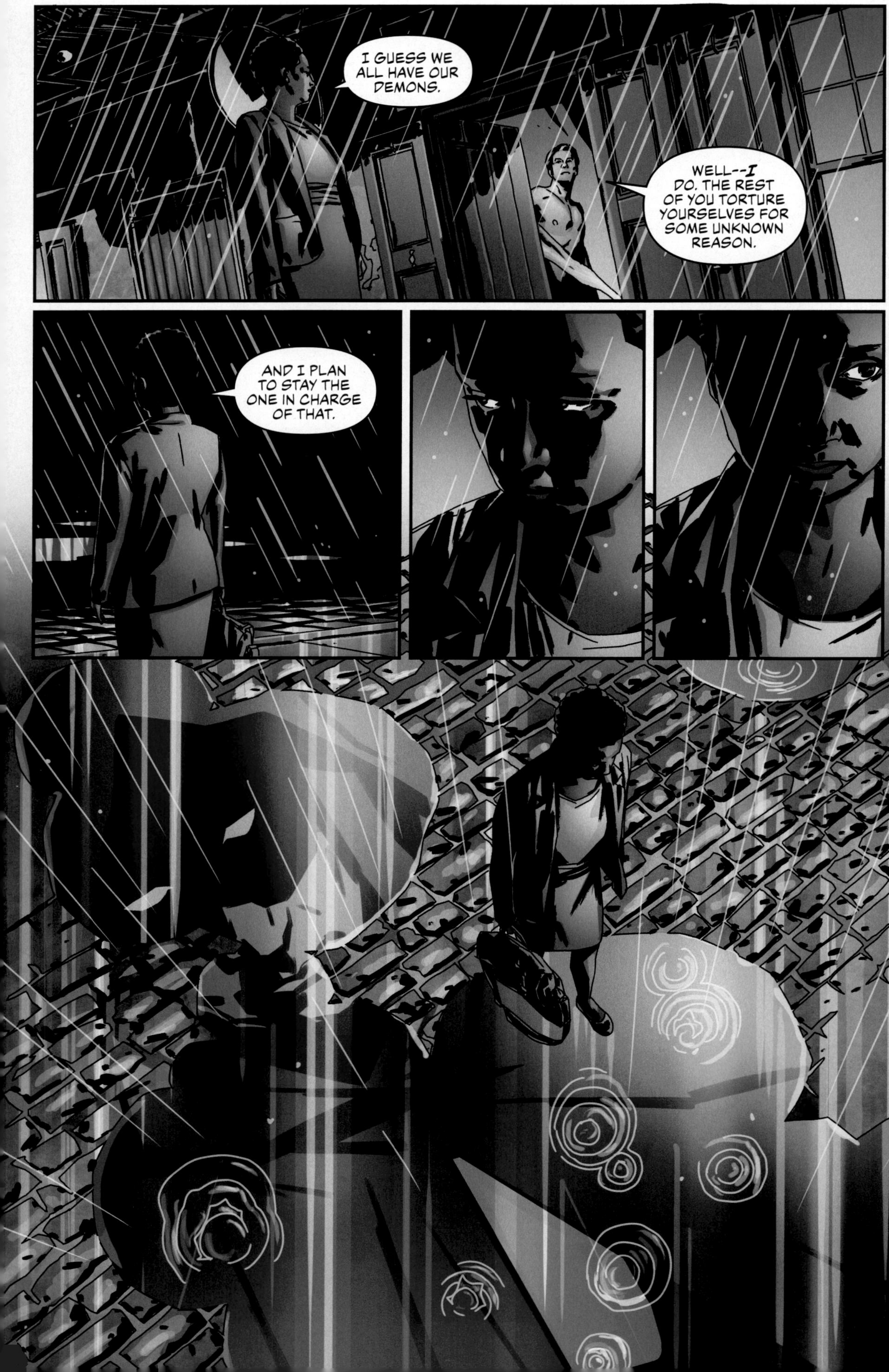
I GUESS WE ALL HAVE OUR DEMONS.
WELL--I DO. THE REST OF YOU TORTURE YOURSELVES FOR SOME UNKNOWN REASON.
AND I PLAN TO STAY THE ONE IN CHARGE OF THAT.

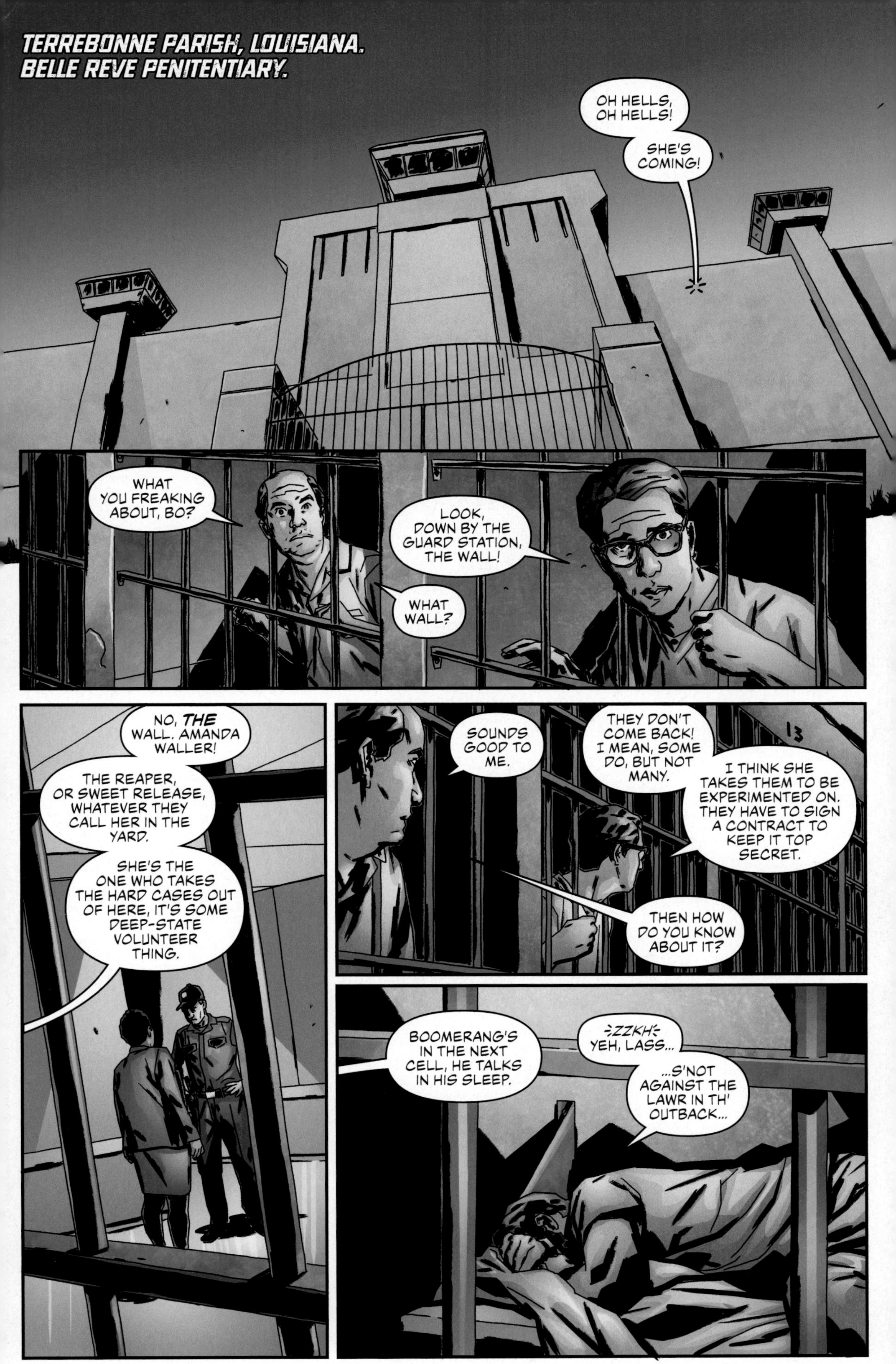
TERREBONNE PARISH, LOUISIANA.
BELLE REVE PENITENTIARY.
OH HELLS, OH HELLS!
SHE'S COMING!
WHAT YOU FREAKING ABOUT, BO?
LOOK, DOWN BY THE GUARD STATION, THE WALL!
WHAT WALL?
NO, THE WALL. AMANDA WALLER!
THE REAPER, OR SWEET RELEASE, WHATEVER THEY CALL HER IN THE YARD.
SHE'S THE ONE WHO TAKES THE HARD CASES OUT OF HERE, IT'S SOME DEEP-STATE VOLUNTEER THING.
SOUNDS GOOD TO ME.
THEY DON'T COME BACK! I MEAN, SOME DO, BUT NOT MANY.
I THINK SHE TAKES THEM TO BE EXPERIMENTED ON. THEY HAVE TO SIGN A CONTRACT TO KEEP IT TOP SECRET.
THEN HOW DO YOU KNOW ABOUT IT?
BOOMERANG'S IN THE NEXT CELL, HE TALKS IN HIS SLEEP.
ZZKH YEH, LASS...
...S'NOT AGAINST THE LAWR IN TH' OUTBACK...

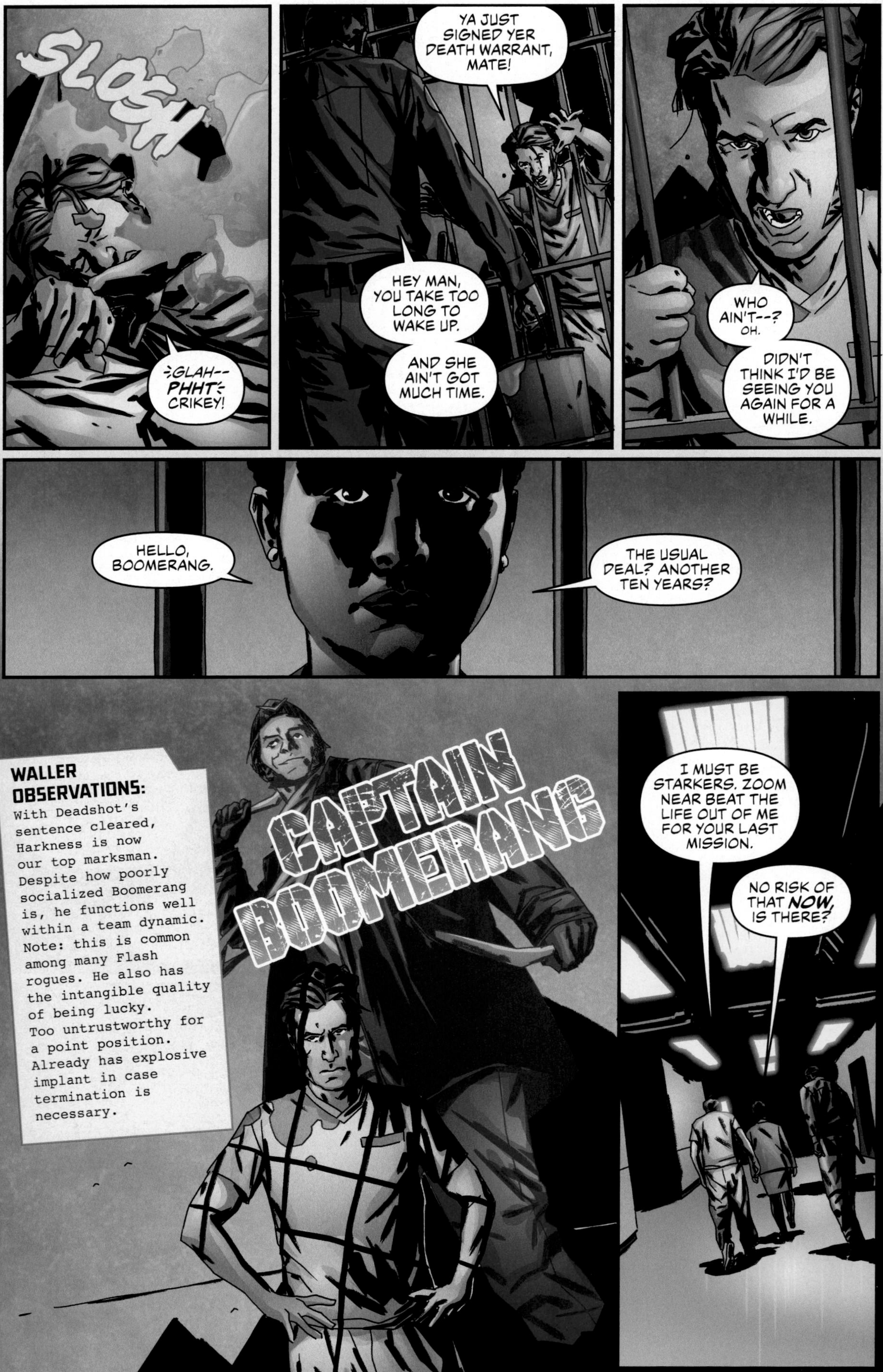
SLOSH
GLAH--PHHT-- CRIKEY!
YA JUST SIGNED YER DEATH WARRANT, MATE!
HEY MAN, YOU TAKE TOO LONG TO WAKE UP.
AND SHE AIN'T GOT MUCH TIME.
WHO AIN'T--? OH.
DIDN'T THINK I'D BE SEEING YOU AGAIN FOR A WHILE.
HELLO, BOOMERANG.
THE USUAL DEAL? ANOTHER TEN YEARS?
CAPTAIN BOOMERANG
WALLER OBSERVATIONS:
With Deadshot's sentence cleared, Harkness is now our top marksman. Despite how poorly socialized Boomerang is, he functions well within a team dynamic. Note: this is common among many Flash rogues. He also has the intangible quality of being lucky. Too untrustworthy for a point position. Already has explosive implant in case termination is necessary.
I MUST BE STARKERS. ZOOM NEAR BEAT THE LIFE OUT OF ME FOR YOUR LAST MISSION.
NO RISK OF THAT NOW, IS THERE?

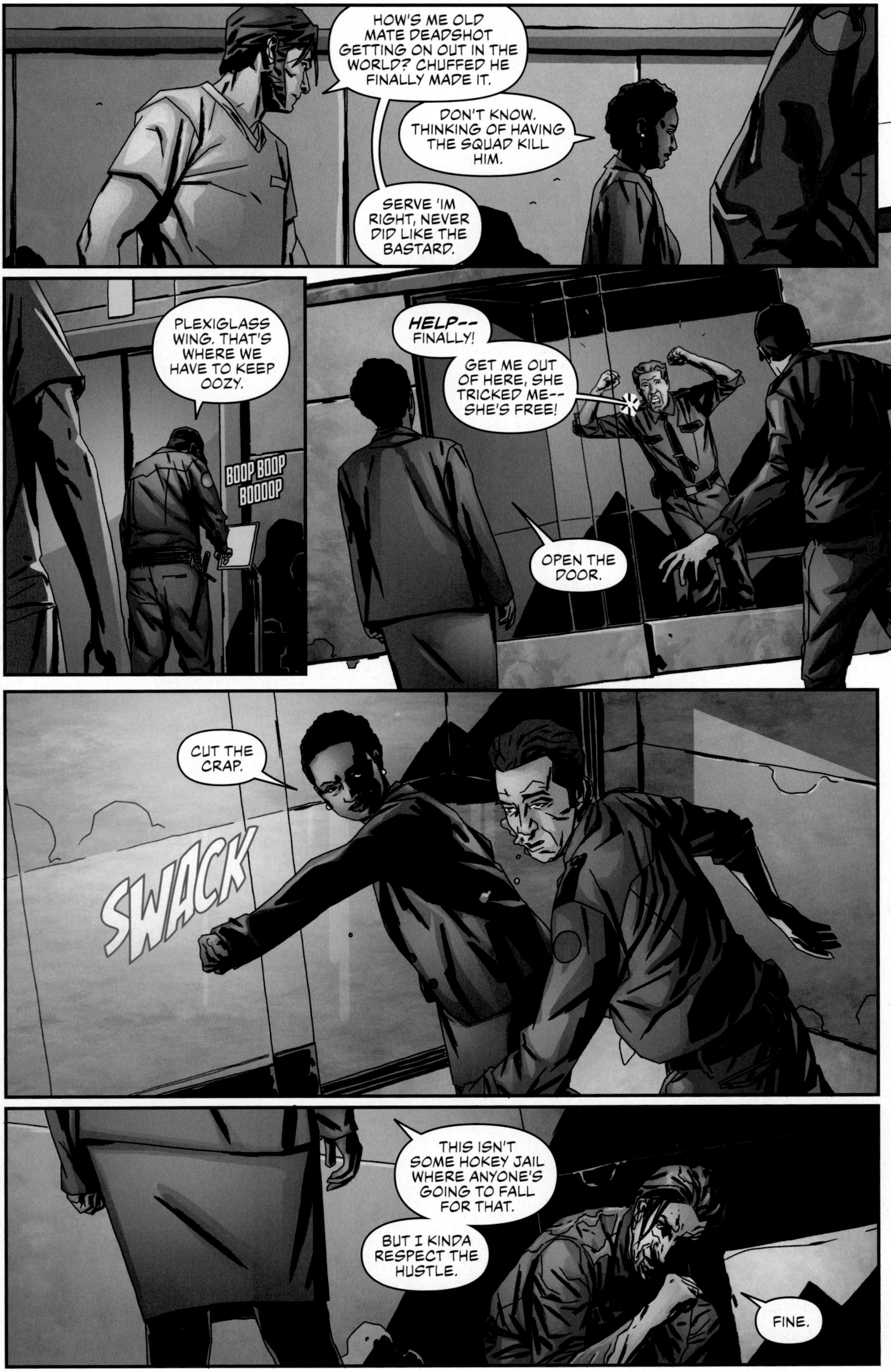
HOW'S ME OLD MATE DEADSHOT GETTING ON OUT IN THE WORLD? CHUFFED HE FINALLY MADE IT.
DON'T KNOW. THINKING OF HAVING THE SQUAD KILL HIM.
SERVE 'IM RIGHT, NEVER DID LIKE THE BASTARD.
PLEXIGLASS WING. THAT'S WHERE WE HAVE TO KEEP OOZY.
BOOP BOOP BOOOOP
HELP-- FINALLY!
GET ME OUT OF HERE, SHE TRICKED ME-- SHE'S FREE!
OPEN THE DOOR.
CUT THE CRAP.
SWACK
THIS ISN'T SOME HOKEY JAIL WHERE ANYONE'S GOING TO FALL FOR THAT.
BUT I KINDA RESPECT THE HUSTLE.
FINE.

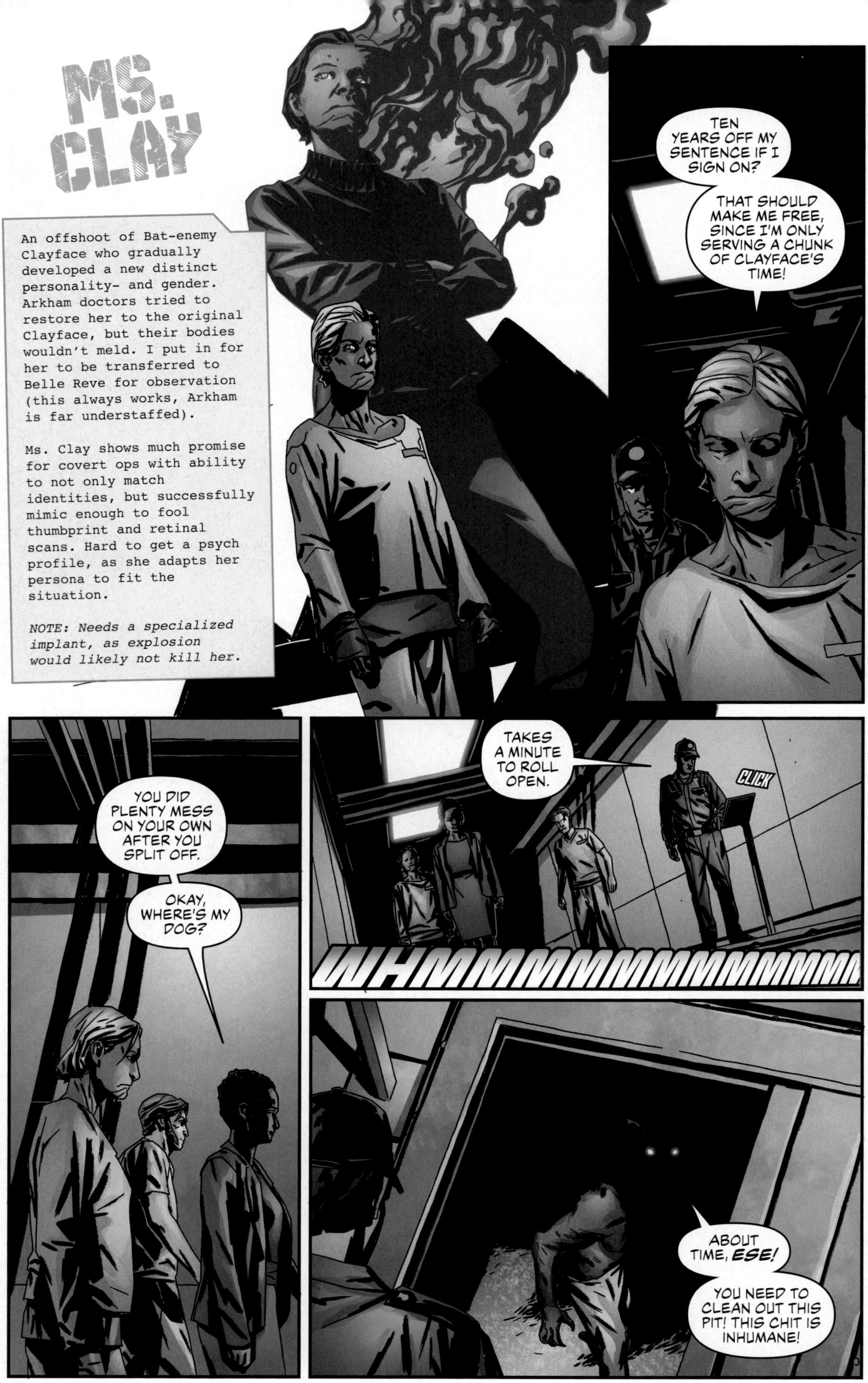
MS. CLAY
An offshoot of Bat-enemy Clayface who gradually developed a new distinct personality- and gender. Arkham doctors tried to restore her to the original Clayface, but their bodies wouldn't meld. I put in for her to be transferred to Belle Reve for observation (this always works, Arkham is far understaffed).
Ms. Clay shows much promise for covert ops with ability to not only match identities, but successfully mimic enough to fool thumbprint and retinal scans. Hard to get a psych profile, as she adapts her persona to fit the situation.
NOTE: Needs a specialized implant, as explosion would likely not kill her.
TEN YEARS OFF MY SENTENCE IF I SIGN ON?
THAT SHOULD MAKE ME FREE, SINCE I'M ONLY SERVING A CHUNK OF CLAYFACE'S TIME!
YOU DID PLENTY MESS ON YOUR OWN AFTER YOU SPLIT OFF.
OKAY, WHERE'S MY DOG?
TAKES A MINUTE TO ROLL OPEN.
CLICK
WHMMMMMMMMMMMMMM
ABOUT TIME, ESE!
YOU NEED TO CLEAN OUT THIS PIT! THIS CHIT IS INHUMANE!

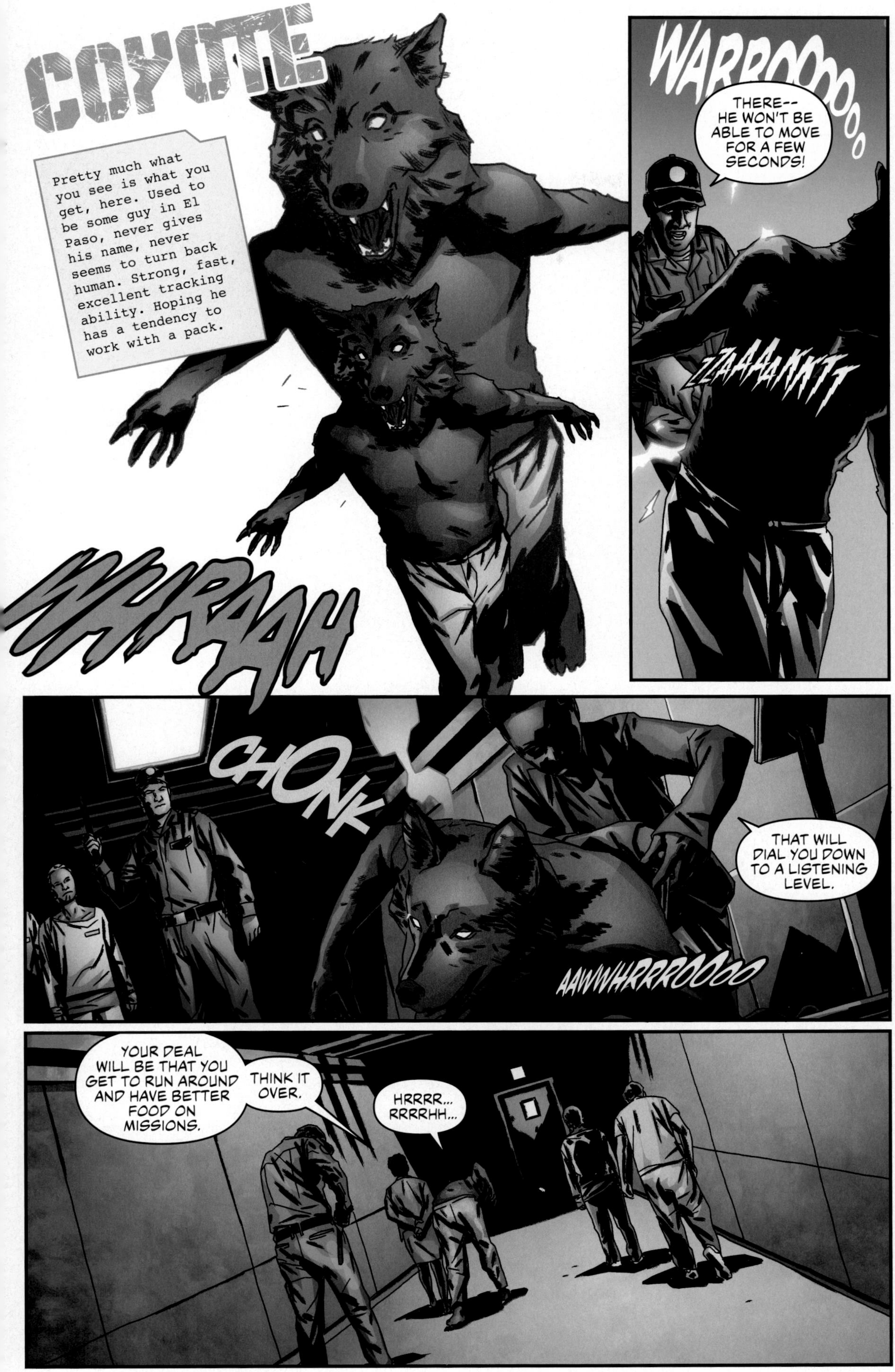
COYOTE
Pretty much what you see is what you get, here. Used to be some guy in El Paso, never gives his name, never seems to turn back human. Strong, fast, excellent tracking ability. Hoping he has a tendency to work with a pack.
WHRAAH
WARROOOOOOO
THERE-- HE WON'T BE ABLE TO MOVE FOR A FEW SECONDS!
ZZAAAAKKTT
CHONK
THAT WILL DIAL YOU DOWN TO A LISTENING LEVEL.
AAWWHRRROOOOO
YOUR DEAL WILL BE THAT YOU GET TO RUN AROUND AND HAVE BETTER FOOD ON MISSIONS.
THINK IT OVER.
HRRRR... RRRRHH...

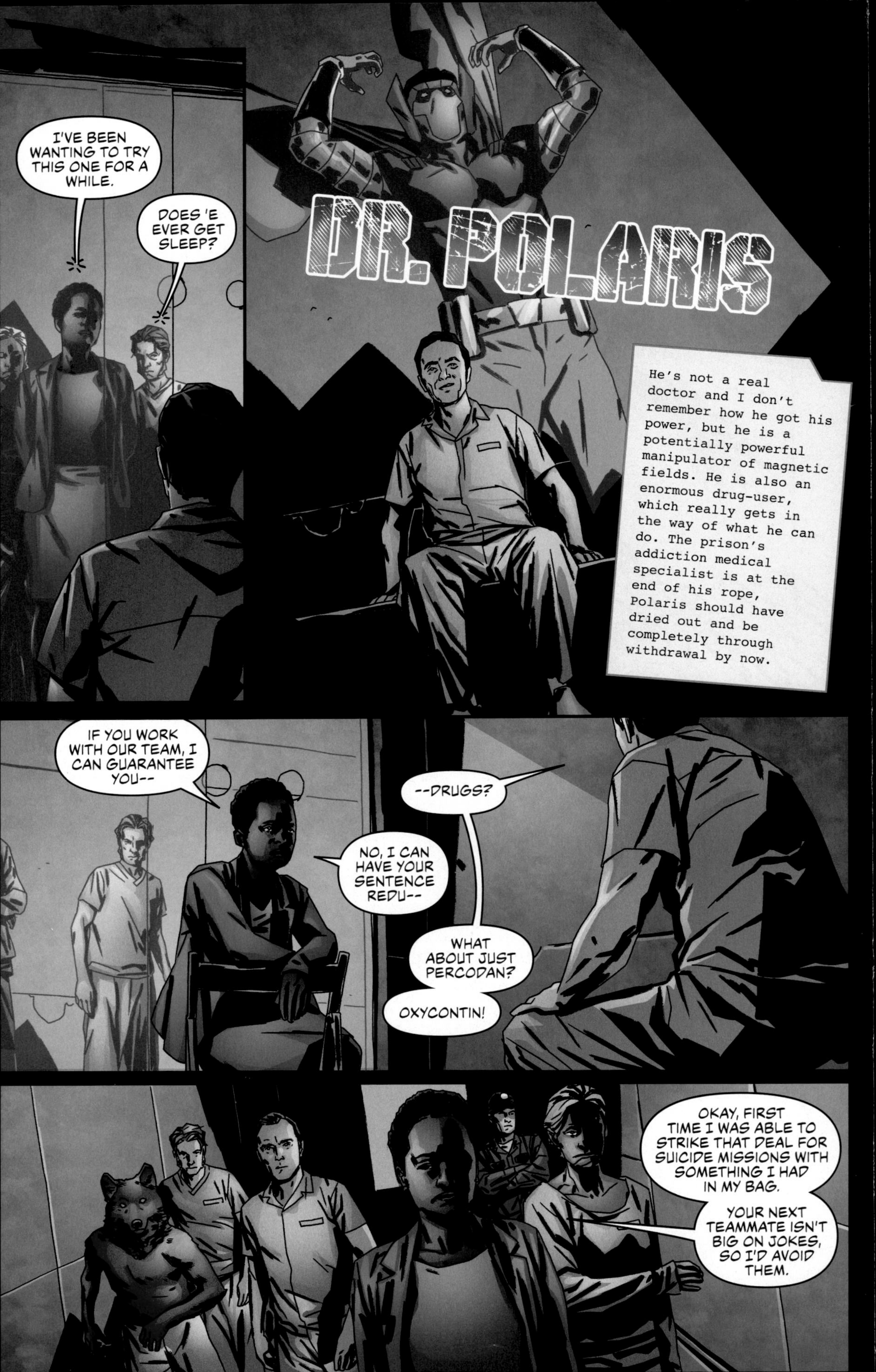
I'VE BEEN WANTING TO TRY THIS ONE FOR A WHILE.
DOES 'E EVER GET SLEEP?
DR. POLARIS
He's not a real doctor and I don't remember how he got his power, but he is a potentially powerful manipulator of magnetic fields. He is also an enormous drug-user, which really gets in the way of what he can do. The prison's addiction medical specialist is at the end of his rope, Polaris should have dried out and be completely through withdrawal by now.
IF YOU WORK WITH OUR TEAM, I CAN GUARANTEE YOU--
--DRUGS?
NO, I CAN HAVE YOUR SENTENCE REDU--
WHAT ABOUT JUST PERCODAN?
OXYCONTIN!
OKAY, FIRST TIME I WAS ABLE TO STRIKE THAT DEAL FOR SUICIDE MISSIONS WITH SOMETHING I HAD IN MY BAG.
YOUR NEXT TEAMMATE ISN'T BIG ON JOKES, SO I'D AVOID THEM.

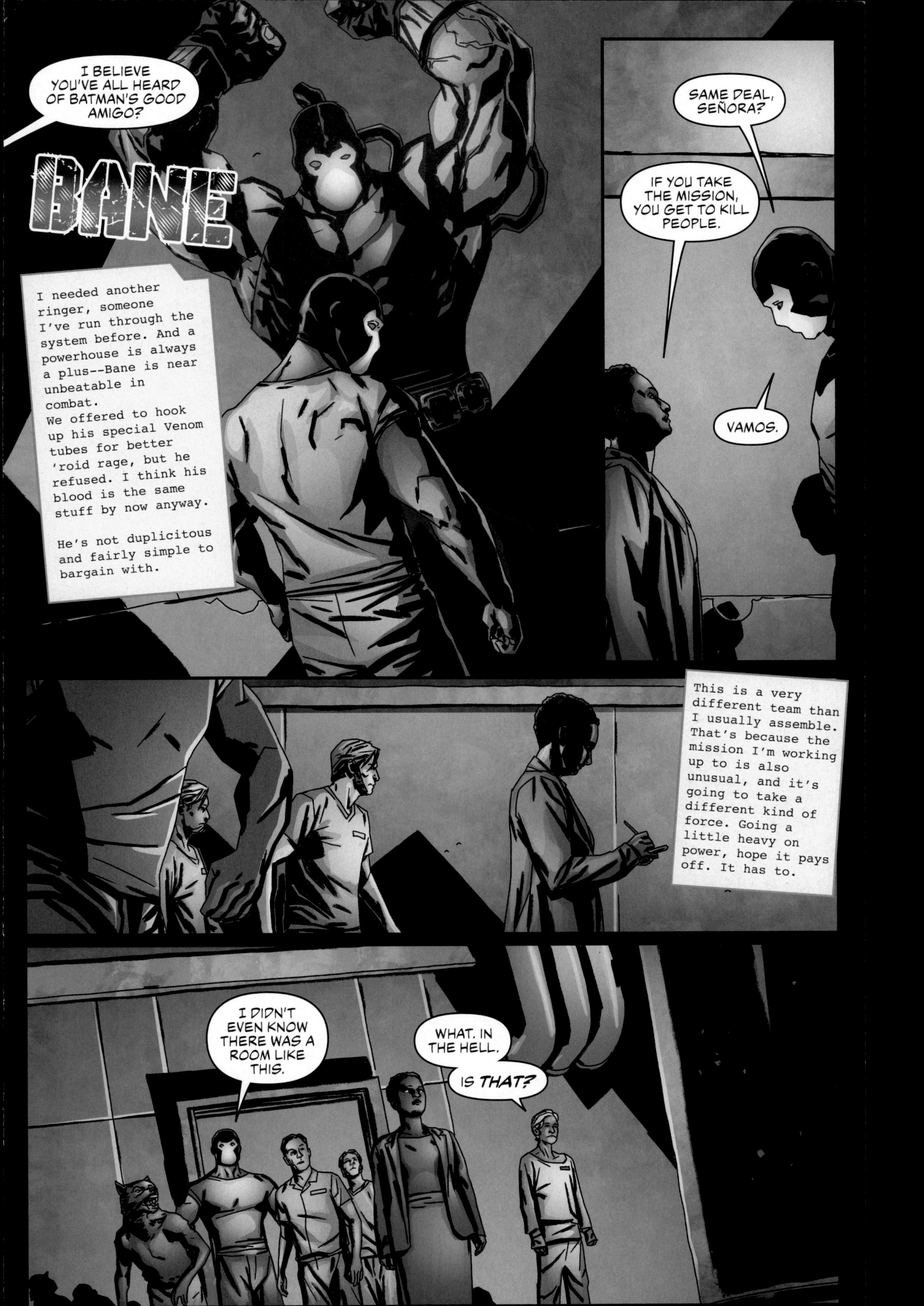
I BELIEVE YOU'VE ALL HEARD OF BATMAN'S GOOD AMIGO?
BANE
I needed another ringer, someone I've run through the system before. And a powerhouse is always a plus--Bane is near unbeatable in combat.
We offered to hook up his special Venom tubes for better 'roid rage, but he refused. I think his blood is the same stuff by now anyway.
He's not duplicitous and fairly simple to bargain with.
SAME DEAL, SEÑORA?
IF YOU TAKE THE MISSION, YOU GET TO KILL PEOPLE.
VAMOS.
This is a very different team than I usually assemble. That's because the mission I'm working up to is also unusual, and it's going to take a different kind of force. Going a little heavy on power, hope it pays off. It has to.
I DIDN'T EVEN KNOW THERE WAS A ROOM LIKE THIS.
WHAT. IN THE HELL.
IS *THAT?*

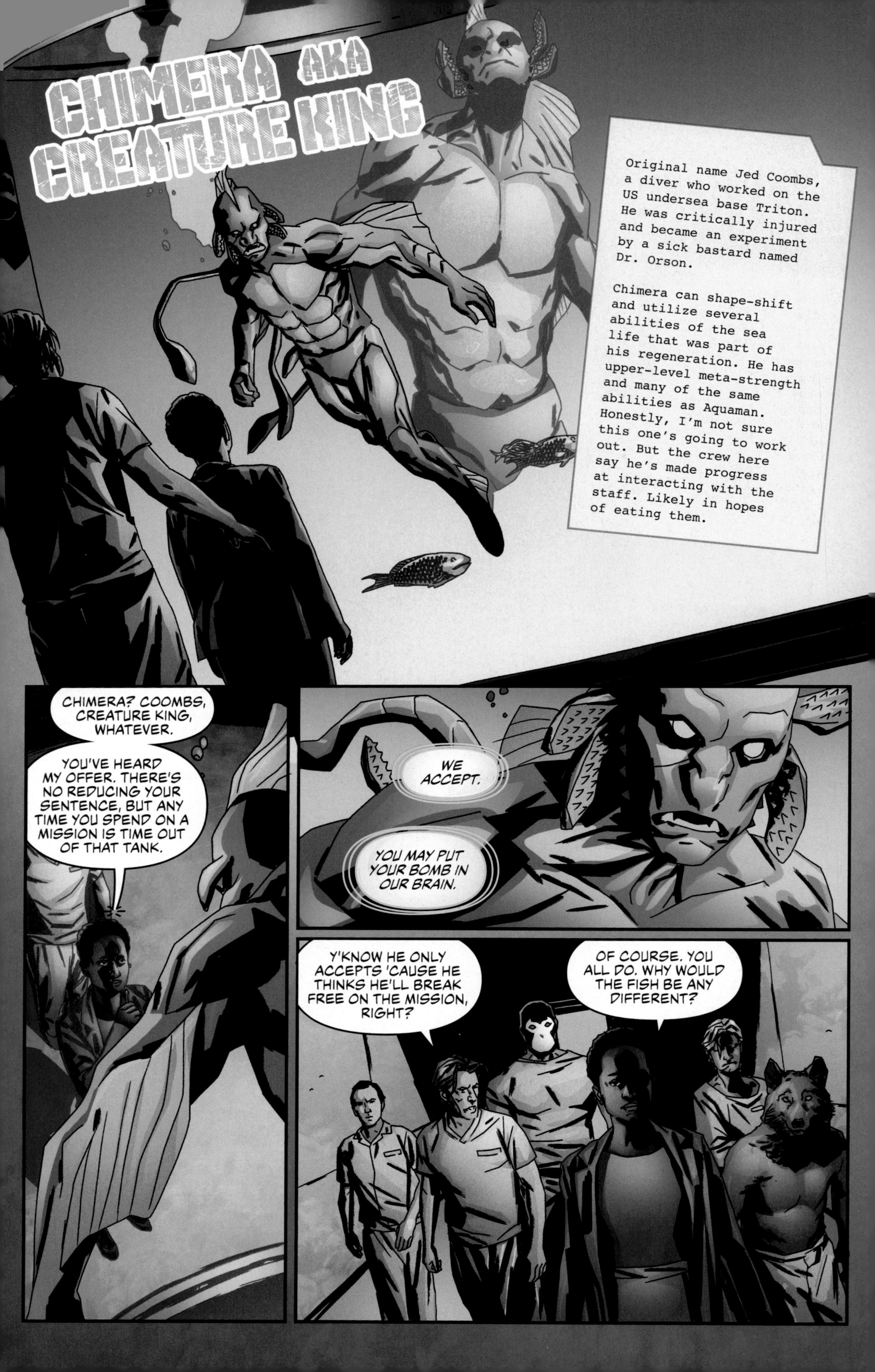
CHIMERA AKA CREATURE KING
Original name Jed Coombs, a diver who worked on the US undersea base Triton. He was critically injured and became an experiment by a sick bastard named Dr. Orson.
Chimera can shape-shift and utilize several abilities of the sea life that was part of his regeneration. He has upper-level meta-strength and many of the same abilities as Aquaman. Honestly, I'm not sure this one's going to work out. But the crew here say he's made progress at interacting with the staff. Likely in hopes of eating them.
CHIMERA? COOMBS, CREATURE KING, WHATEVER.
YOU'VE HEARD MY OFFER. THERE'S NO REDUCING YOUR SENTENCE, BUT ANY TIME YOU SPEND ON A MISSION IS TIME OUT OF THAT TANK.
WE ACCEPT.
YOU MAY PUT YOUR BOMB IN OUR BRAIN.
Y'KNOW HE ONLY ACCEPTS 'CAUSE HE THINKS HE'LL BREAK FREE ON THE MISSION, RIGHT?
OF COURSE. YOU ALL DO. WHY WOULD THE FISH BE ANY DIFFERENT?

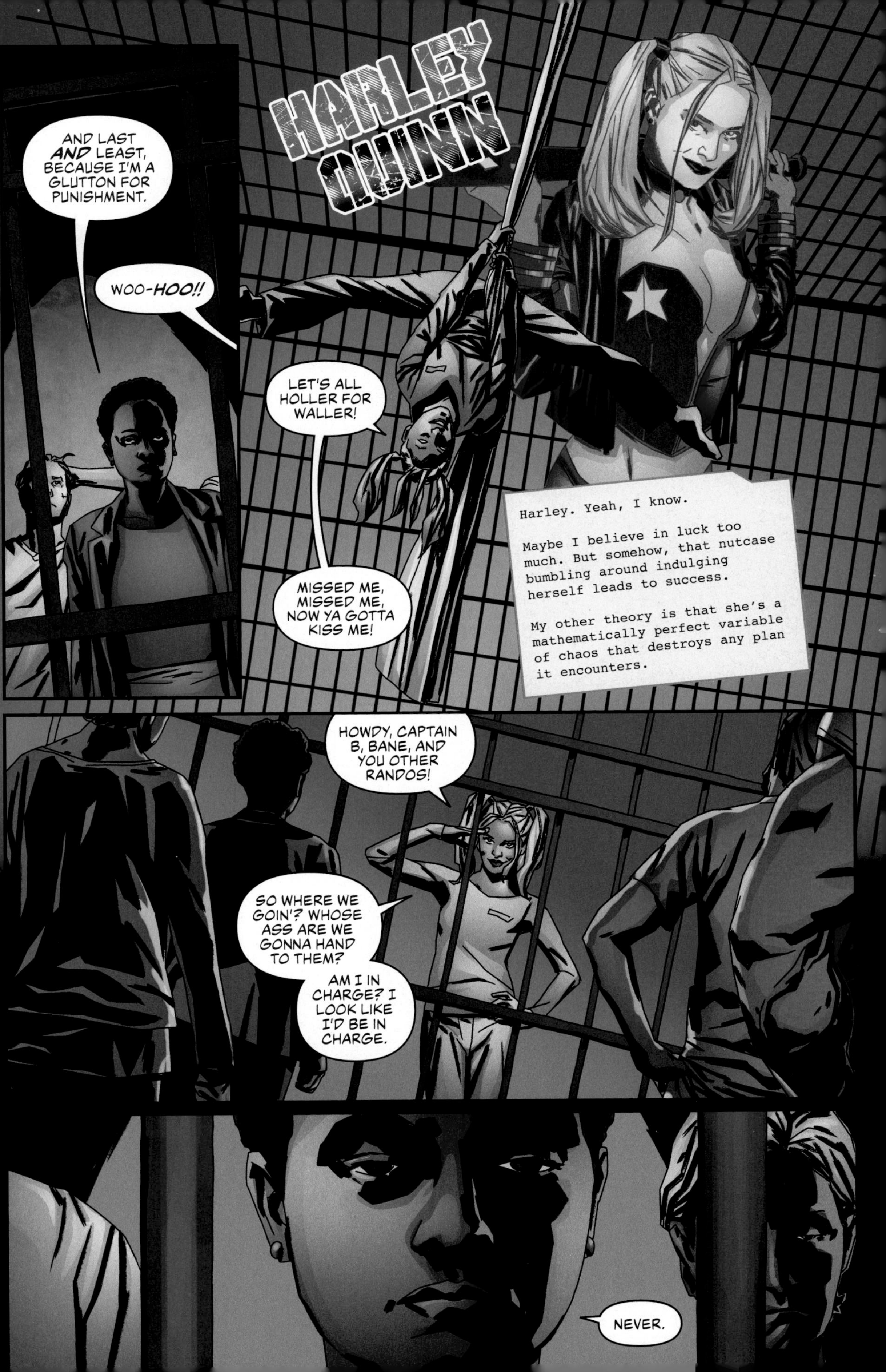
AND LAST AND LEAST, BECAUSE I'M A GLUTTON FOR PUNISHMENT.
WOO-HOO!!
HARLEY QUINN
LET'S ALL HOLLER FOR WALLER!
MISSED ME, MISSED ME, NOW YA GOTTA KISS ME!
Harley. Yeah, I know.
Maybe I believe in luck too much. But somehow, that nutcase bumbling around indulging herself leads to success.
My other theory is that she's a mathematically perfect variable of chaos that destroys any plan it encounters.
HOWDY, CAPTAIN B, BANE, AND YOU OTHER RANDOS!
SO WHERE WE GOIN'? WHOSE ASS ARE WE GONNA HAND TO THEM?
AM I IN CHARGE? I LOOK LIKE I'D BE IN CHARGE.
NEVER.

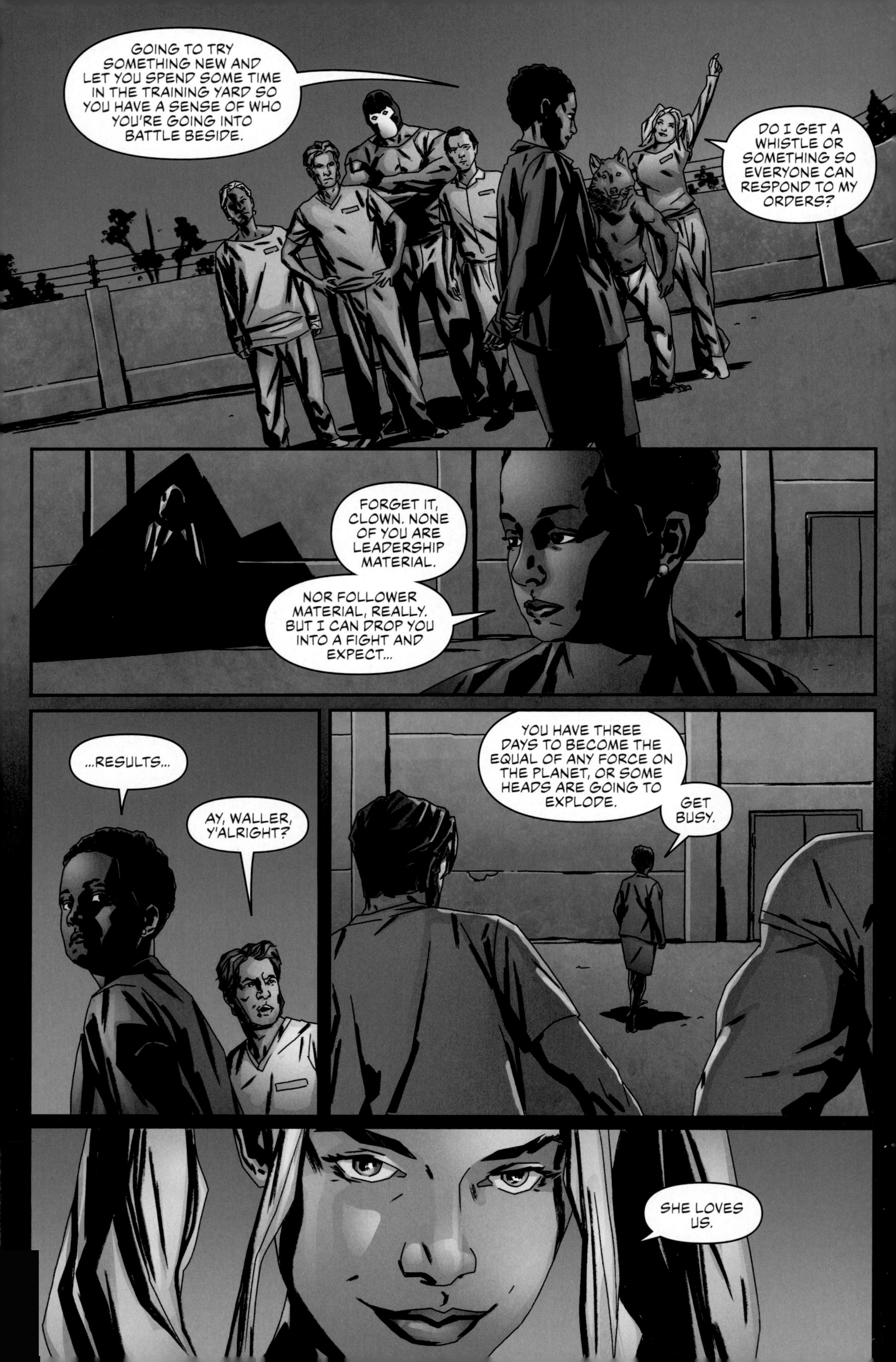
GOING TO TRY SOMETHING NEW AND LET YOU SPEND SOME TIME IN THE TRAINING YARD SO YOU HAVE A SENSE OF WHO YOU'RE GOING INTO BATTLE BESIDE.
DO I GET A WHISTLE OR SOMETHING SO EVERYONE CAN RESPOND TO MY ORDERS?
FORGET IT, CLOWN. NONE OF YOU ARE LEADERSHIP MATERIAL.
NOR FOLLOWER MATERIAL, REALLY. BUT I CAN DROP YOU INTO A FIGHT AND EXPECT...
...RESULTS...
AY, WALLER, Y'ALRIGHT?
YOU HAVE THREE DAYS TO BECOME THE EQUAL OF ANY FORCE ON THE PLANET, OR SOME HEADS ARE GOING TO EXPLODE.
GET BUSY.
SHE LOVES US.

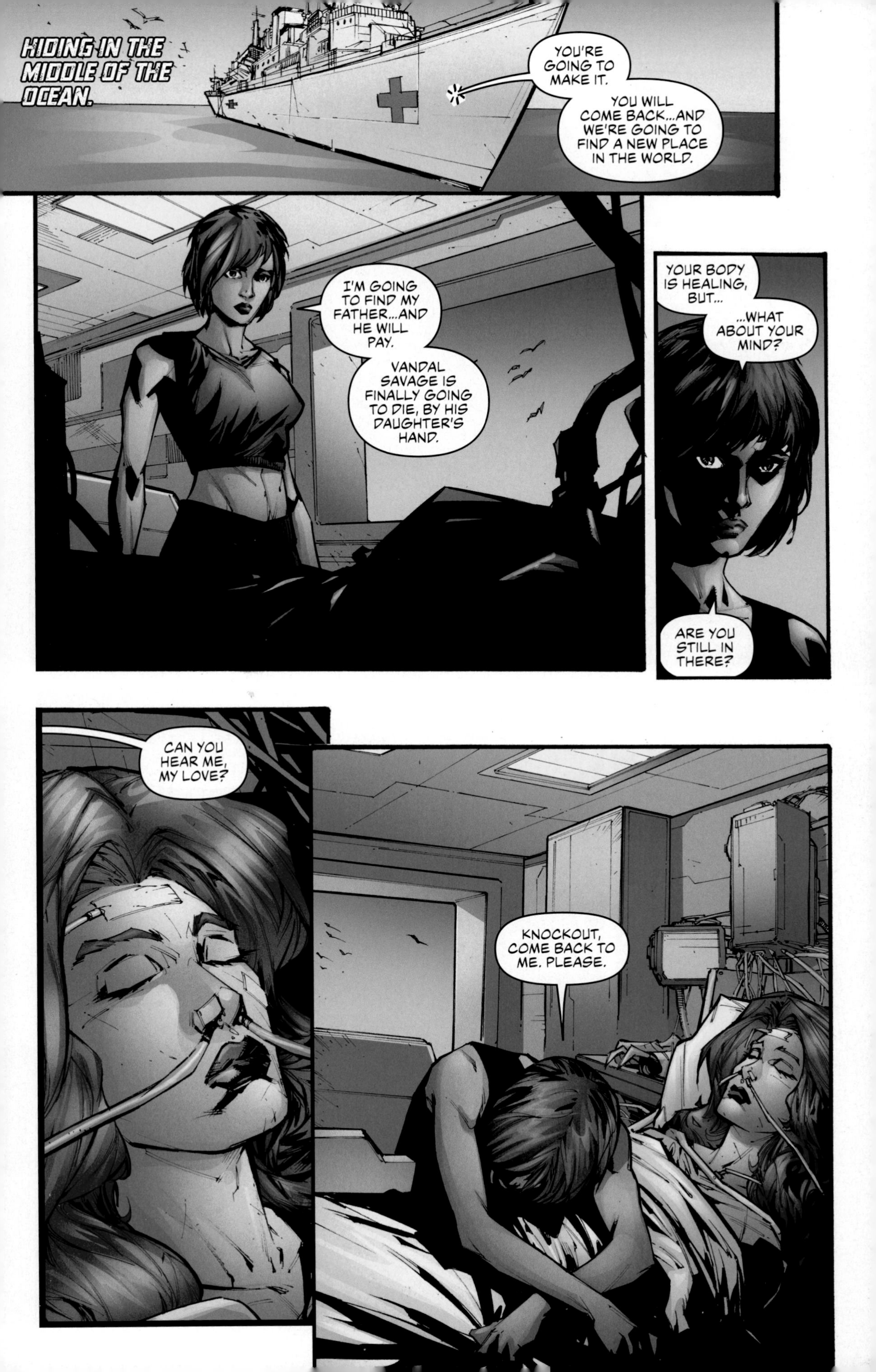
HIDING IN THE MIDDLE OF THE OCEAN.
YOU'RE GOING TO MAKE IT.
YOU WILL COME BACK...AND WE'RE GOING TO FIND A NEW PLACE IN THE WORLD.
I'M GOING TO FIND MY FATHER...AND HE WILL PAY.
VANDAL SAVAGE IS FINALLY GOING TO DIE, BY HIS DAUGHTER'S HAND.
YOUR BODY IS HEALING, BUT...
...WHAT ABOUT YOUR MIND?
ARE YOU STILL IN THERE?
CAN YOU HEAR ME, MY LOVE?
KNOCKOUT, COME BACK TO ME. PLEASE.

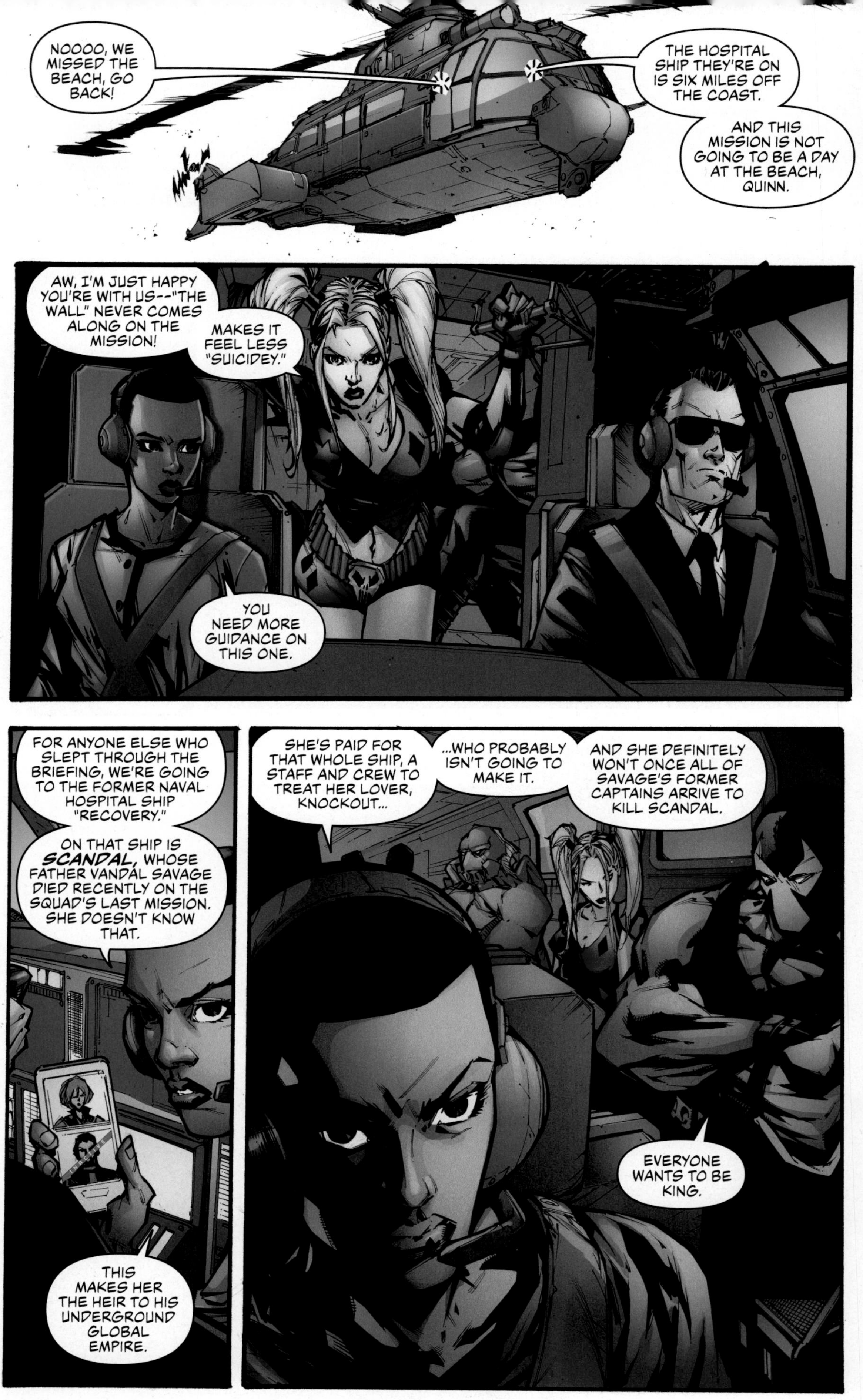
NOOOO, WE MISSED THE BEACH, GO BACK!
THE HOSPITAL SHIP THEY'RE ON IS SIX MILES OFF THE COAST.
AND THIS MISSION IS NOT GOING TO BE A DAY AT THE BEACH, QUINN.
AW, I'M JUST HAPPY YOU'RE WITH US--"THE WALL" NEVER COMES ALONG ON THE MISSION!
MAKES IT FEEL LESS "SUICIDEY."
YOU NEED MORE GUIDANCE ON THIS ONE.
FOR ANYONE ELSE WHO SLEPT THROUGH THE BRIEFING, WE'RE GOING TO THE FORMER NAVAL HOSPITAL SHIP "RECOVERY."
ON THAT SHIP IS SCANDAL, WHOSE FATHER VANDAL SAVAGE DIED RECENTLY ON THE SQUAD'S LAST MISSION. SHE DOESN'T KNOW THAT.
THIS MAKES HER THE HEIR TO HIS UNDERGROUND GLOBAL EMPIRE.
SHE'S PAID FOR THAT WHOLE SHIP, A STAFF AND CREW TO TREAT HER LOVER, KNOCKOUT...
...WHO PROBABLY ISN'T GOING TO MAKE IT.
AND SHE DEFINITELY WON'T ONCE ALL OF SAVAGE'S FORMER CAPTAINS ARRIVE TO KILL SCANDAL.
EVERYONE WANTS TO BE KING.

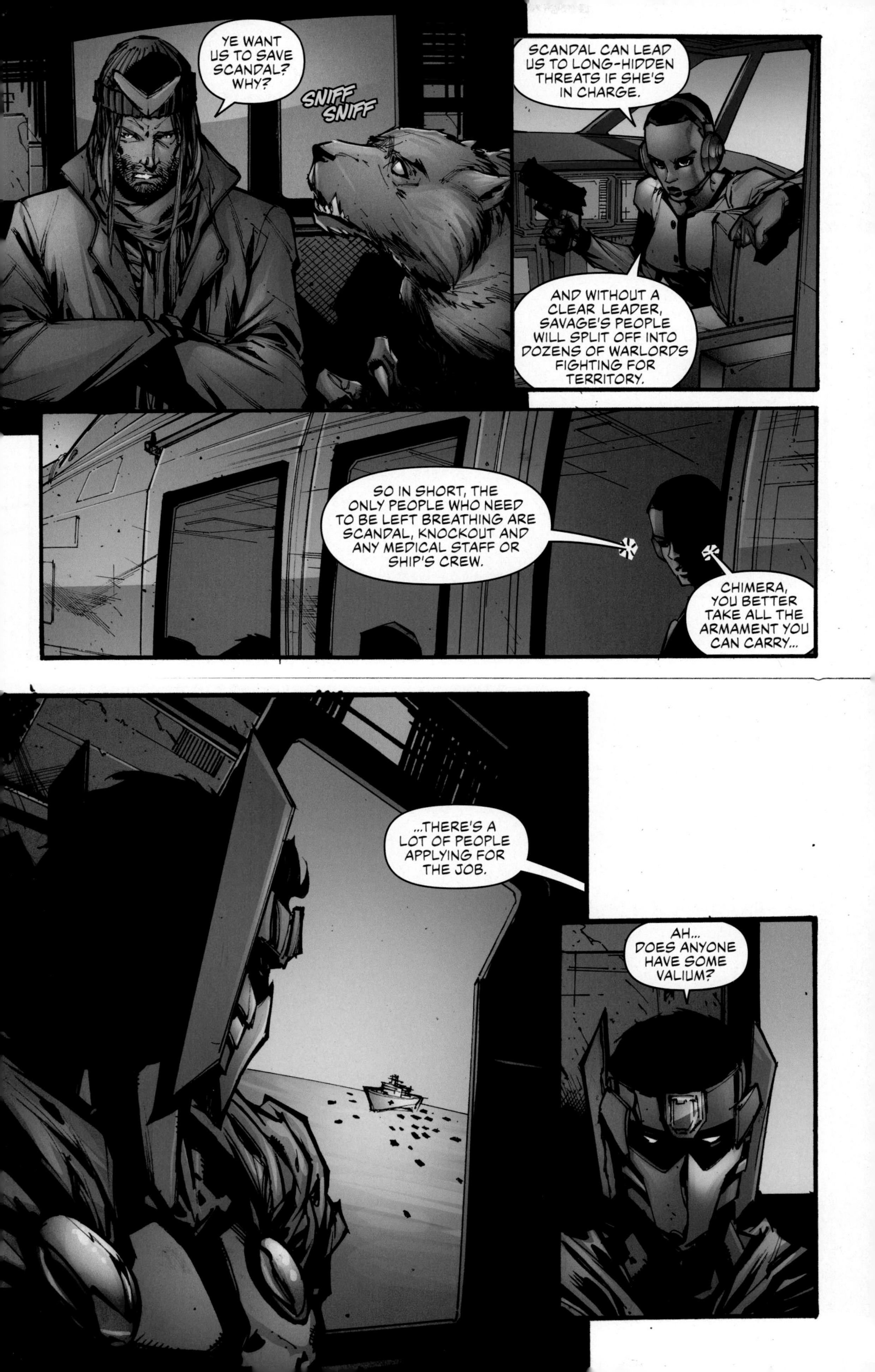
YE WANT US TO SAVE SCANDAL? WHY?
SNIFF SNIFF
SCANDAL CAN LEAD US TO LONG-HIDDEN THREATS IF SHE'S IN CHARGE.
AND WITHOUT A CLEAR LEADER, SAVAGE'S PEOPLE WILL SPLIT OFF INTO DOZENS OF WARLORDS FIGHTING FOR TERRITORY.
SO IN SHORT, THE ONLY PEOPLE WHO NEED TO BE LEFT BREATHING ARE SCANDAL, KNOCKOUT AND ANY MEDICAL STAFF OR SHIP'S CREW.
CHIMERA, YOU BETTER TAKE ALL THE ARMAMENT YOU CAN CARRY...
...THERE'S A LOT OF PEOPLE APPLYING FOR THE JOB.
AH... DOES ANYONE HAVE SOME VALIUM?

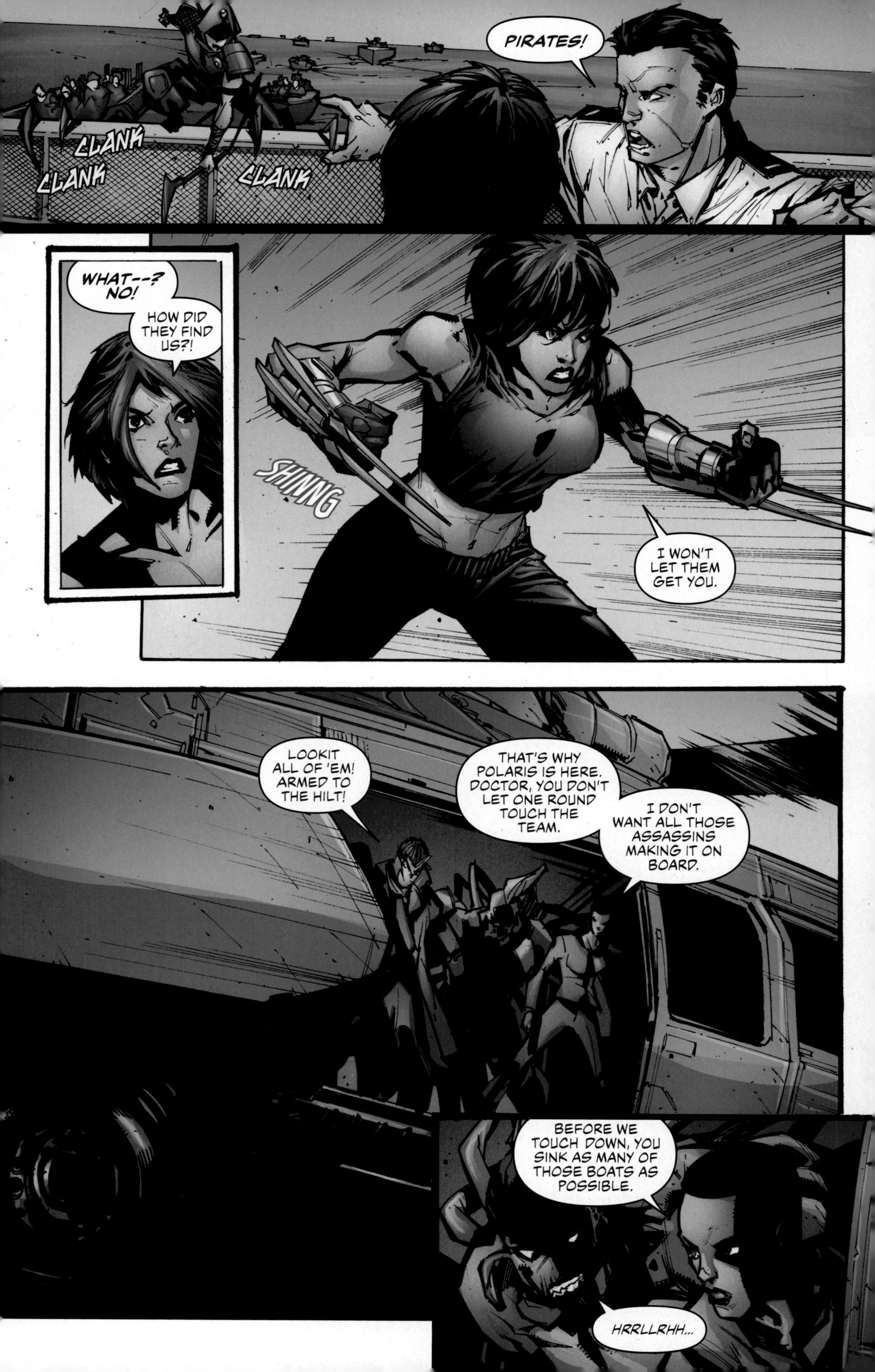
PIRATES!
CLANK
CLANK
CLANK
WHAT--? NO!
HOW DID THEY FIND US?!
SHING
I WON'T LET THEM GET YOU.
LOOKIT ALL OF 'EM! ARMED TO THE HILT!
THAT'S WHY POLARIS IS HERE. DOCTOR, YOU DON'T LET ONE ROUND TOUCH THE TEAM.
I DON'T WANT ALL THOSE ASSASSINS MAKING IT ON BOARD.
BEFORE WE TOUCH DOWN, YOU SINK AS MANY OF THOSE BOATS AS POSSIBLE.
HRRLLRHH...

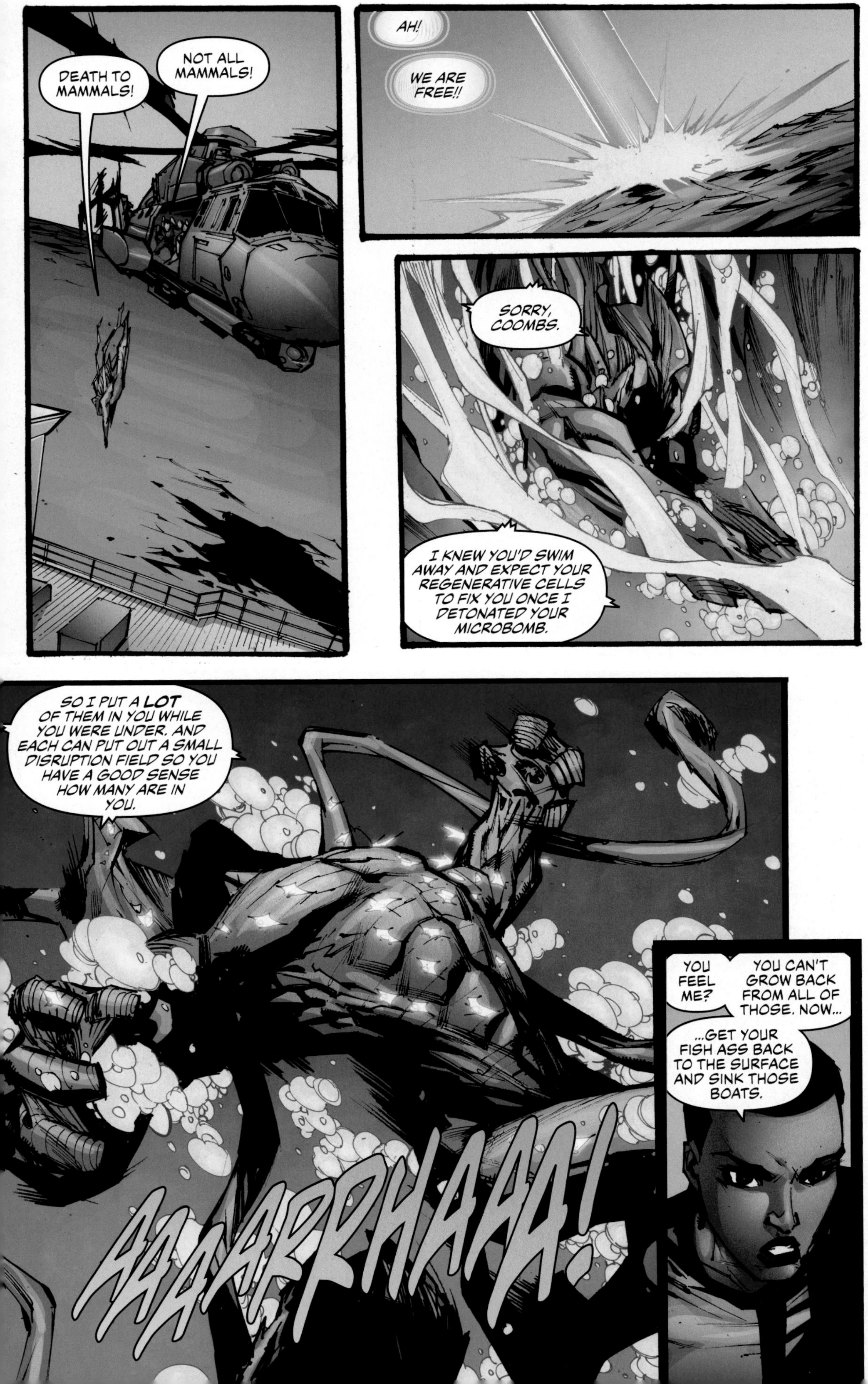

DEATH TO MAMMALS!
NOT ALL MAMMALS!
AH!
WE ARE FREE!!
SORRY, COOMBS.
I KNEW YOU'D SWIM AWAY AND EXPECT YOUR REGENERATIVE CELLS TO FIX YOU ONCE I DETONATED YOUR MICROBOMB.
SO I PUT A **LOT** OF THEM IN YOU WHILE YOU WERE UNDER. AND EACH CAN PUT OUT A SMALL DISRUPTION FIELD SO YOU HAVE A GOOD SENSE HOW MANY ARE IN YOU.
AAAARRHAAAA!
YOU FEEL ME?
YOU CAN'T GROW BACK FROM ALL OF THOSE. NOW...
...GET YOUR FISH ASS BACK TO THE SURFACE AND SINK THOSE BOATS.

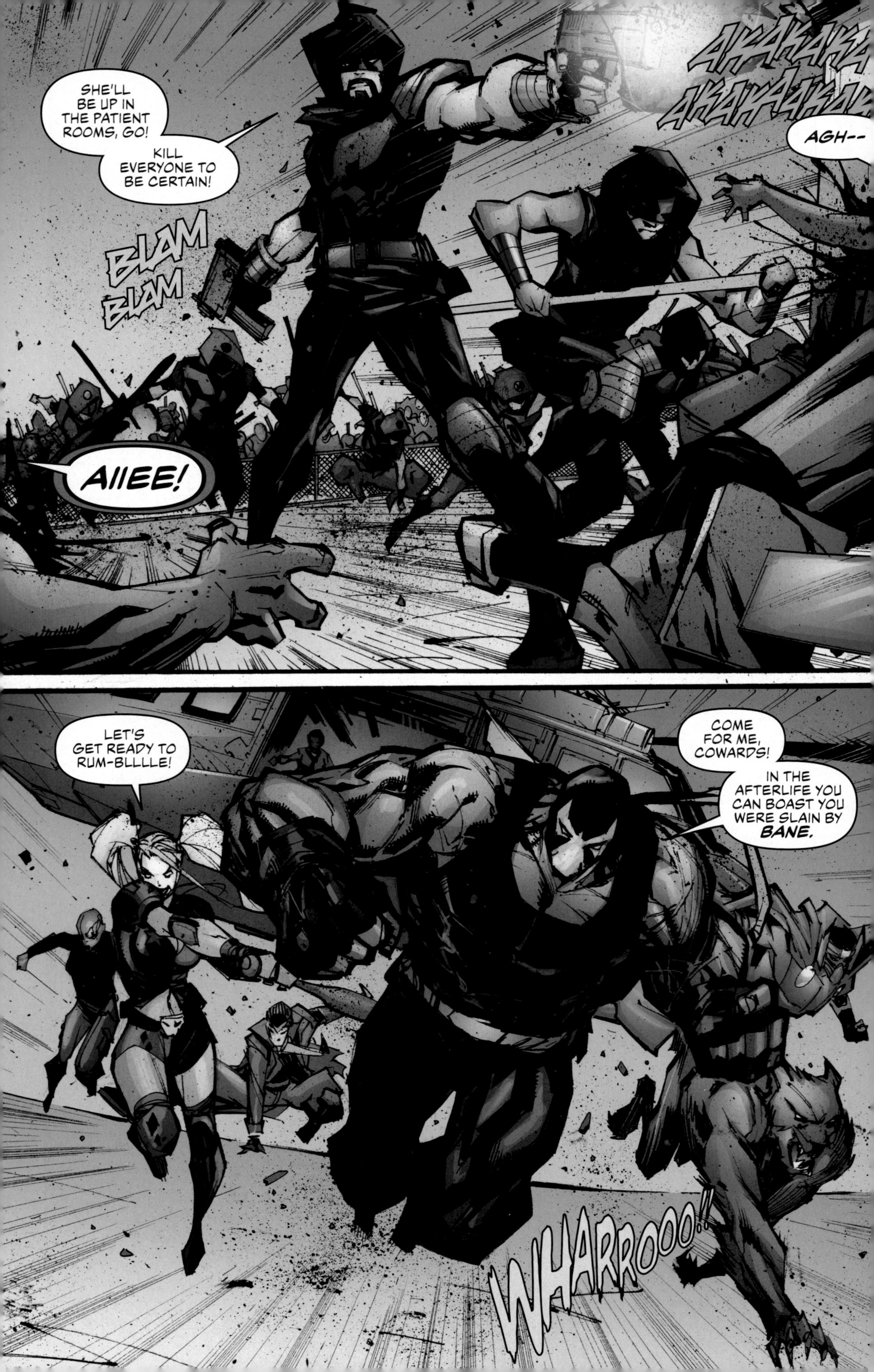
SHE'LL BE UP IN THE PATIENT ROOMS, GO!
KILL EVERYONE TO BE CERTAIN!
BLAM BLAM
AGH--
AIIEE!
LET'S GET READY TO RUM-BLLLLE!
COME FOR ME, COWARDS!
IN THE AFTERLIFE YOU CAN BOAST YOU WERE SLAIN BY BANE.
WHARROOO!!

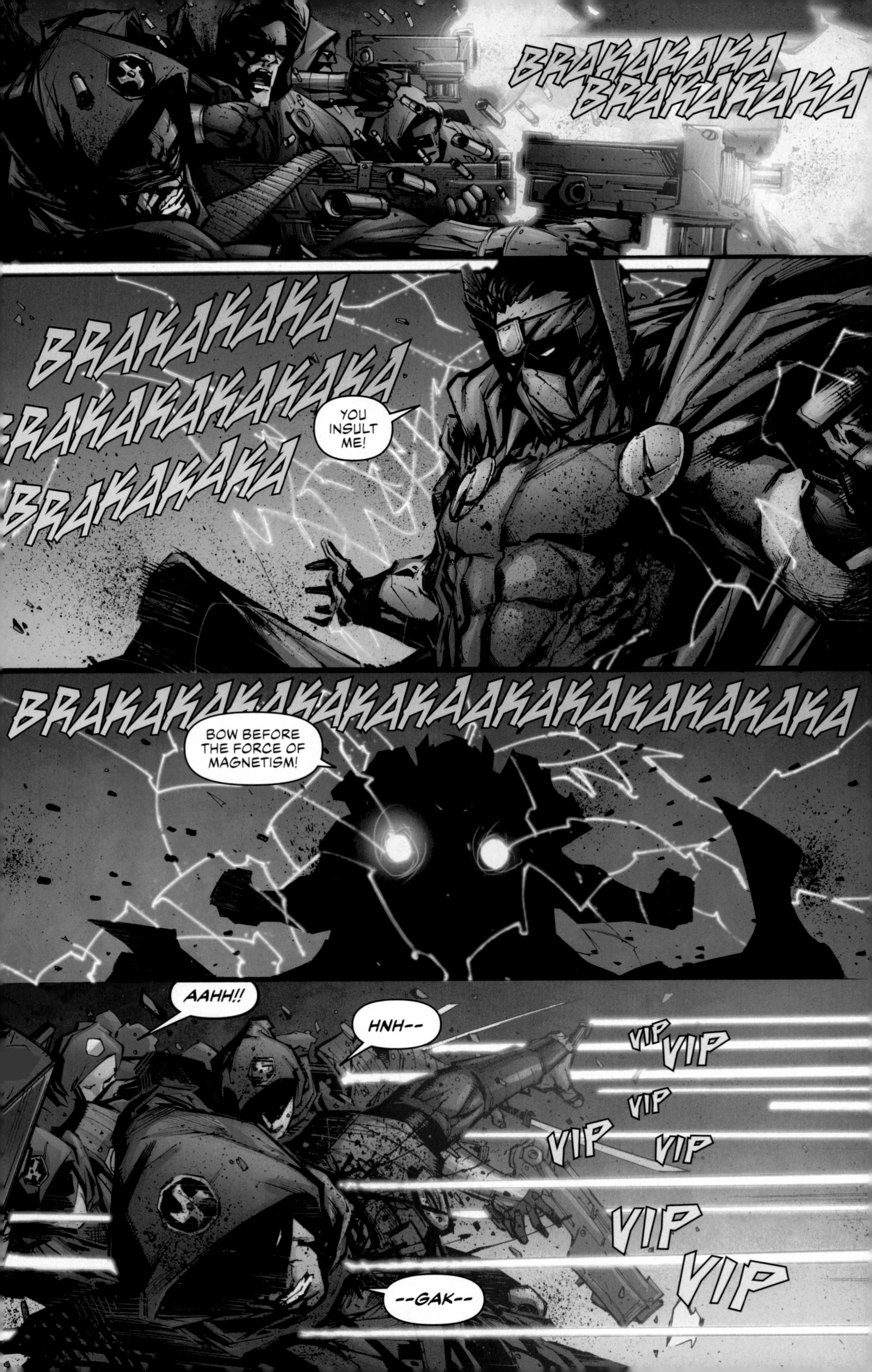
BRAKAKAKA
BRAKAKAKA
BRAKAKAKA
BRAKAKAKAKAKA
YOU INSULT ME!
BRAKAKAKA
BRAKAKAKAKAKAKAAKAKAKAKAKAKA
BOW BEFORE THE FORCE OF MAGNETISM!
AAHH!!
HNH--
VIP VIP
VIP
VIP
VIP
VIP
VIP
--GAK--

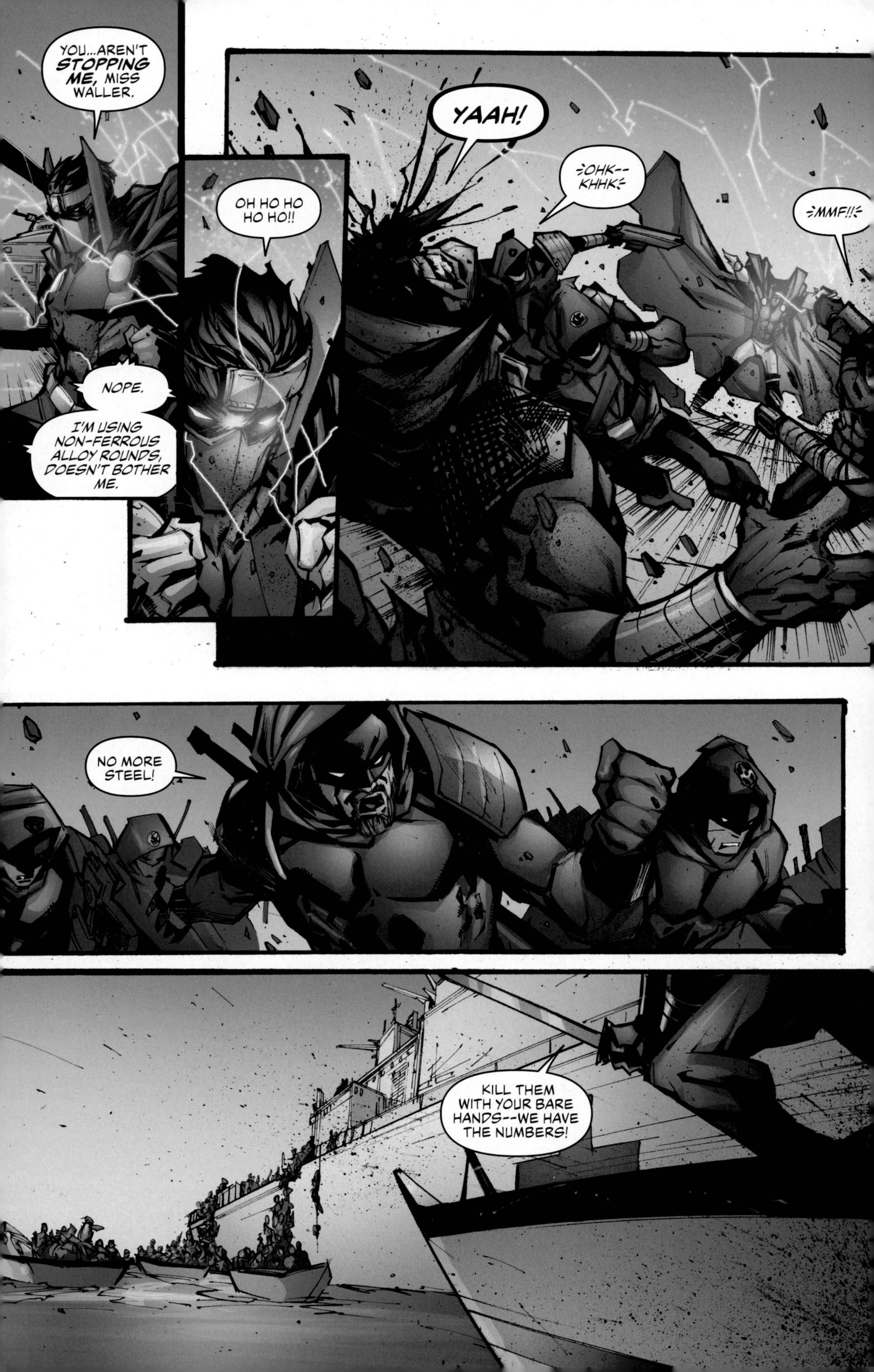

YOU...AREN'T STOPPING ME, MISS WALLER.
OH HO HO HO HO!!
NOPE.
I'M USING NON-FERROUS ALLOY ROUNDS, DOESN'T BOTHER ME.
YAAH!
OHK-- KHHK
MMF!!
NO MORE STEEL!
KILL THEM WITH YOUR BARE HANDS--WE HAVE THE NUMBERS!

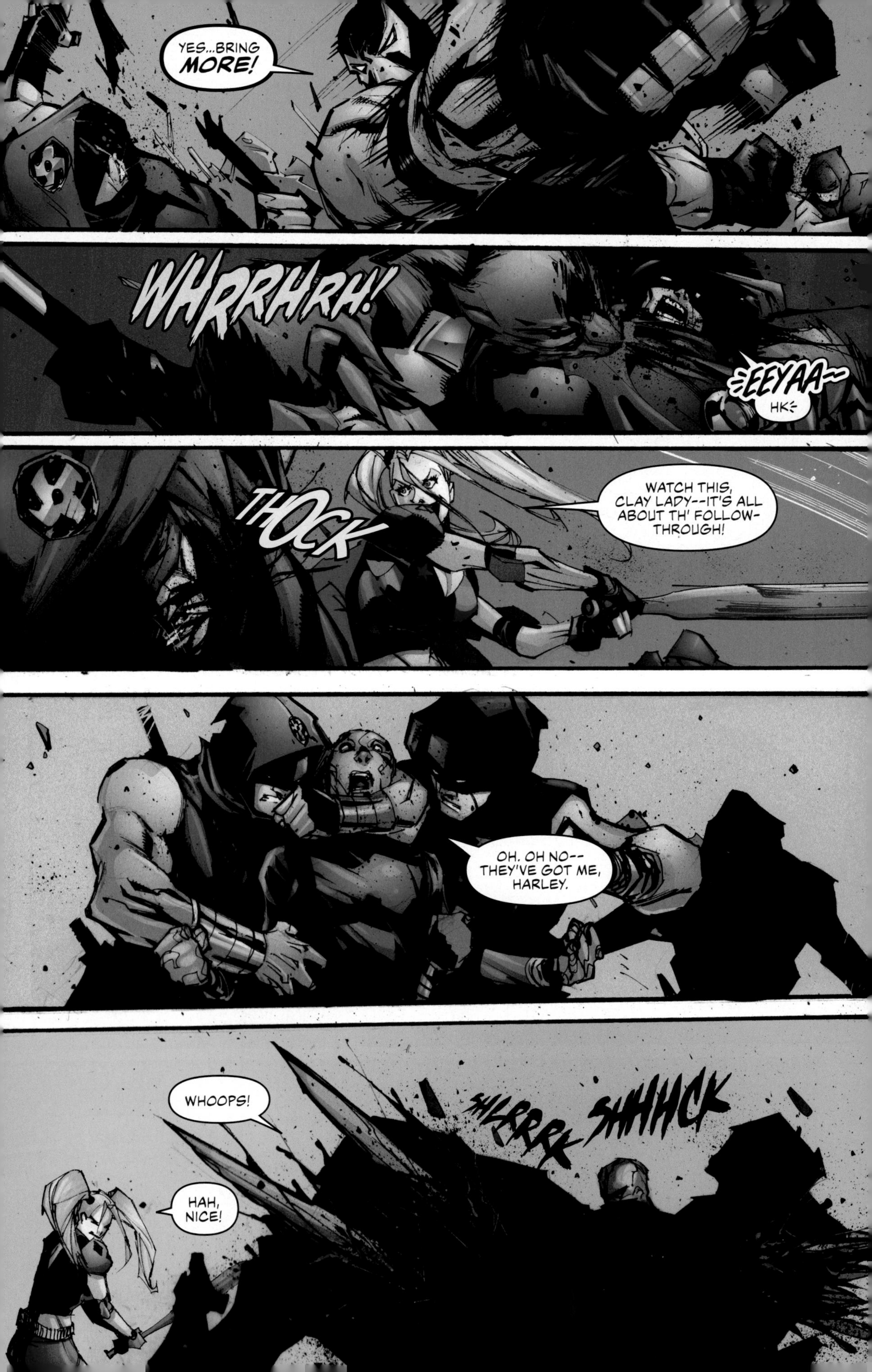

YES...BRING MORE!
WHRRHRH!
EEYAA
HK
THOCK
WATCH THIS, CLAY LADY--IT'S ALL ABOUT TH' FOLLOW-THROUGH!
OH. OH NO--THEY'VE GOT ME, HARLEY.
WHOOPS!
SHLRRRK
SHHHCK
HAH, NICE!

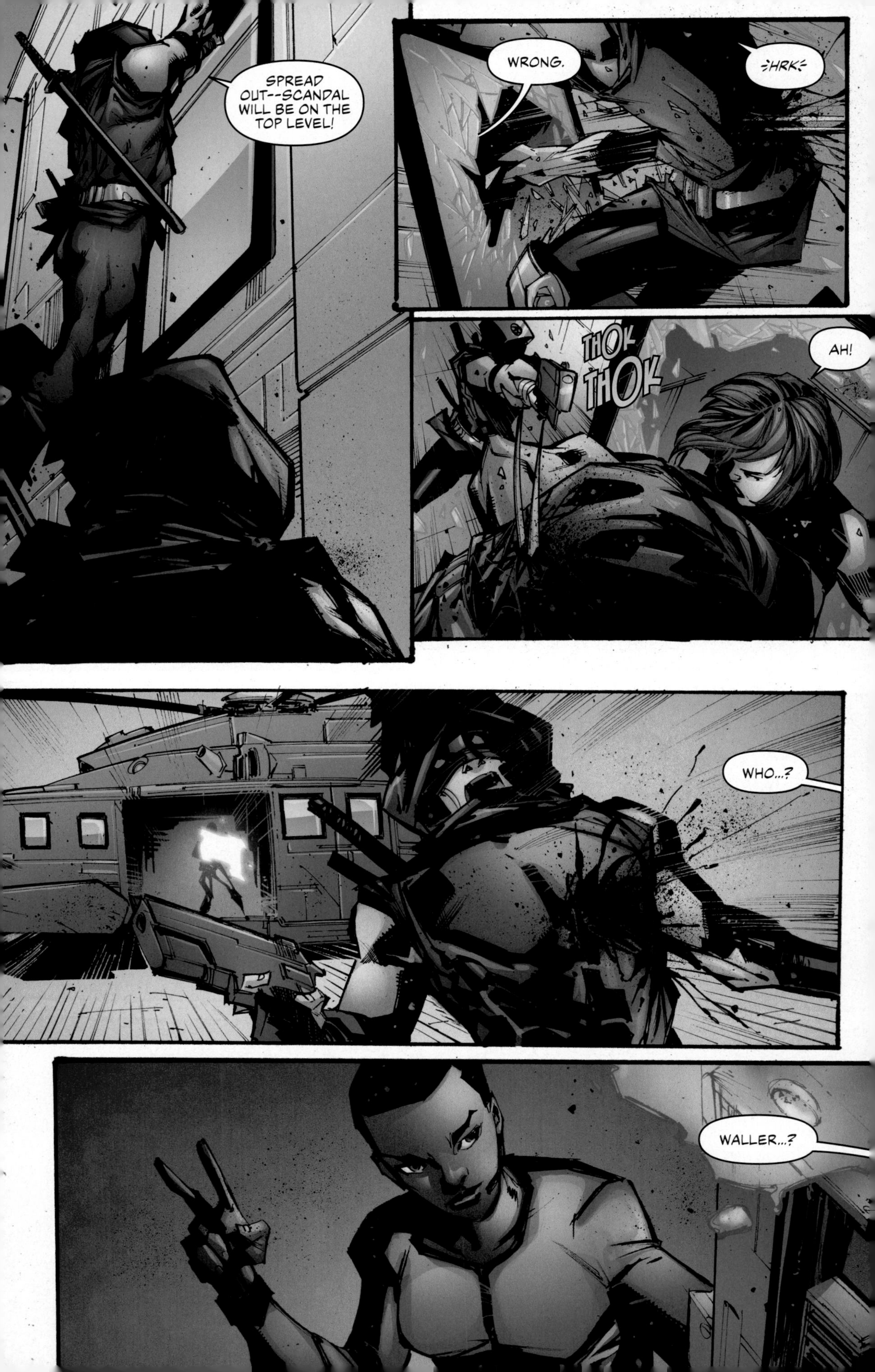
SPREAD OUT--SCANDAL WILL BE ON THE TOP LEVEL!
WRONG.
HRK
THOK
THOK
AH!
WHO...?
WALLER...?

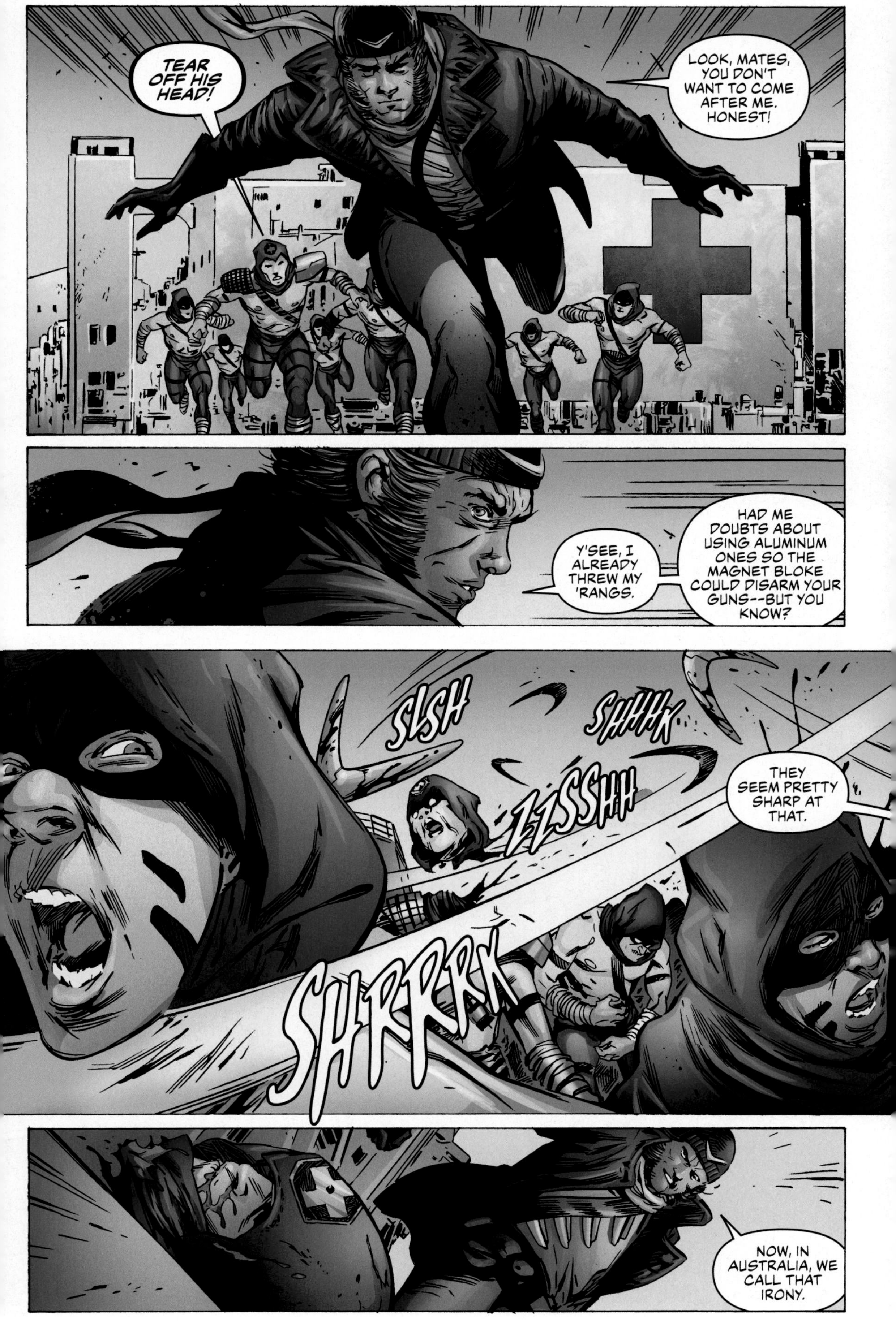
TEAR OFF HIS HEAD!
LOOK, MATES, YOU DON'T WANT TO COME AFTER ME. HONEST!
Y'SEE, I ALREADY THREW MY 'RANGS.
HAD ME DOUBTS ABOUT USING ALUMINUM ONES SO THE MAGNET BLOKE COULD DISARM YOUR GUNS--BUT YOU KNOW?
SLSH
SHHHK
ZZSSHH
THEY SEEM PRETTY SHARP AT THAT.
SHRRRK
NOW, IN AUSTRALIA, WE CALL THAT IRONY.

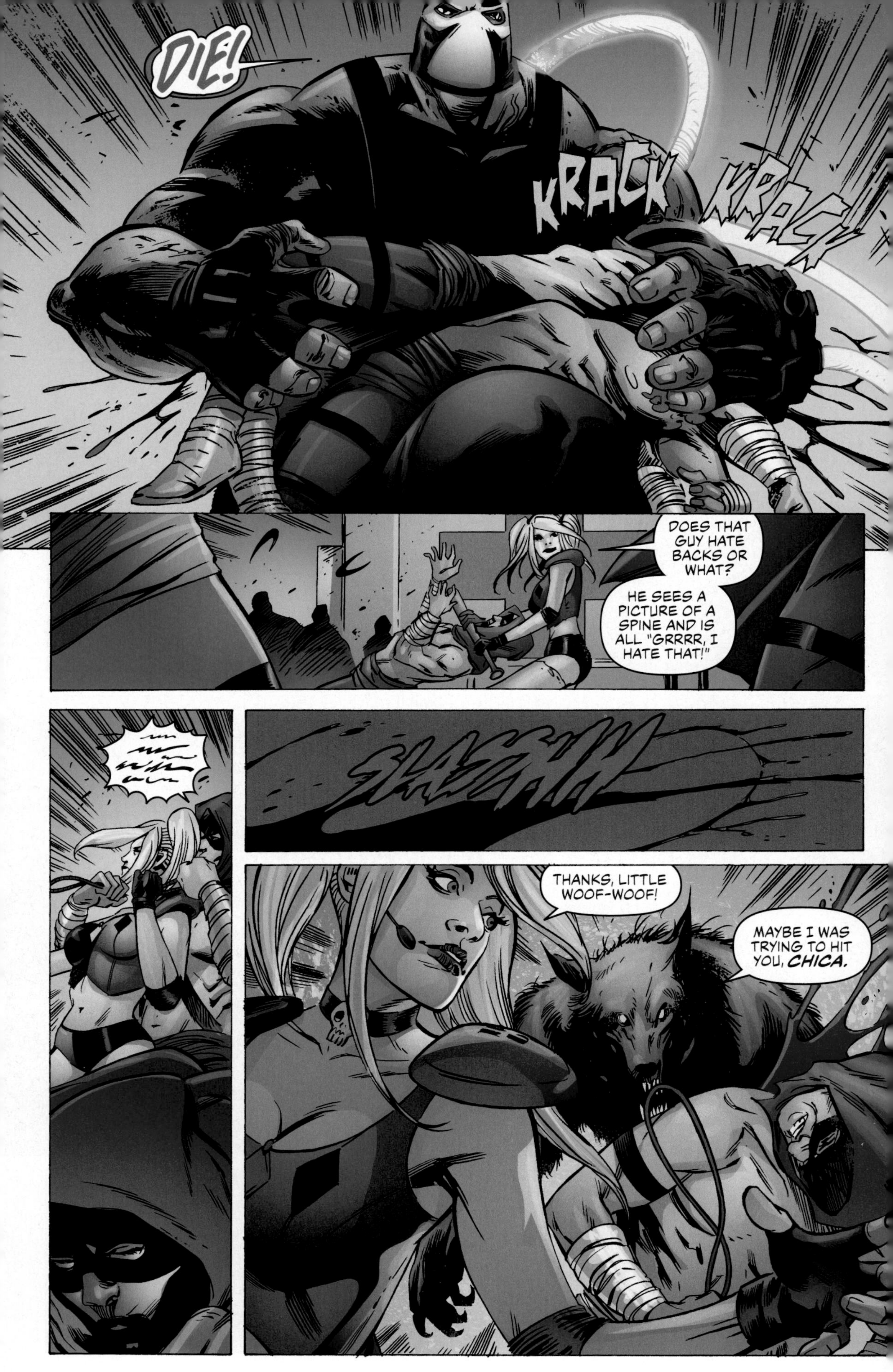
DIE!
KRACK
KRACK
DOES THAT GUY HATE BACKS OR WHAT?
HE SEES A PICTURE OF A SPINE AND IS ALL "GRRRR, I HATE THAT!"
SHASHH
THANKS, LITTLE WOOF-WOOF!
MAYBE I WAS TRYING TO HIT YOU, *CHICA.*

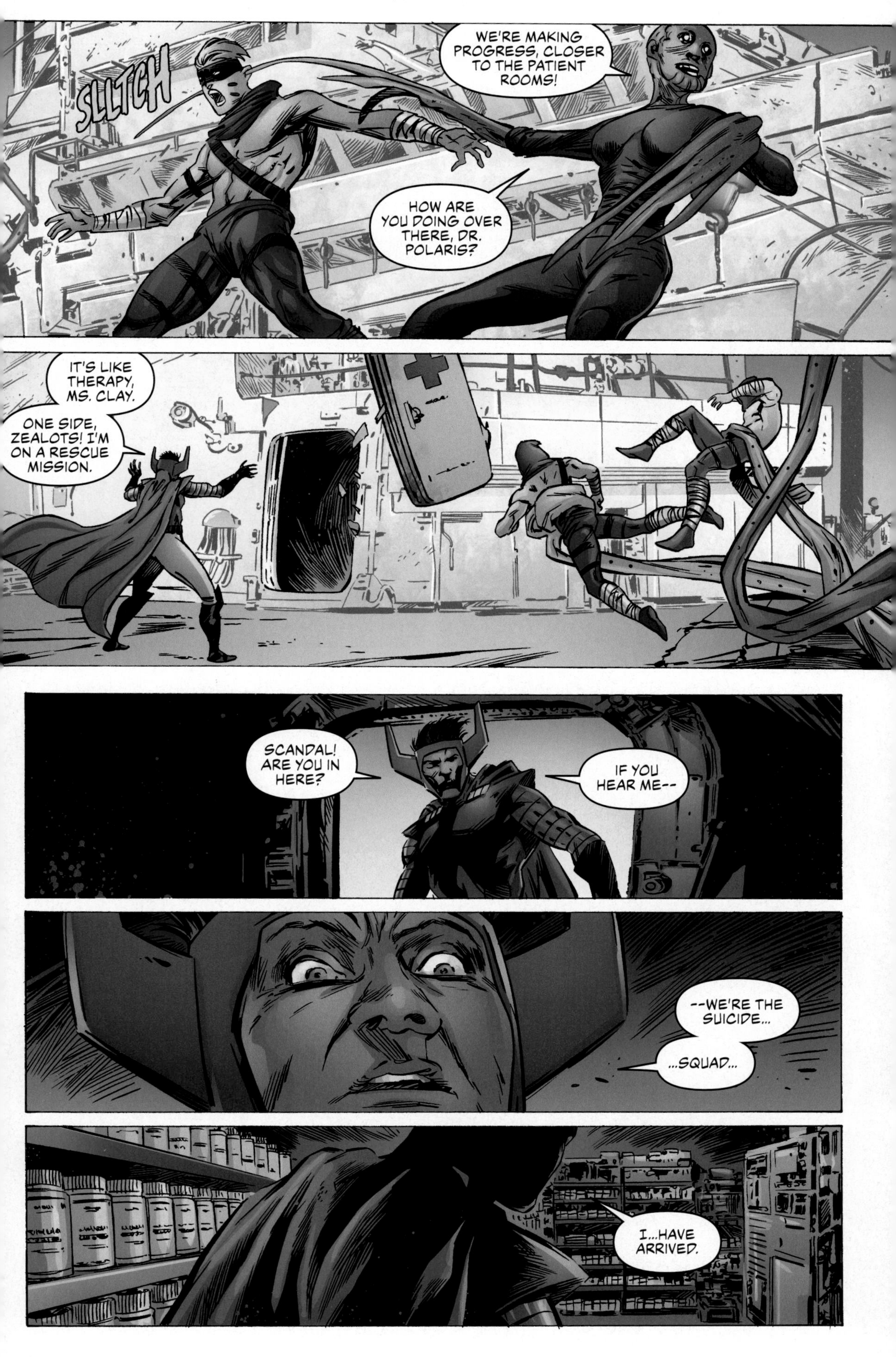
SLLTCH
WE'RE MAKING PROGRESS, CLOSER TO THE PATIENT ROOMS!
HOW ARE YOU DOING OVER THERE, DR. POLARIS?
IT'S LIKE THERAPY, MS. CLAY.
ONE SIDE, ZEALOTS! I'M ON A RESCUE MISSION.
SCANDAL! ARE YOU IN HERE?
IF YOU HEAR ME--
--WE'RE THE SUICIDE...
...SQUAD...
I...HAVE ARRIVED.

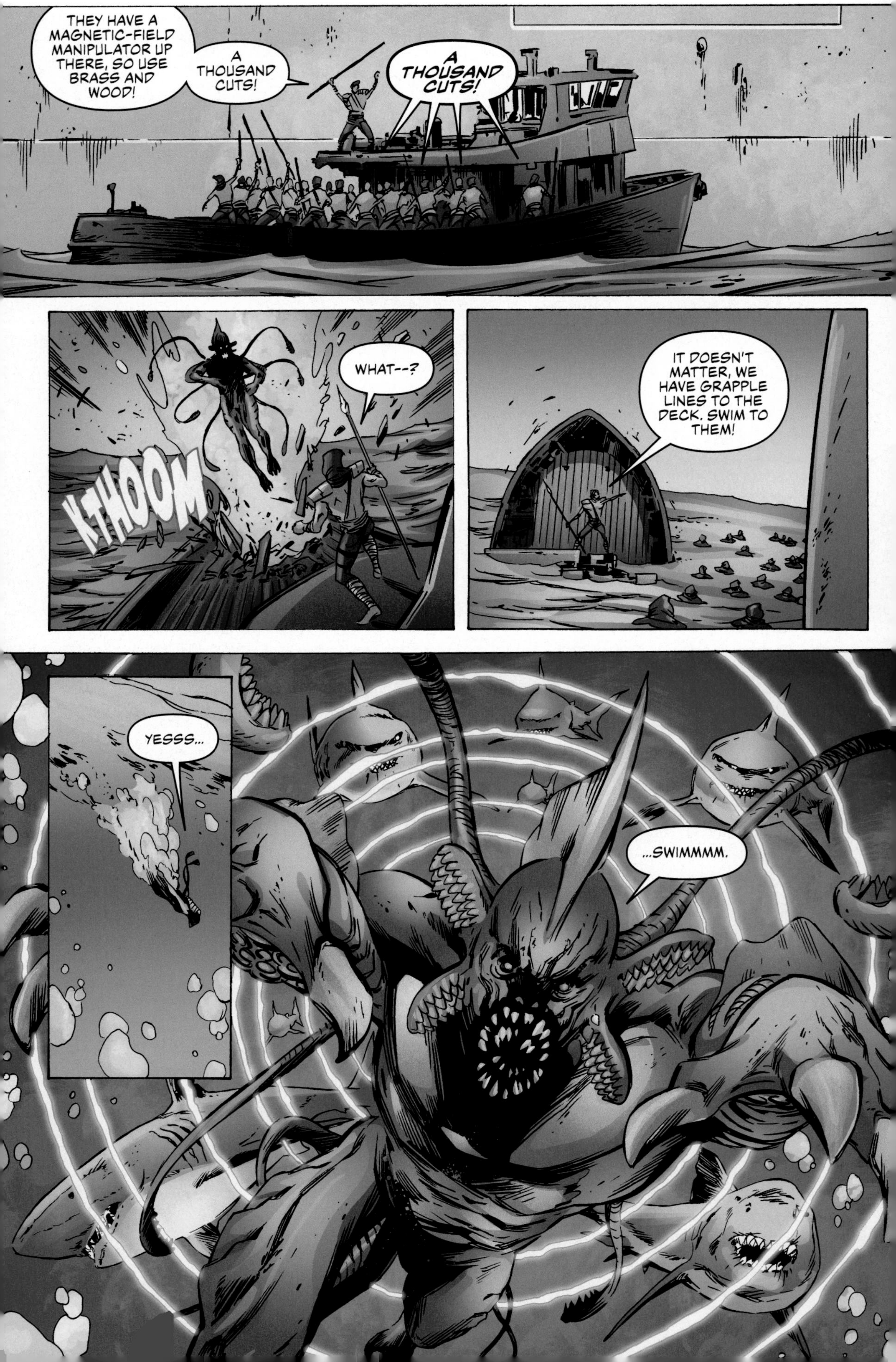
THEY HAVE A MAGNETIC-FIELD MANIPULATOR UP THERE, SO USE BRASS AND WOOD!
A THOUSAND CUTS!
A THOUSAND CUTS!
WHAT--?
KTHOOM
IT DOESN'T MATTER, WE HAVE GRAPPLE LINES TO THE DECK. SWIM TO THEM!
YESSS...
...SWIMMMM.

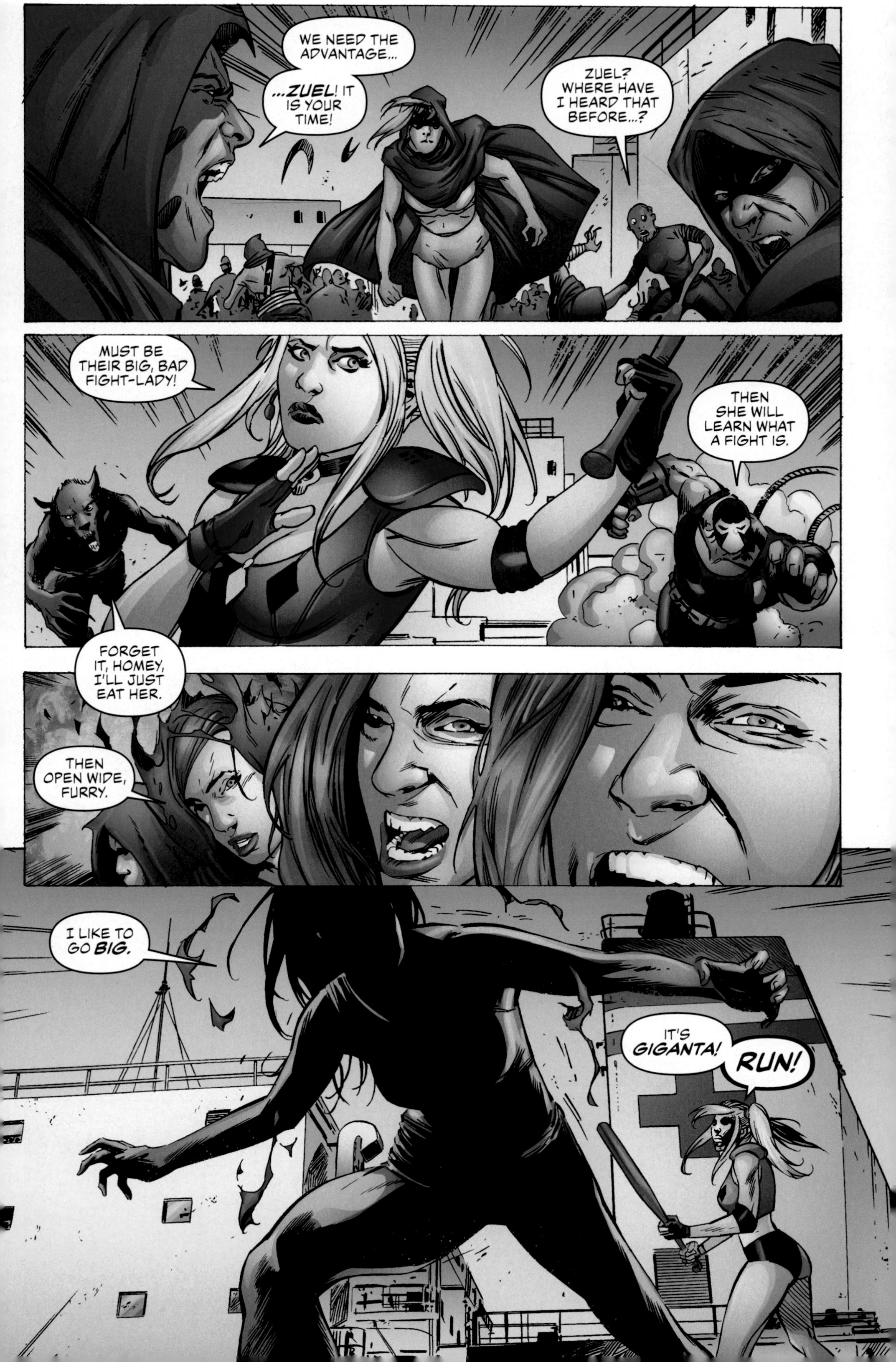
WE NEED THE ADVANTAGE...
...ZUEL! IT IS YOUR TIME!
ZUEL? WHERE HAVE I HEARD THAT BEFORE...?
MUST BE THEIR BIG, BAD FIGHT-LADY!
THEN SHE WILL LEARN WHAT A FIGHT IS.
FORGET IT, HOMEY, I'LL JUST EAT HER.
THEN OPEN WIDE, FURRY.
I LIKE TO GO BIG.
IT'S GIGANTA!
RUN!

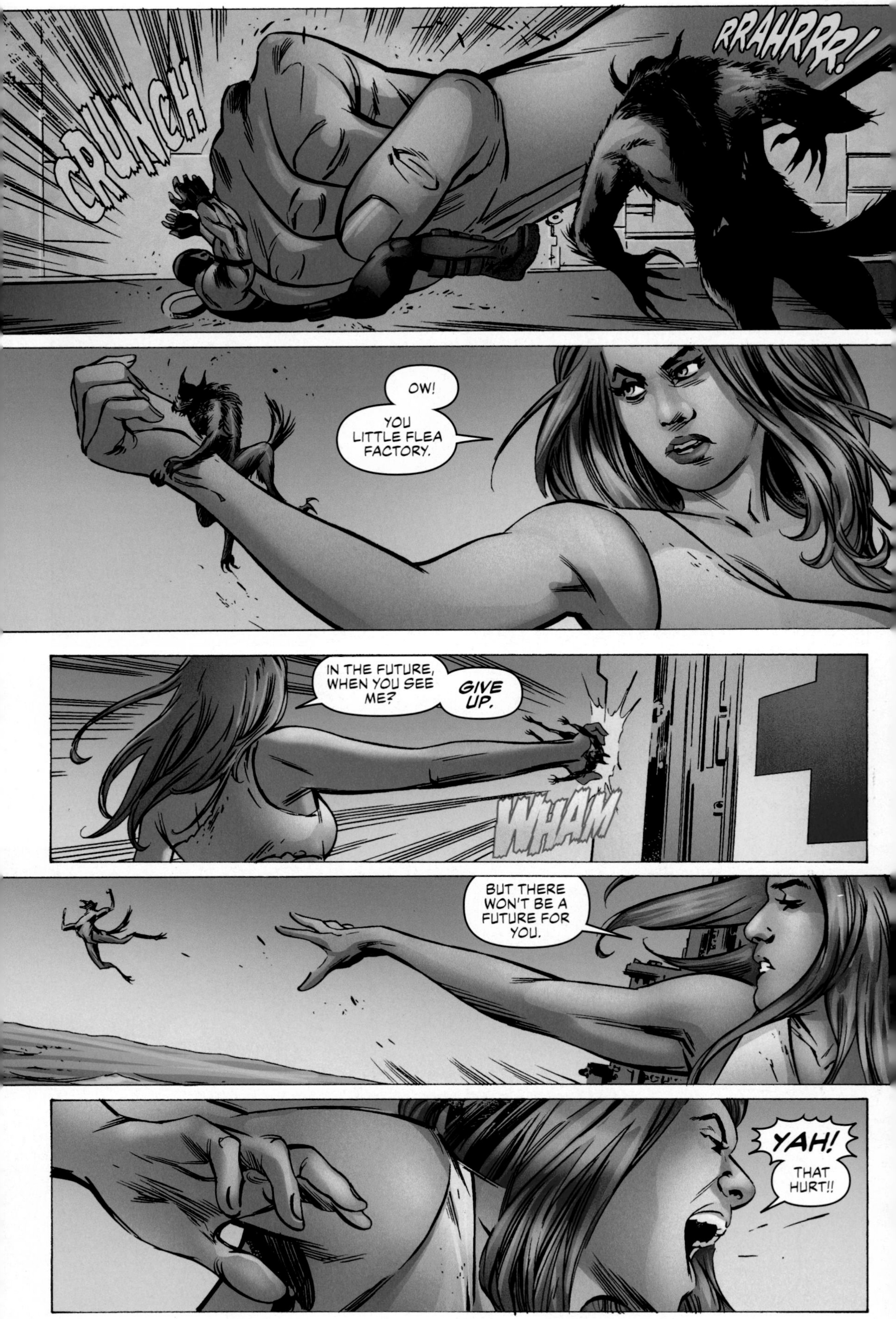
CRUNCH
RRAHRRR!
OW!
YOU LITTLE FLEA FACTORY.
IN THE FUTURE, WHEN YOU SEE ME?
GIVE UP.
WHAM
BUT THERE WON'T BE A FUTURE FOR YOU.
YAH!
THAT HURT!!

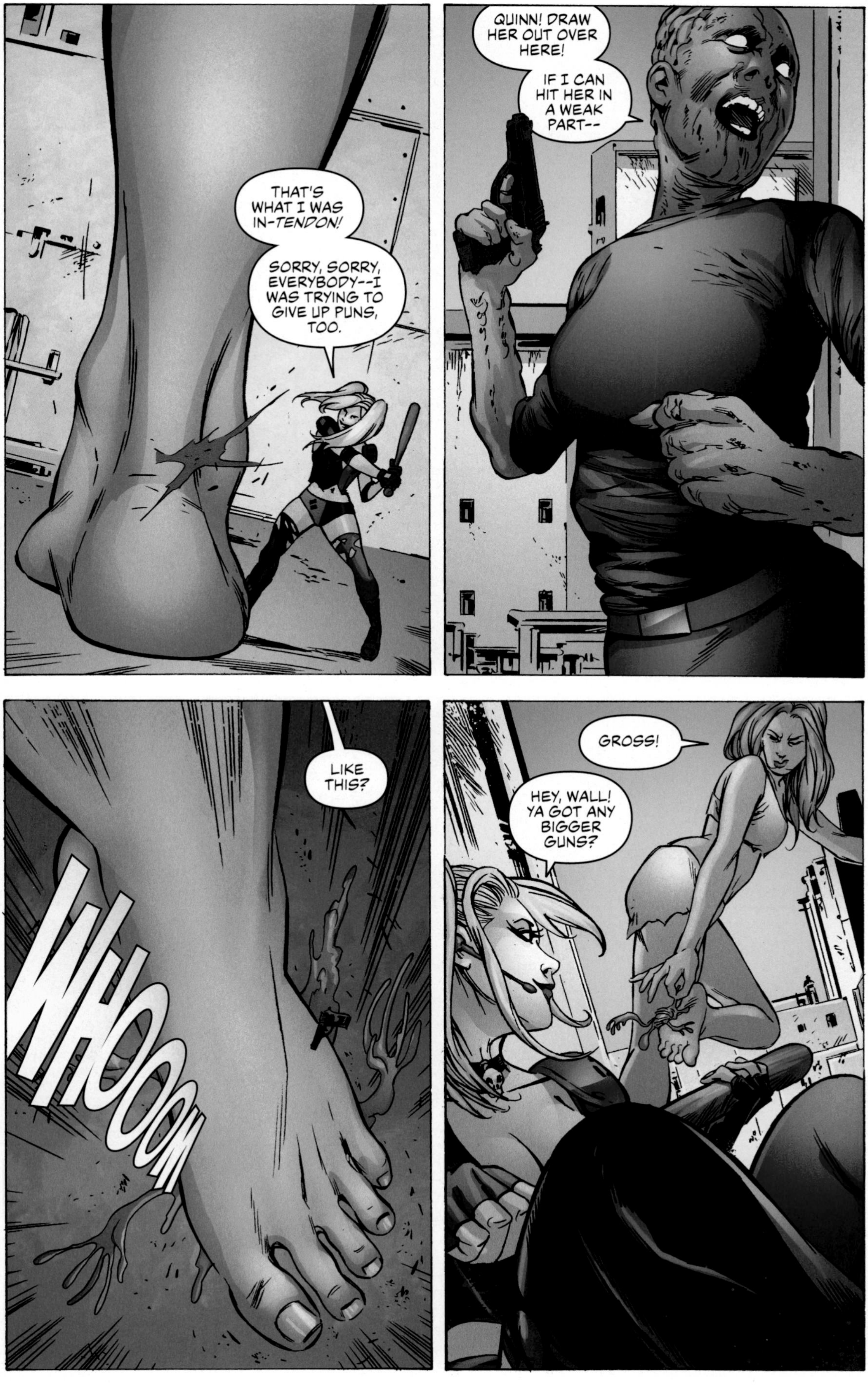
THAT'S WHAT I WAS IN-*TENDON!*
SORRY, SORRY, EVERYBODY--I WAS TRYING TO GIVE UP PUNS, TOO.
QUINN! DRAW HER OUT OVER HERE!
IF I CAN HIT HER IN A WEAK PART--
LIKE THIS?
WHOOOM
GROSS!
HEY, WALL! YA GOT ANY BIGGER GUNS?

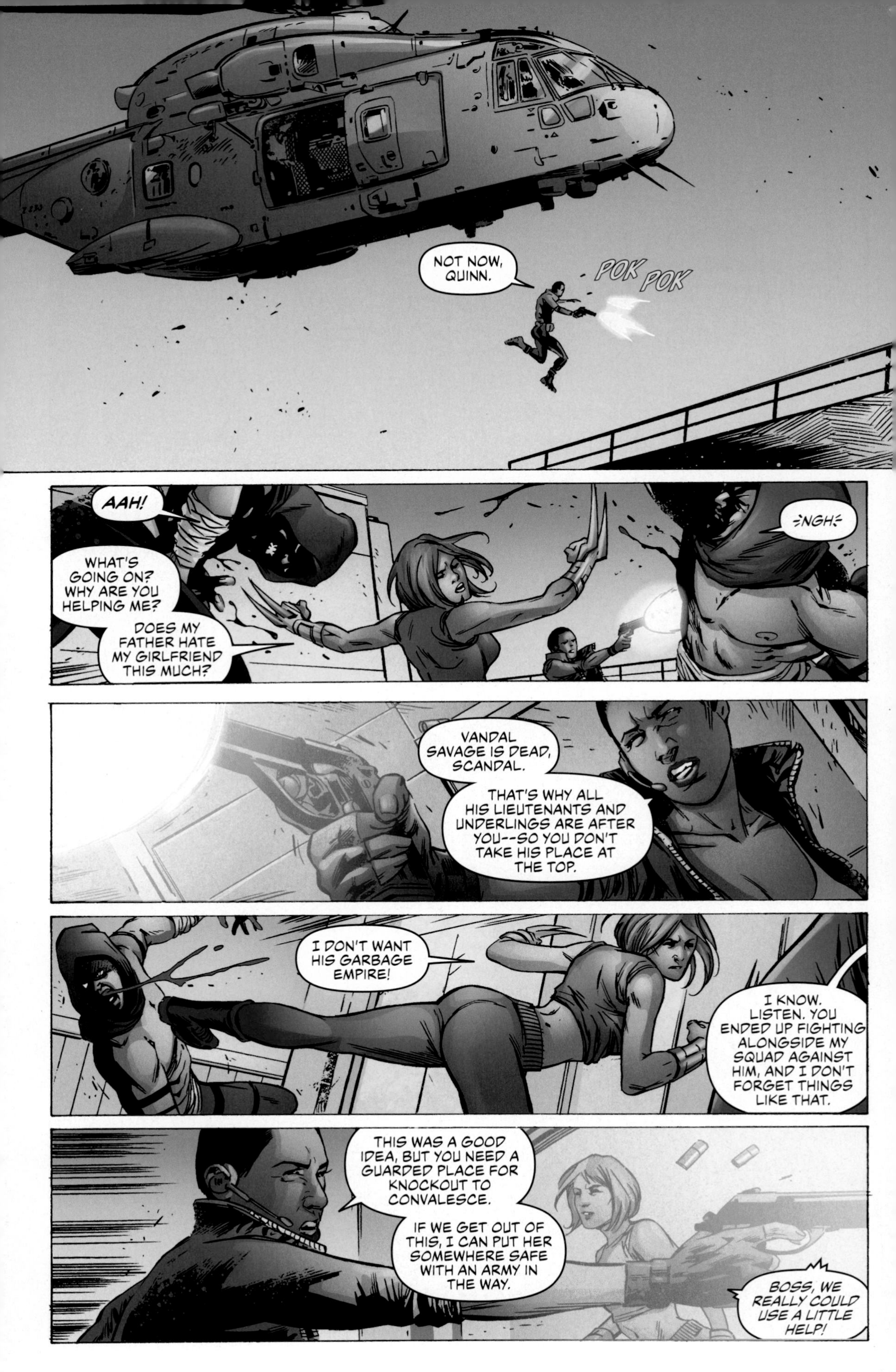
NOT NOW, QUINN.
POK POK
AAH!
NGH
WHAT'S GOING ON? WHY ARE YOU HELPING ME?
DOES MY FATHER HATE MY GIRLFRIEND THIS MUCH?
VANDAL SAVAGE IS DEAD, SCANDAL.
THAT'S WHY ALL HIS LIEUTENANTS AND UNDERLINGS ARE AFTER YOU--SO YOU DON'T TAKE HIS PLACE AT THE TOP.
I DON'T WANT HIS GARBAGE EMPIRE!
I KNOW. LISTEN. YOU ENDED UP FIGHTING ALONGSIDE MY SQUAD AGAINST HIM, AND I DON'T FORGET THINGS LIKE THAT.
THIS WAS A GOOD IDEA, BUT YOU NEED A GUARDED PLACE FOR KNOCKOUT TO CONVALESCE.
IF WE GET OUT OF THIS, I CAN PUT HER SOMEWHERE SAFE WITH AN ARMY IN THE WAY.
BOSS, WE REALLY COULD USE A LITTLE HELP!

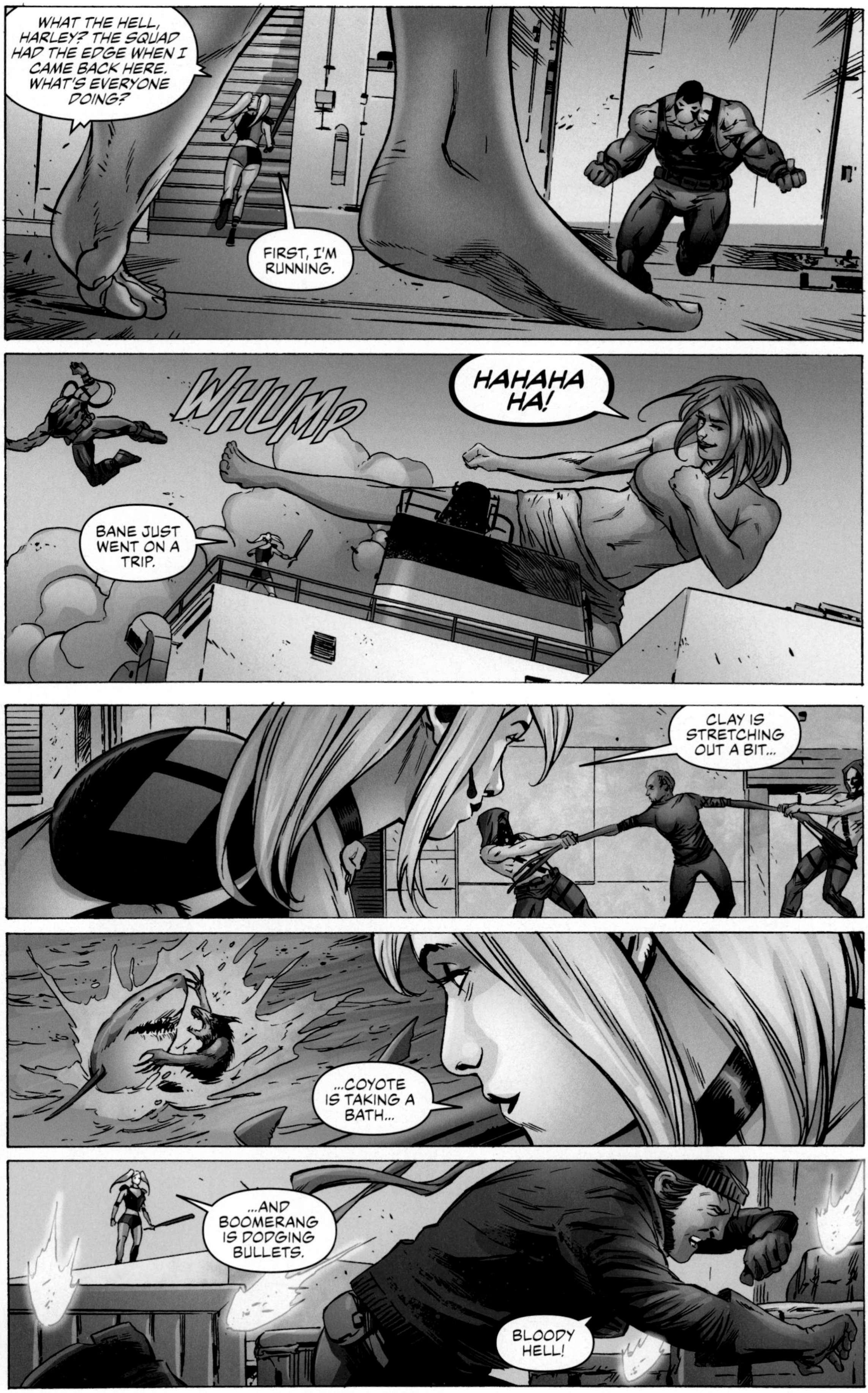
WHAT THE HELL, HARLEY? THE SQUAD HAD THE EDGE WHEN I CAME BACK HERE. WHAT'S EVERYONE DOING?
FIRST, I'M RUNNING.
WHUMP
HAHAHA HA!
BANE JUST WENT ON A TRIP.
CLAY IS STRETCHING OUT A BIT...
...COYOTE IS TAKING A BATH...
...AND BOOMERANG IS DODGING BULLETS.
BLOODY HELL!

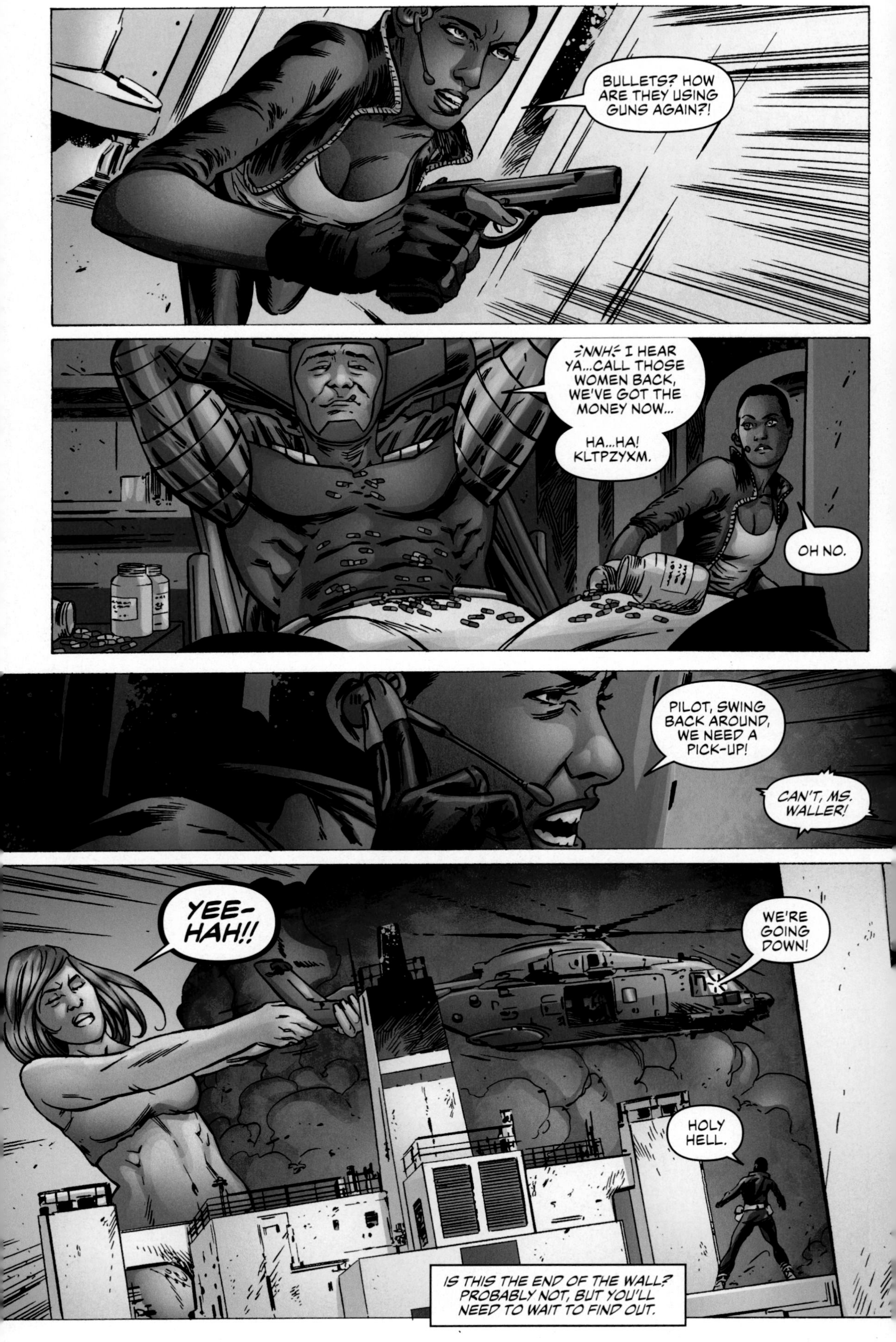
BULLETS? HOW ARE THEY USING GUNS AGAIN?!
=NNH= I HEAR YA...CALL THOSE WOMEN BACK, WE'VE GOT THE MONEY NOW...
HA...HA! KLTPZYXM.
OH NO.
PILOT, SWING BACK AROUND, WE NEED A PICK-UP!
CAN'T, MS. WALLER!
YEE-HAH!!
WE'RE GOING DOWN!
HOLY HELL.
IS THIS THE END OF THE WALL? PROBABLY NOT, BUT YOU'LL NEED TO WAIT TO FIND OUT.

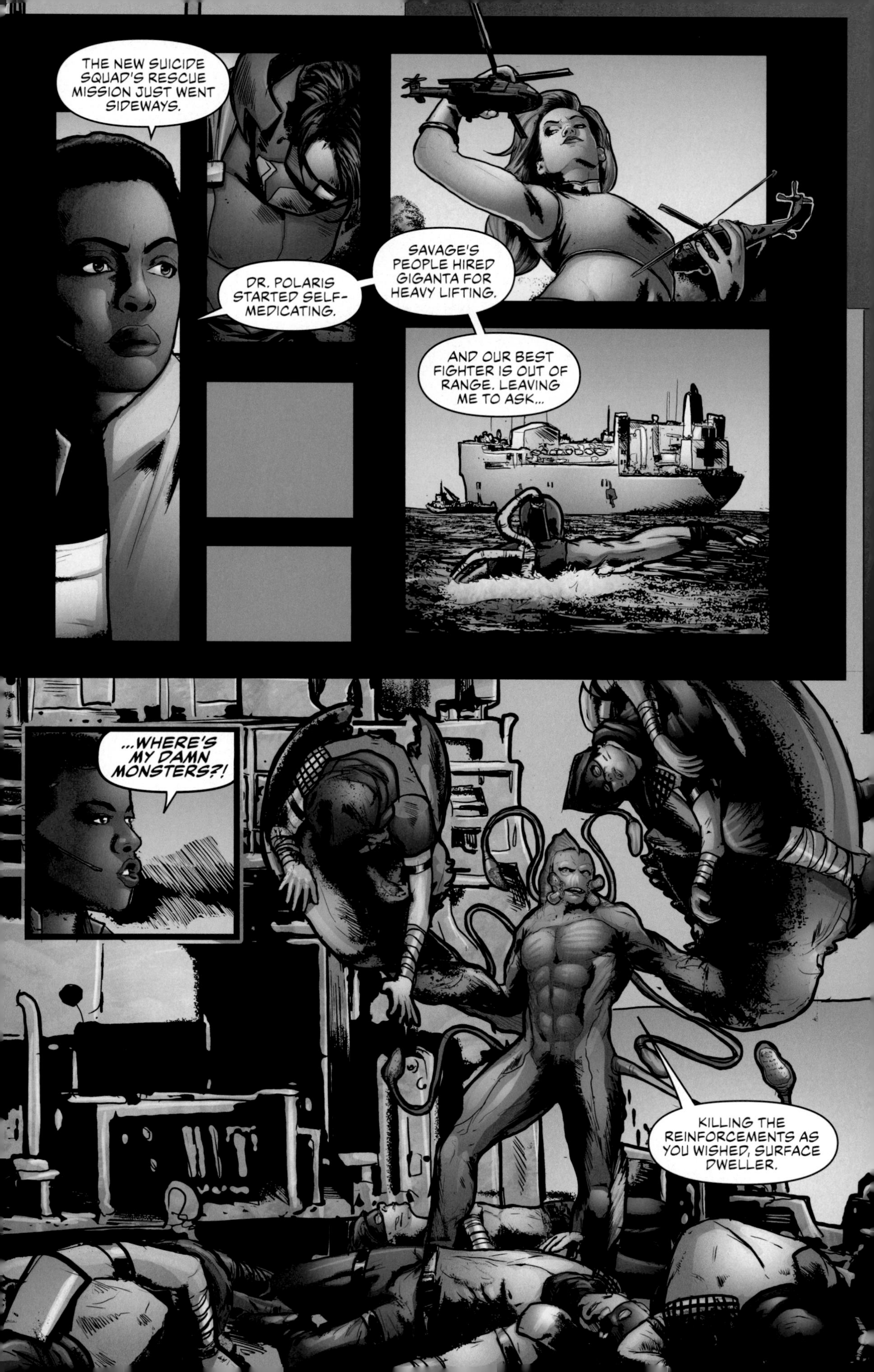
THE NEW SUICIDE SQUAD'S RESCUE MISSION JUST WENT SIDEWAYS.
DR. POLARIS STARTED SELF-MEDICATING.
SAVAGE'S PEOPLE HIRED GIGANTA FOR HEAVY LIFTING.
AND OUR BEST FIGHTER IS OUT OF RANGE. LEAVING ME TO ASK...
...WHERE'S MY DAMN MONSTERS?!
KILLING THE REINFORCEMENTS AS YOU WISHED, SURFACE DWELLER.

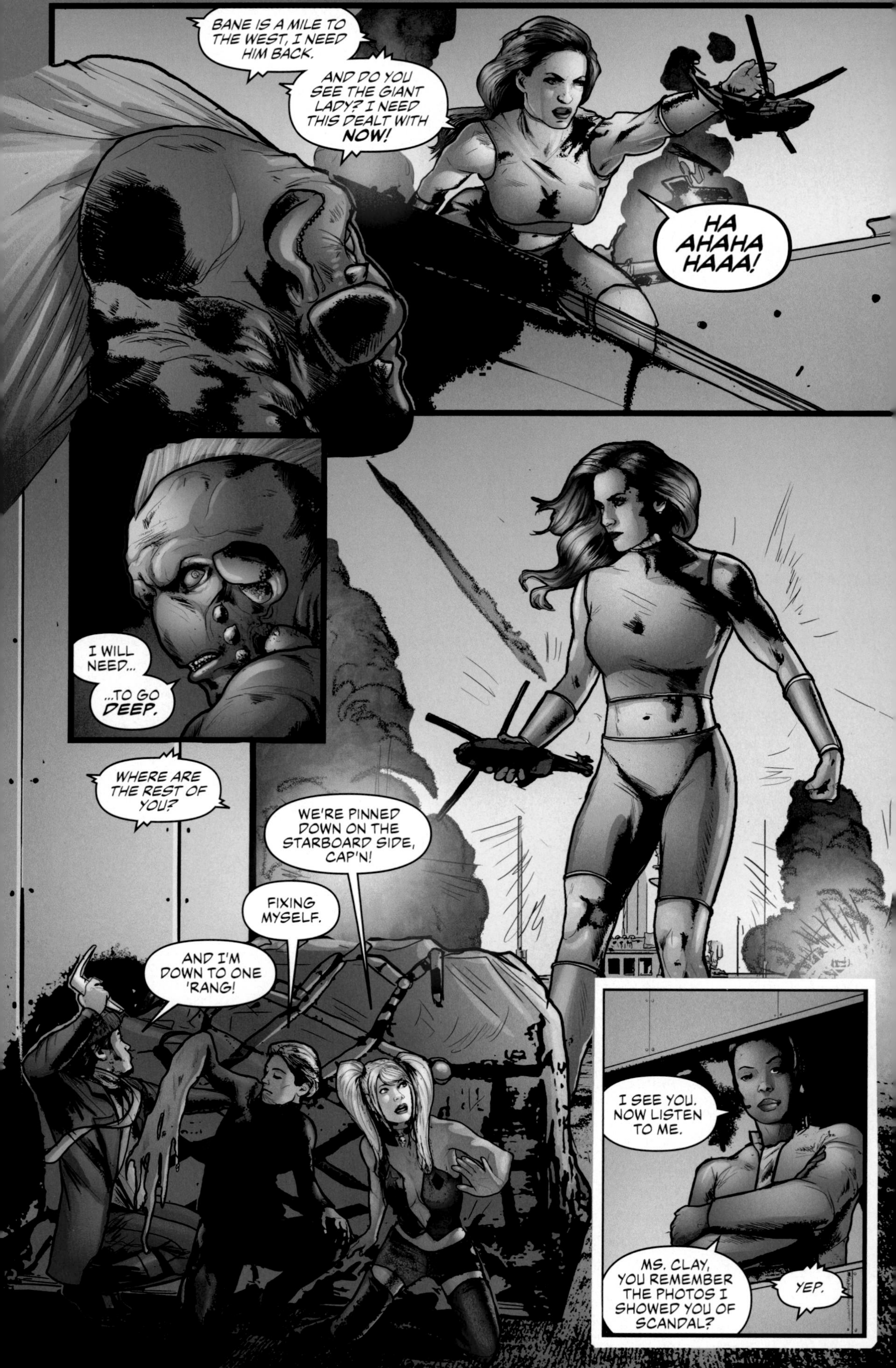
BANE IS A MILE TO THE WEST, I NEED HIM BACK.
AND DO YOU SEE THE GIANT LADY? I NEED THIS DEALT WITH NOW!
HA AHAHA HAAA!
I WILL NEED...
...TO GO DEEP.
WHERE ARE THE REST OF YOU?
WE'RE PINNED DOWN ON THE STARBOARD SIDE, CAP'N!
FIXING MYSELF.
AND I'M DOWN TO ONE 'RANG!
I SEE YOU. NOW LISTEN TO ME.
MS. CLAY, YOU REMEMBER THE PHOTOS I SHOWED YOU OF SCANDAL?
YEP.

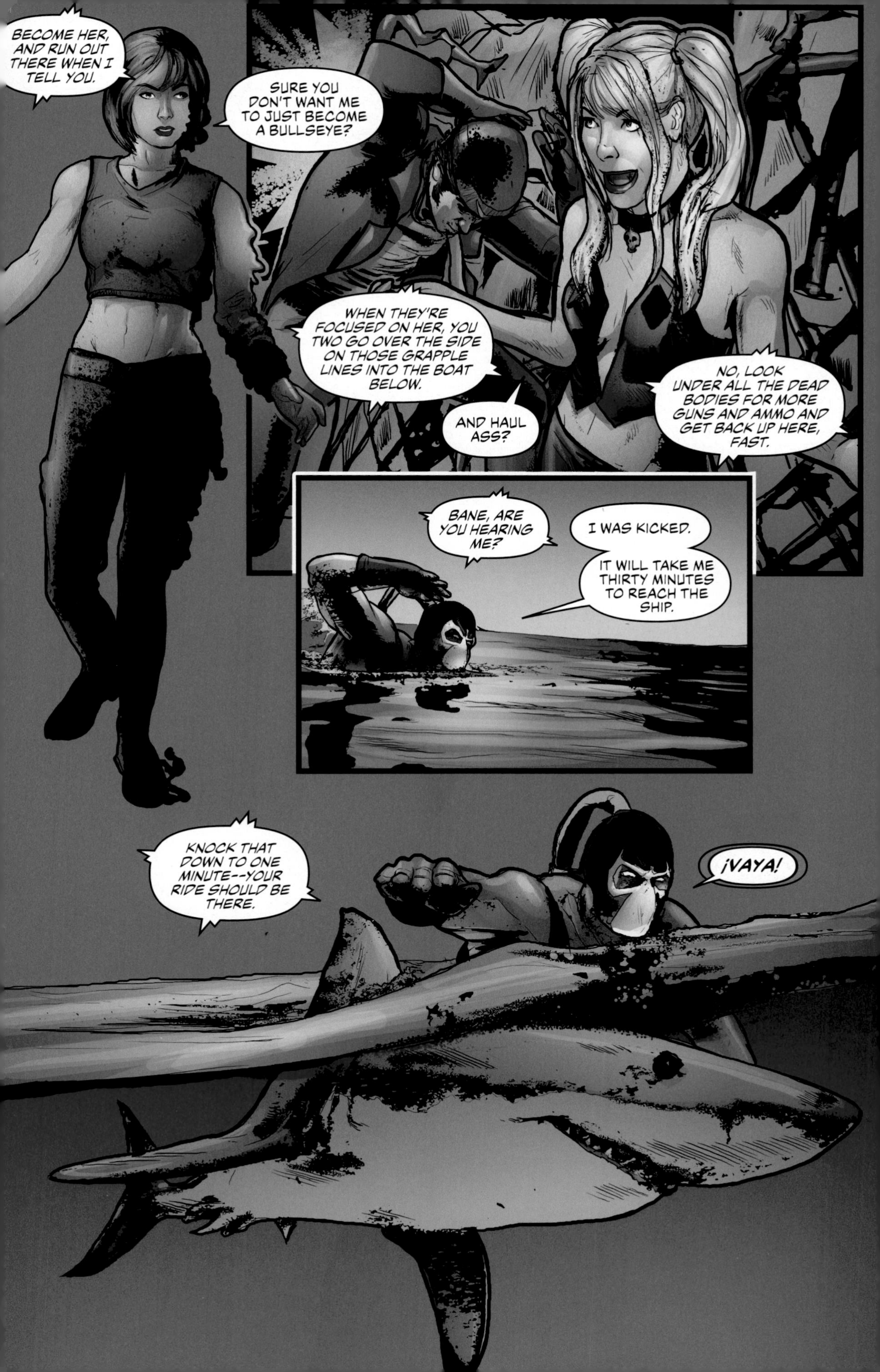
BECOME HER, AND RUN OUT THERE WHEN I TELL YOU.
SURE YOU DON'T WANT ME TO JUST BECOME A BULLSEYE?
WHEN THEY'RE FOCUSED ON HER, YOU TWO GO OVER THE SIDE ON THOSE GRAPPLE LINES INTO THE BOAT BELOW.
AND HAUL ASS?
NO, LOOK UNDER ALL THE DEAD BODIES FOR MORE GUNS AND AMMO AND GET BACK UP HERE, FAST.
BANE, ARE YOU HEARING ME?
I WAS KICKED.
IT WILL TAKE ME THIRTY MINUTES TO REACH THE SHIP.
KNOCK THAT DOWN TO ONE MINUTE--YOUR RIDE SHOULD BE THERE.
¡VAYA!

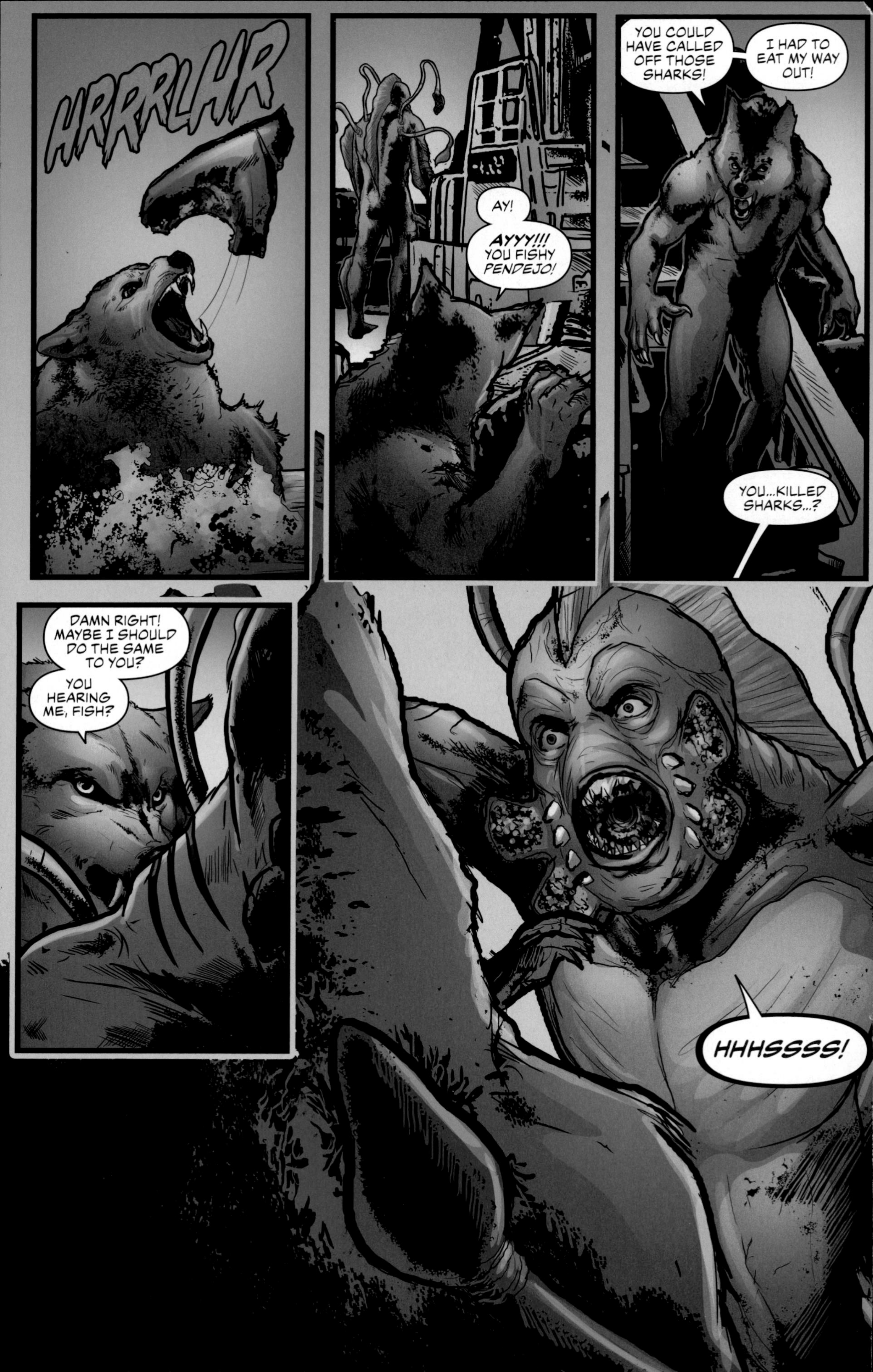
HRRRLHR
AY!
AYYY!!! YOU FISHY PENDEJO!
YOU COULD HAVE CALLED OFF THOSE SHARKS!
I HAD TO EAT MY WAY OUT!
YOU...KILLED SHARKS...?
DAMN RIGHT! MAYBE I SHOULD DO THE SAME TO YOU?
YOU HEARING ME, FISH?
HHHSSSS!

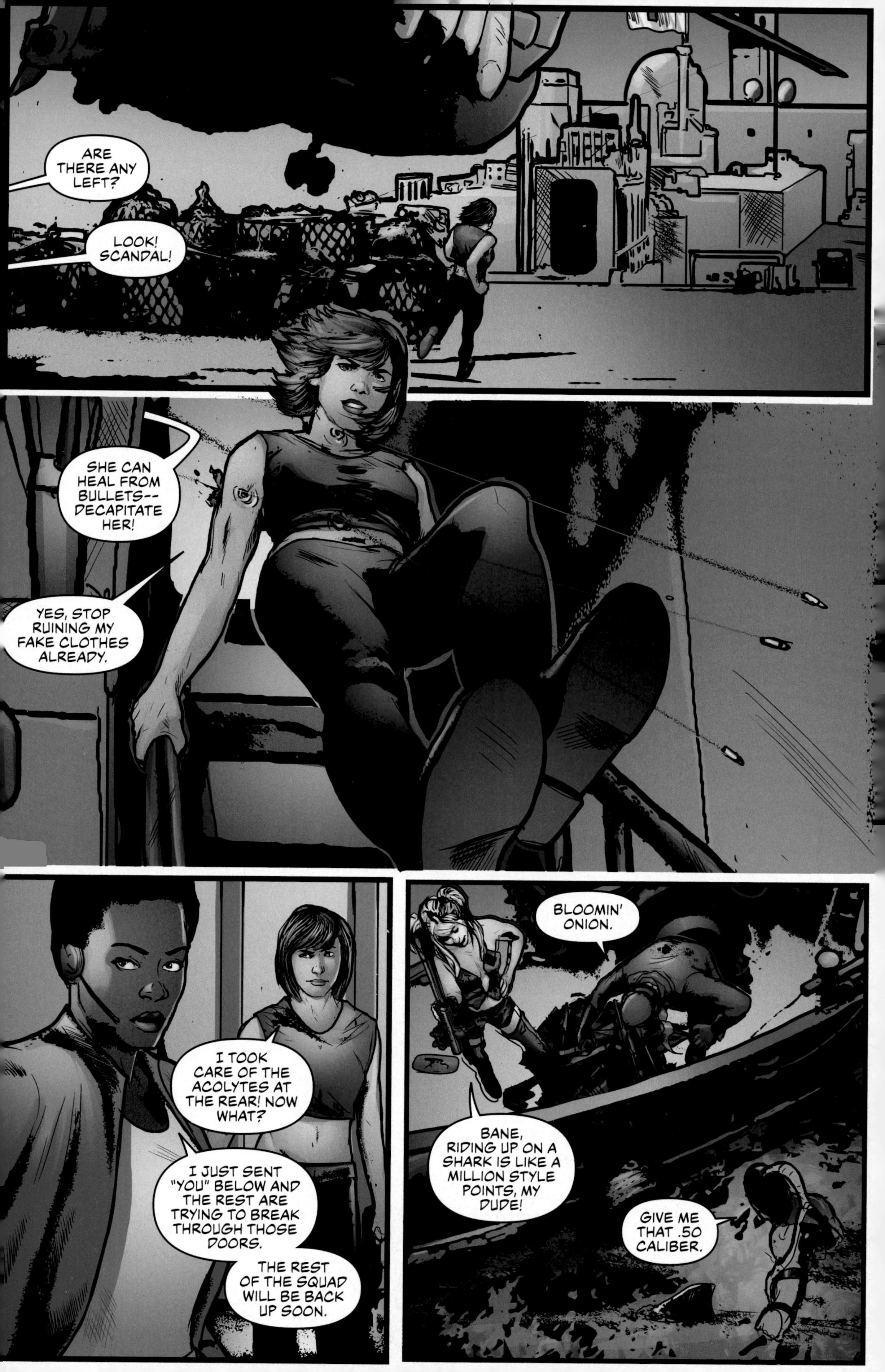

ARE THERE ANY LEFT?
LOOK! SCANDAL!
SHE CAN HEAL FROM BULLETS-- DECAPITATE HER!
YES, STOP RUINING MY FAKE CLOTHES ALREADY.
I TOOK CARE OF THE ACOLYTES AT THE REAR! NOW WHAT?
I JUST SENT "YOU" BELOW AND THE REST ARE TRYING TO BREAK THROUGH THOSE DOORS.
THE REST OF THE SQUAD WILL BE BACK UP SOON.
BLOOMIN' ONION.
BANE, RIDING UP ON A SHARK IS LIKE A MILLION STYLE POINTS, MY DUDE!
GIVE ME THAT .50 CALIBER.

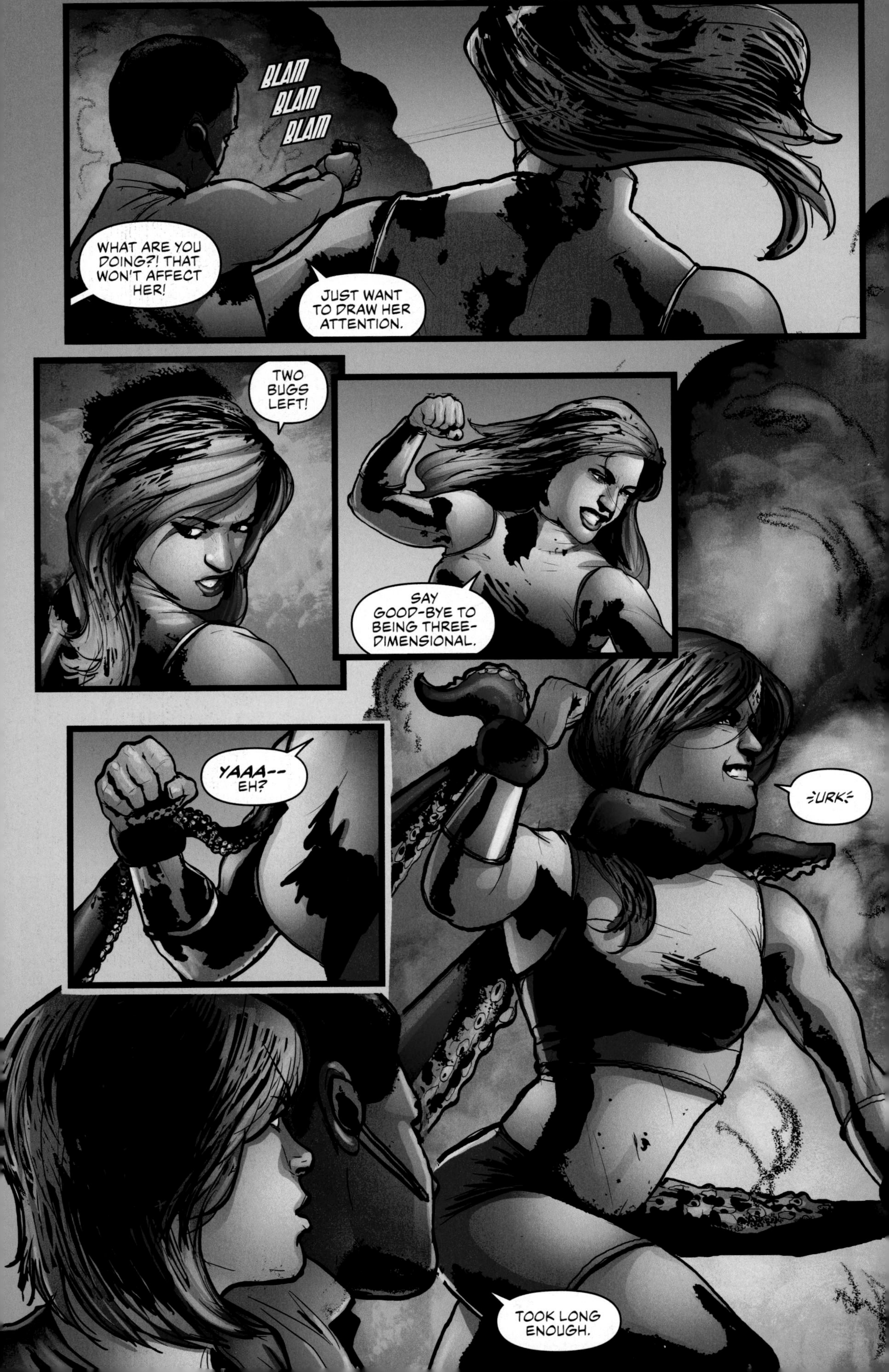
BLAM
BLAM
BLAM
WHAT ARE YOU DOING?! THAT WON'T AFFECT HER!
JUST WANT TO DRAW HER ATTENTION.
TWO BUGS LEFT!
SAY GOOD-BYE TO BEING THREE-DIMENSIONAL.
YAAA-- EH?
URK
TOOK LONG ENOUGH.

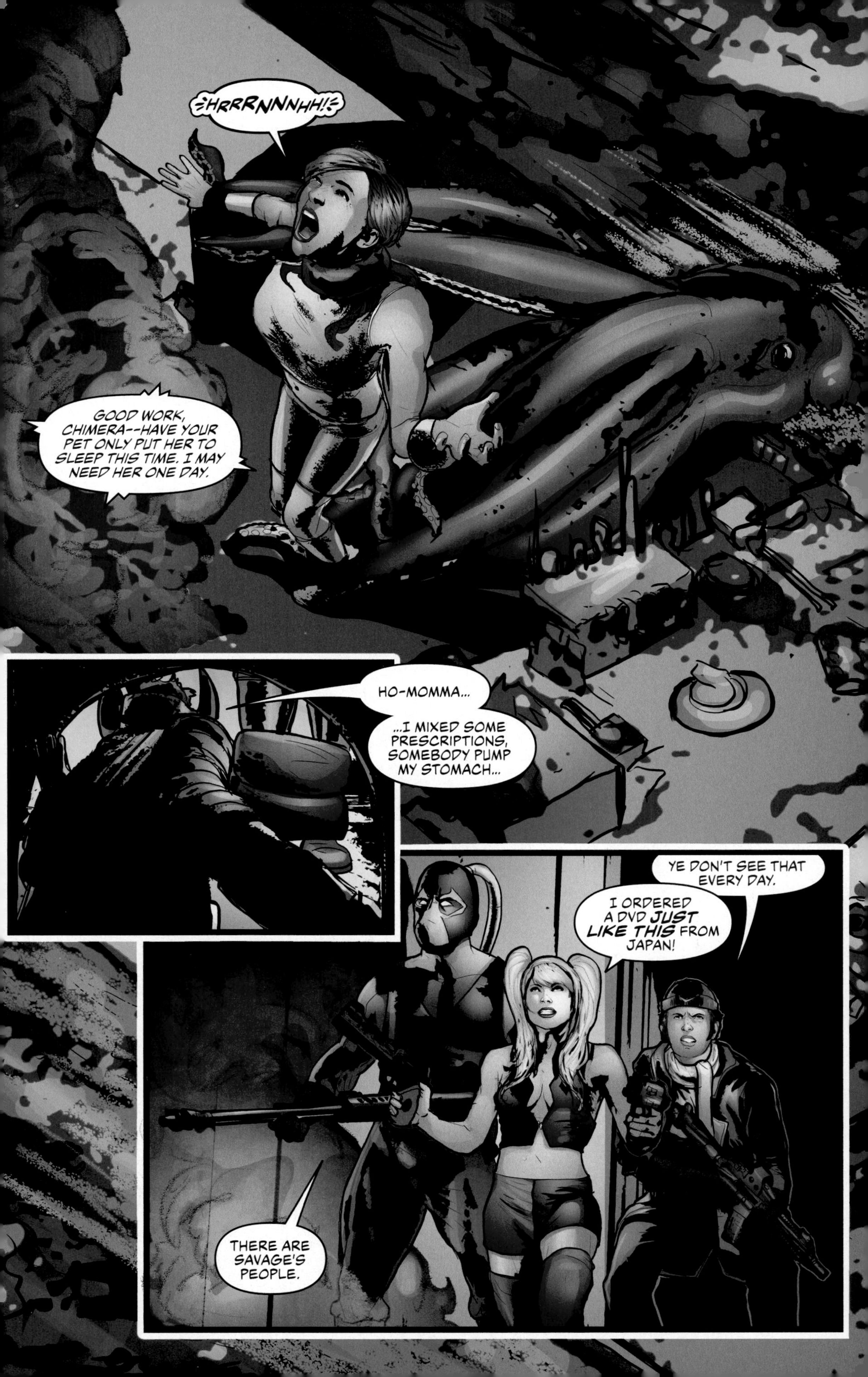
HRRRNNNHH!
GOOD WORK, CHIMERA--HAVE YOUR PET ONLY PUT HER TO SLEEP THIS TIME. I MAY NEED HER ONE DAY.
HO-MOMMA...
...I MIXED SOME PRESCRIPTIONS, SOMEBODY PUMP MY STOMACH...
YE DON'T SEE THAT EVERY DAY.
I ORDERED A DVD JUST LIKE THIS FROM JAPAN!
THERE ARE SAVAGE'S PEOPLE.

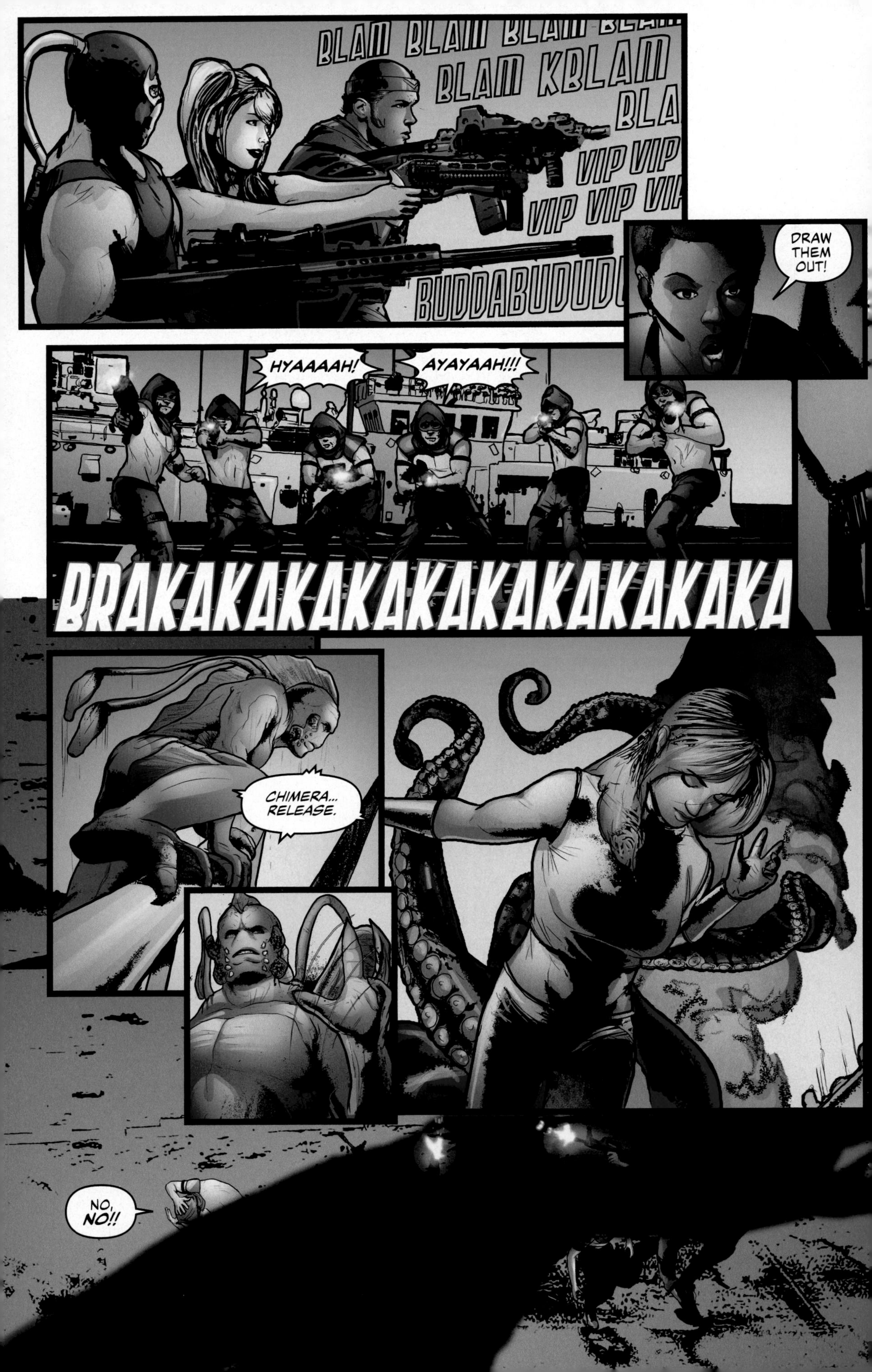
BLAM BLAM BLAM BLAM
BLAM KBLAM
BLA
VIP VIP
VIP VIP VIP
BUDDABUDUDU
DRAW THEM OUT!
HYAAAAH!
AYAYAAH!!!
BRAKAKAKAKAKAKAKAKAKAKAKAKA
CHIMERA... RELEASE.
NO, NO!!

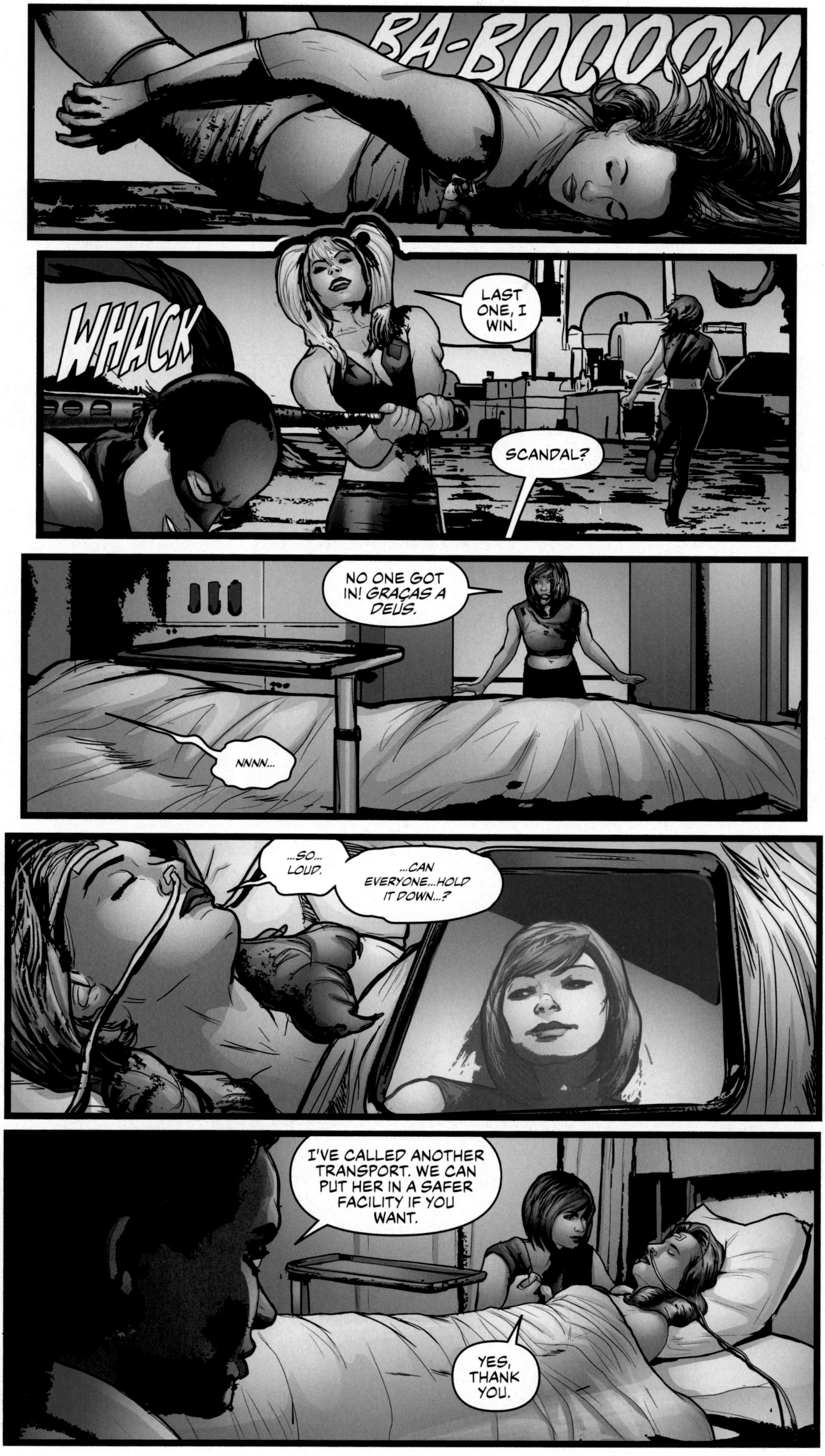
BA-BOOOOOM
WHACK
LAST ONE, I WIN.
SCANDAL?
NO ONE GOT IN! GRAÇAS A DEUS.
NNNN...
...SO... LOUD.
...CAN EVERYONE...HOLD IT DOWN...?
I'VE CALLED ANOTHER TRANSPORT. WE CAN PUT HER IN A SAFER FACILITY IF YOU WANT.
YES, THANK YOU.

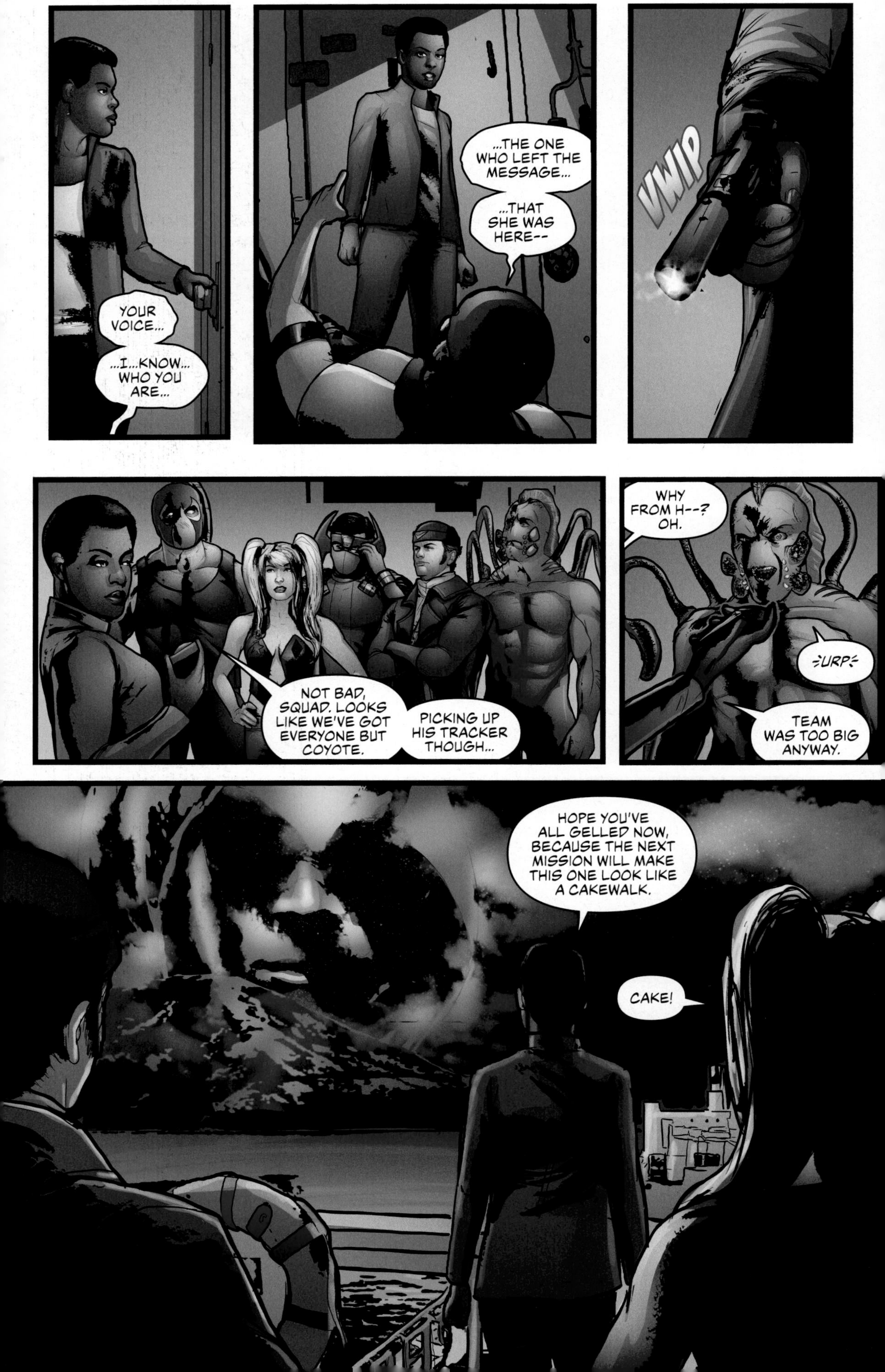
YOUR VOICE...
...I...KNOW... WHO YOU ARE...
...THE ONE WHO LEFT THE MESSAGE...
...THAT SHE WAS HERE--
VWIP
NOT BAD, SQUAD. LOOKS LIKE WE'VE GOT EVERYONE BUT COYOTE.
PICKING UP HIS TRACKER THOUGH...
WHY FROM H--? OH.
=URP=
TEAM WAS TOO BIG ANYWAY.
HOPE YOU'VE ALL GELLED NOW, BECAUSE THE NEXT MISSION WILL MAKE THIS ONE LOOK LIKE A CAKEWALK.
CAKE!

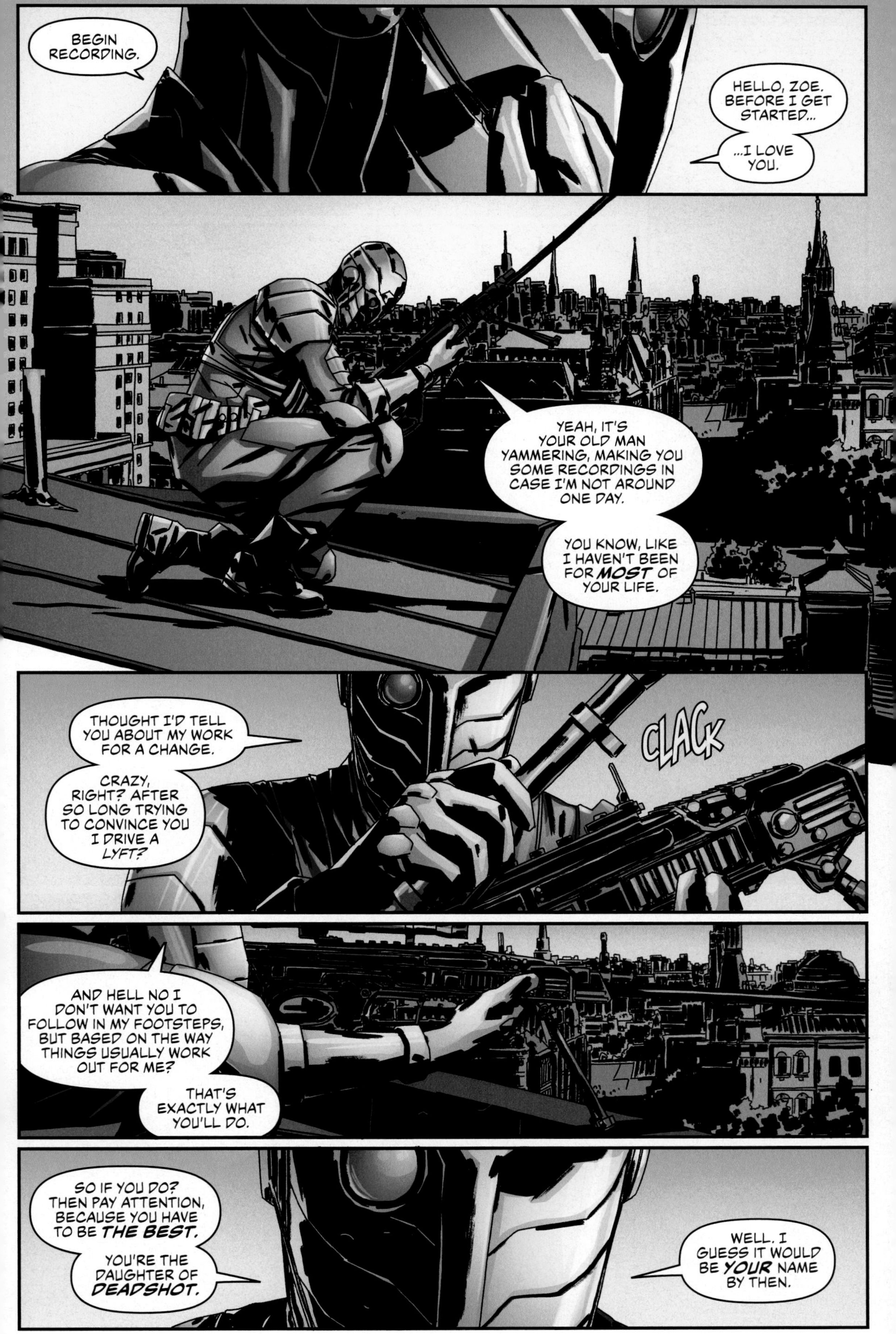
BEGIN RECORDING.
HELLO, ZOE. BEFORE I GET STARTED...
...I LOVE YOU.
YEAH, IT'S YOUR OLD MAN YAMMERING, MAKING YOU SOME RECORDINGS IN CASE I'M NOT AROUND ONE DAY.
YOU KNOW, LIKE I HAVEN'T BEEN FOR MOST OF YOUR LIFE.
THOUGHT I'D TELL YOU ABOUT MY WORK FOR A CHANGE.
CLACK
CRAZY, RIGHT? AFTER SO LONG TRYING TO CONVINCE YOU I DRIVE A LYFT?
AND HELL NO I DON'T WANT YOU TO FOLLOW IN MY FOOTSTEPS, BUT BASED ON THE WAY THINGS USUALLY WORK OUT FOR ME?
THAT'S EXACTLY WHAT YOU'LL DO.
SO IF YOU DO? THEN PAY ATTENTION, BECAUSE YOU HAVE TO BE THE BEST.
YOU'RE THE DAUGHTER OF DEADSHOT.
WELL. I GUESS IT WOULD BE YOUR NAME BY THEN.

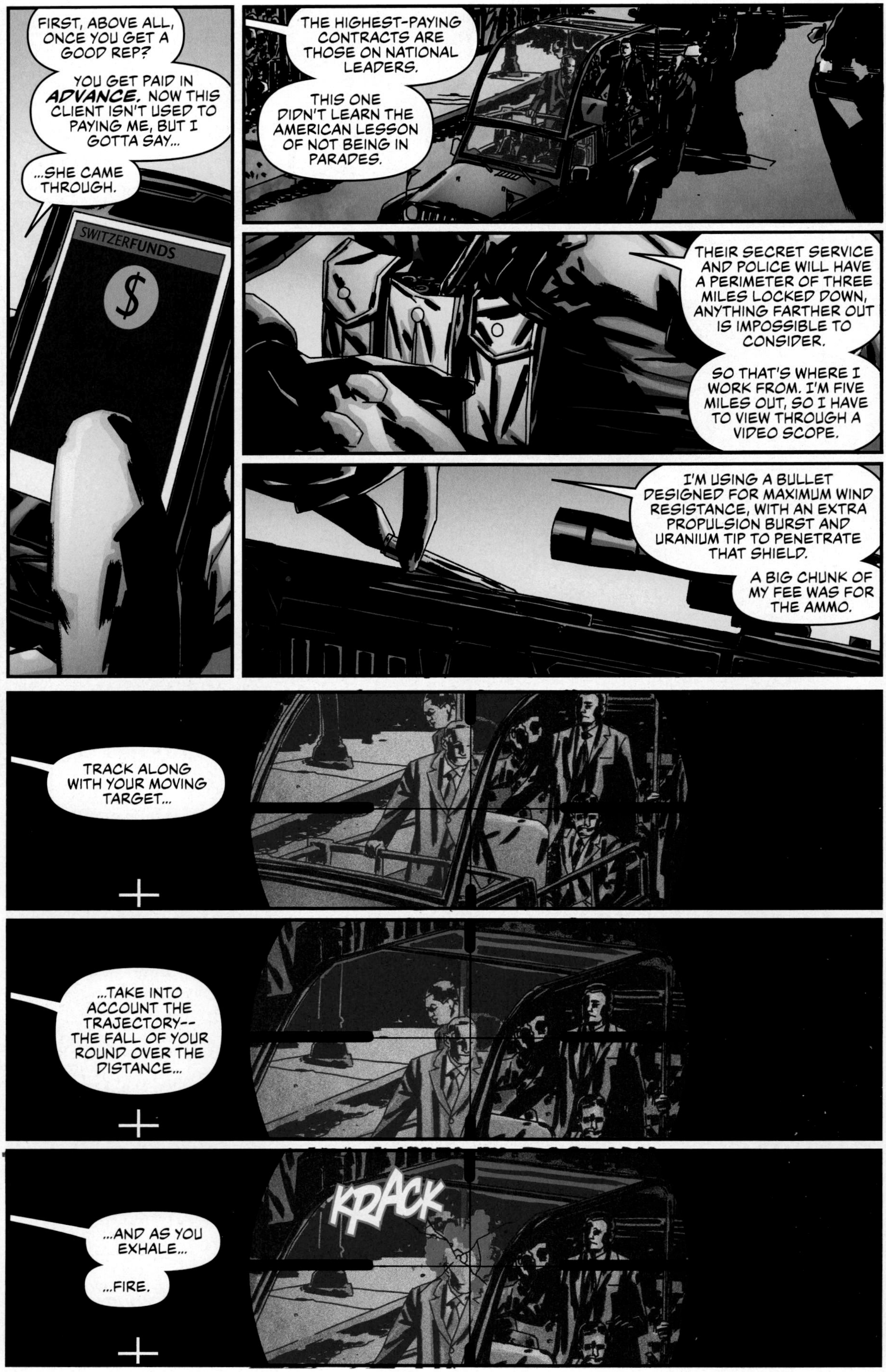
FIRST, ABOVE ALL, ONCE YOU GET A GOOD REP?
YOU GET PAID IN ADVANCE. NOW THIS CLIENT ISN'T USED TO PAYING ME, BUT I GOTTA SAY...
...SHE CAME THROUGH.
SWITZERFUNDS
$
THE HIGHEST-PAYING CONTRACTS ARE THOSE ON NATIONAL LEADERS.
THIS ONE DIDN'T LEARN THE AMERICAN LESSON OF NOT BEING IN PARADES.
THEIR SECRET SERVICE AND POLICE WILL HAVE A PERIMETER OF THREE MILES LOCKED DOWN, ANYTHING FARTHER OUT IS IMPOSSIBLE TO CONSIDER.
SO THAT'S WHERE I WORK FROM. I'M FIVE MILES OUT, SO I HAVE TO VIEW THROUGH A VIDEO SCOPE.
I'M USING A BULLET DESIGNED FOR MAXIMUM WIND RESISTANCE, WITH AN EXTRA PROPULSION BURST AND URANIUM TIP TO PENETRATE THAT SHIELD.
A BIG CHUNK OF MY FEE WAS FOR THE AMMO.
TRACK ALONG WITH YOUR MOVING TARGET...
...TAKE INTO ACCOUNT THE TRAJECTORY-- THE FALL OF YOUR ROUND OVER THE DISTANCE...
KRACK
...AND AS YOU EXHALE...
...FIRE.

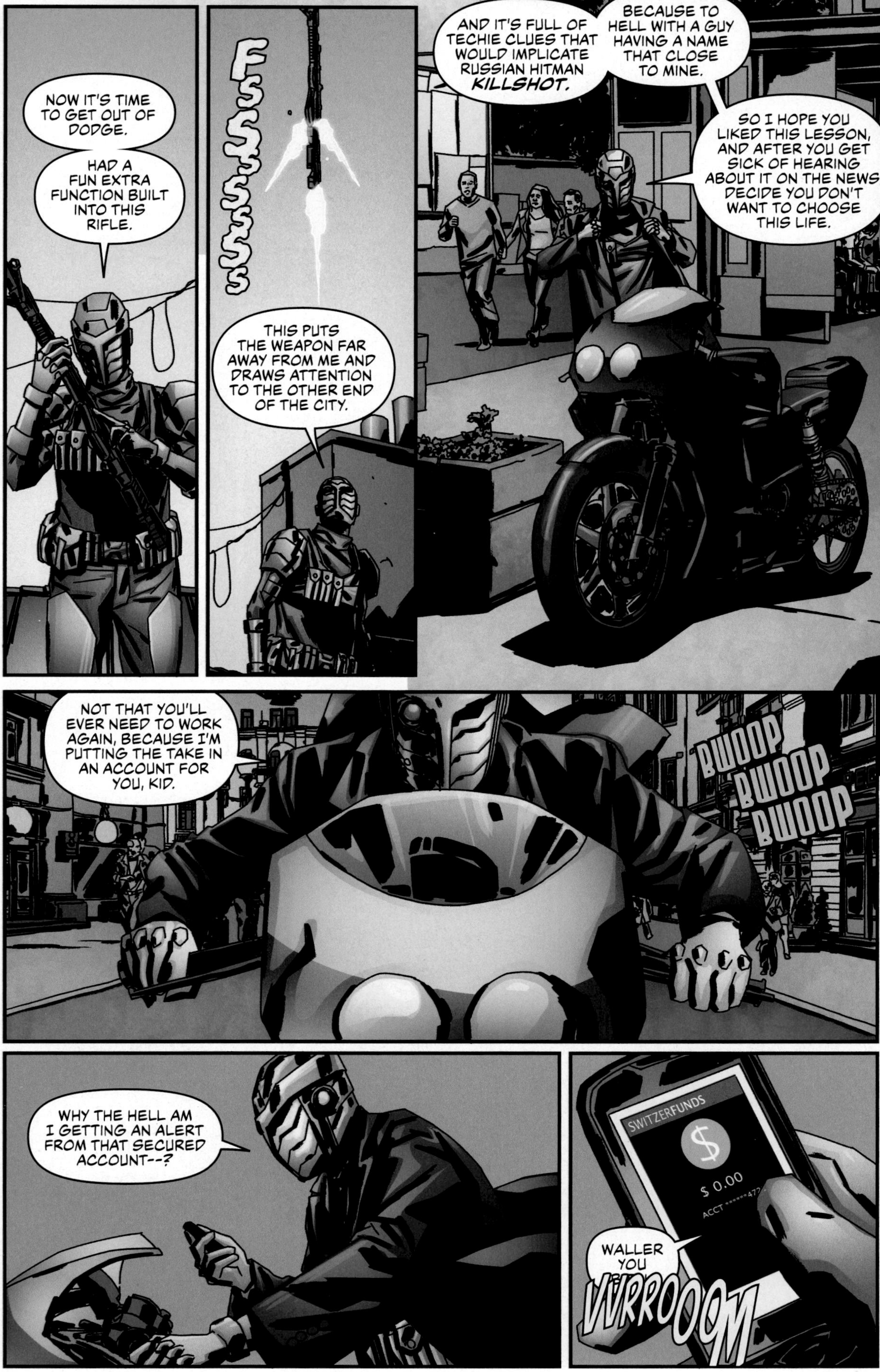

NOW IT'S TIME TO GET OUT OF DODGE.
HAD A FUN EXTRA FUNCTION BUILT INTO THIS RIFLE.
FSSSSSSS
THIS PUTS THE WEAPON FAR AWAY FROM ME AND DRAWS ATTENTION TO THE OTHER END OF THE CITY.
AND IT'S FULL OF TECHIE CLUES THAT WOULD IMPLICATE RUSSIAN HITMAN KILLSHOT.
BECAUSE TO HELL WITH A GUY HAVING A NAME THAT CLOSE TO MINE.
SO I HOPE YOU LIKED THIS LESSON, AND AFTER YOU GET SICK OF HEARING ABOUT IT ON THE NEWS, DECIDE YOU DON'T WANT TO CHOOSE THIS LIFE.
NOT THAT YOU'LL EVER NEED TO WORK AGAIN, BECAUSE I'M PUTTING THE TAKE IN AN ACCOUNT FOR YOU, KID.
BWOOP BWOOP BWOOP
WHY THE HELL AM I GETTING AN ALERT FROM THAT SECURED ACCOUNT--?
SWITZERFUNDS
$ 0.00
WALLER YOU
VVRROOOM

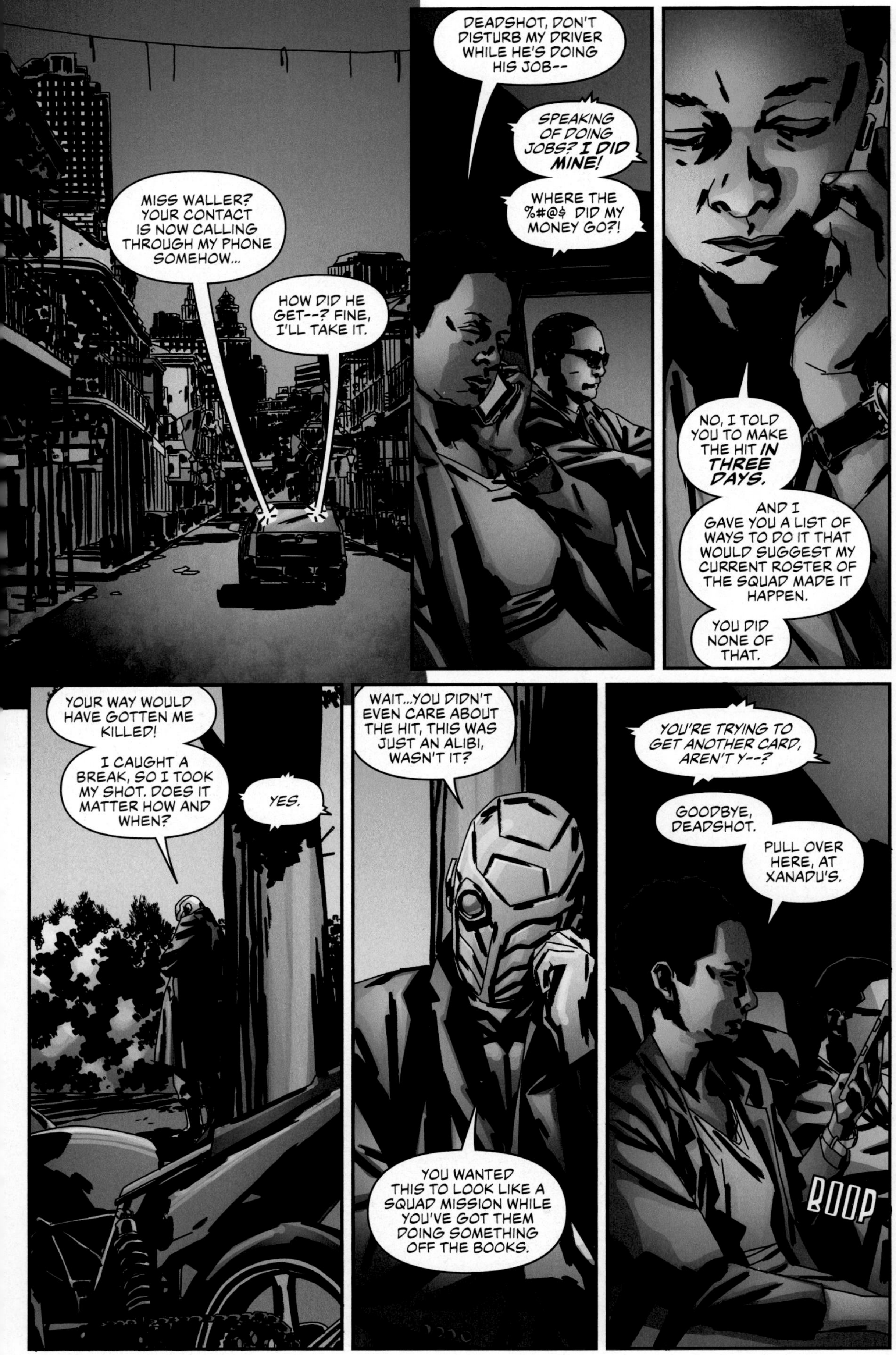
MISS WALLER? YOUR CONTACT IS NOW CALLING THROUGH MY PHONE SOMEHOW...
HOW DID HE GET--? FINE, I'LL TAKE IT.
DEADSHOT, DON'T DISTURB MY DRIVER WHILE HE'S DOING HIS JOB--
SPEAKING OF DOING JOBS? I DID MINE!
WHERE THE %#@$ DID MY MONEY GO?!
NO, I TOLD YOU TO MAKE THE HIT IN THREE DAYS.
AND I GAVE YOU A LIST OF WAYS TO DO IT THAT WOULD SUGGEST MY CURRENT ROSTER OF THE SQUAD MADE IT HAPPEN.
YOU DID NONE OF THAT.
YOUR WAY WOULD HAVE GOTTEN ME KILLED!
I CAUGHT A BREAK, SO I TOOK MY SHOT. DOES IT MATTER HOW AND WHEN?
YES.
WAIT...YOU DIDN'T EVEN CARE ABOUT THE HIT, THIS WAS JUST AN ALIBI, WASN'T IT?
YOU WANTED THIS TO LOOK LIKE A SQUAD MISSION WHILE YOU'VE GOT THEM DOING SOMETHING OFF THE BOOKS.
YOU'RE TRYING TO GET ANOTHER CARD, AREN'T Y--?
GOODBYE, DEADSHOT.
PULL OVER HERE, AT XANADU'S.
BOOP

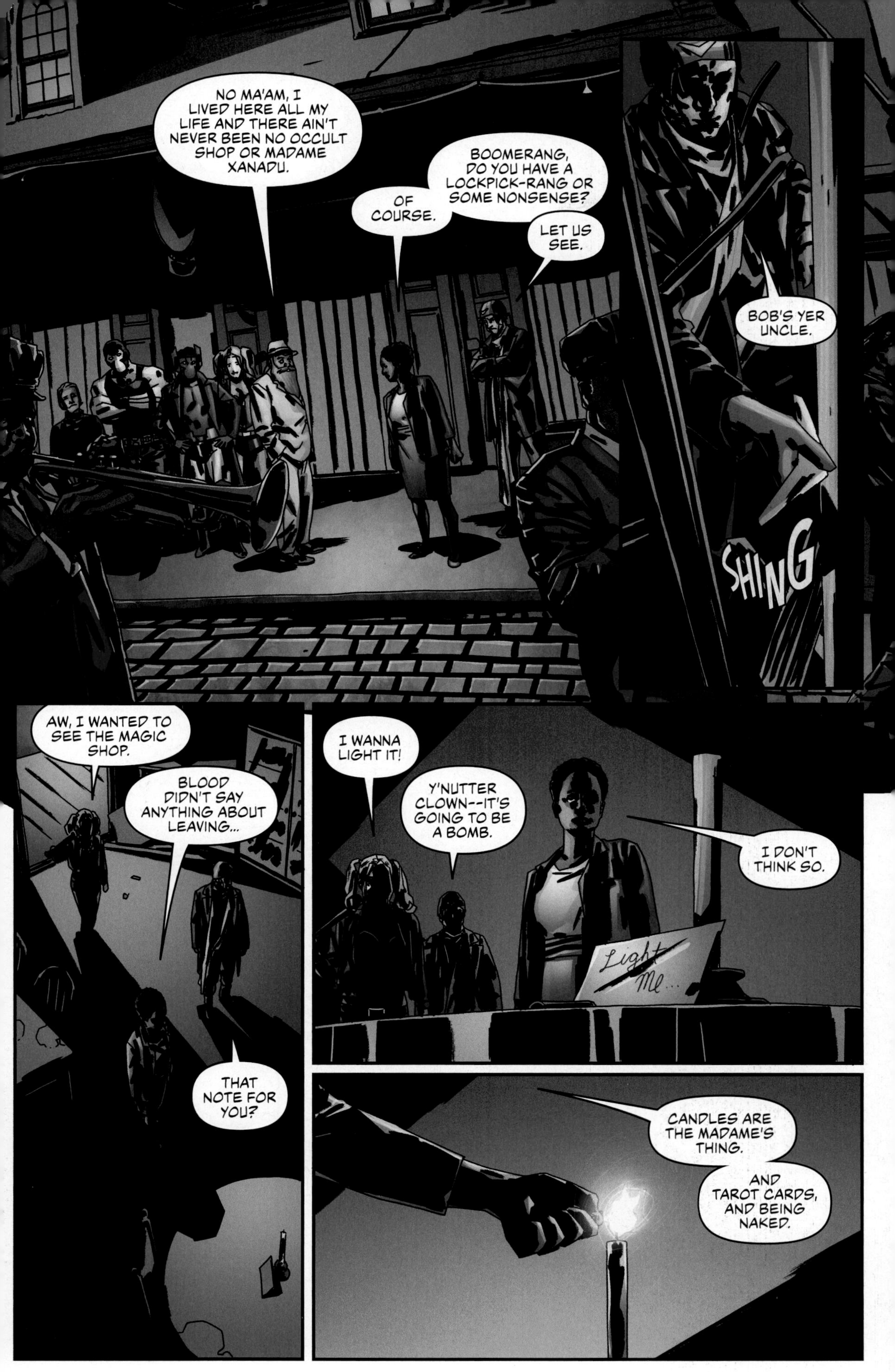
NO MA'AM, I LIVED HERE ALL MY LIFE AND THERE AIN'T NEVER BEEN NO OCCULT SHOP OR MADAME XANADU.
BOOMERANG, DO YOU HAVE A LOCKPICK-RANG OR SOME NONSENSE?
OF COURSE.
LET US SEE.
BOB'S YER UNCLE.
SHING
AW, I WANTED TO SEE THE MAGIC SHOP.
BLOOD DIDN'T SAY ANYTHING ABOUT LEAVING...
THAT NOTE FOR YOU?
I WANNA LIGHT IT!
Y'NUTTER CLOWN--IT'S GOING TO BE A BOMB.
I DON'T THINK SO.
Light Me...
CANDLES ARE THE MADAME'S THING.
AND TAROT CARDS, AND BEING NAKED.

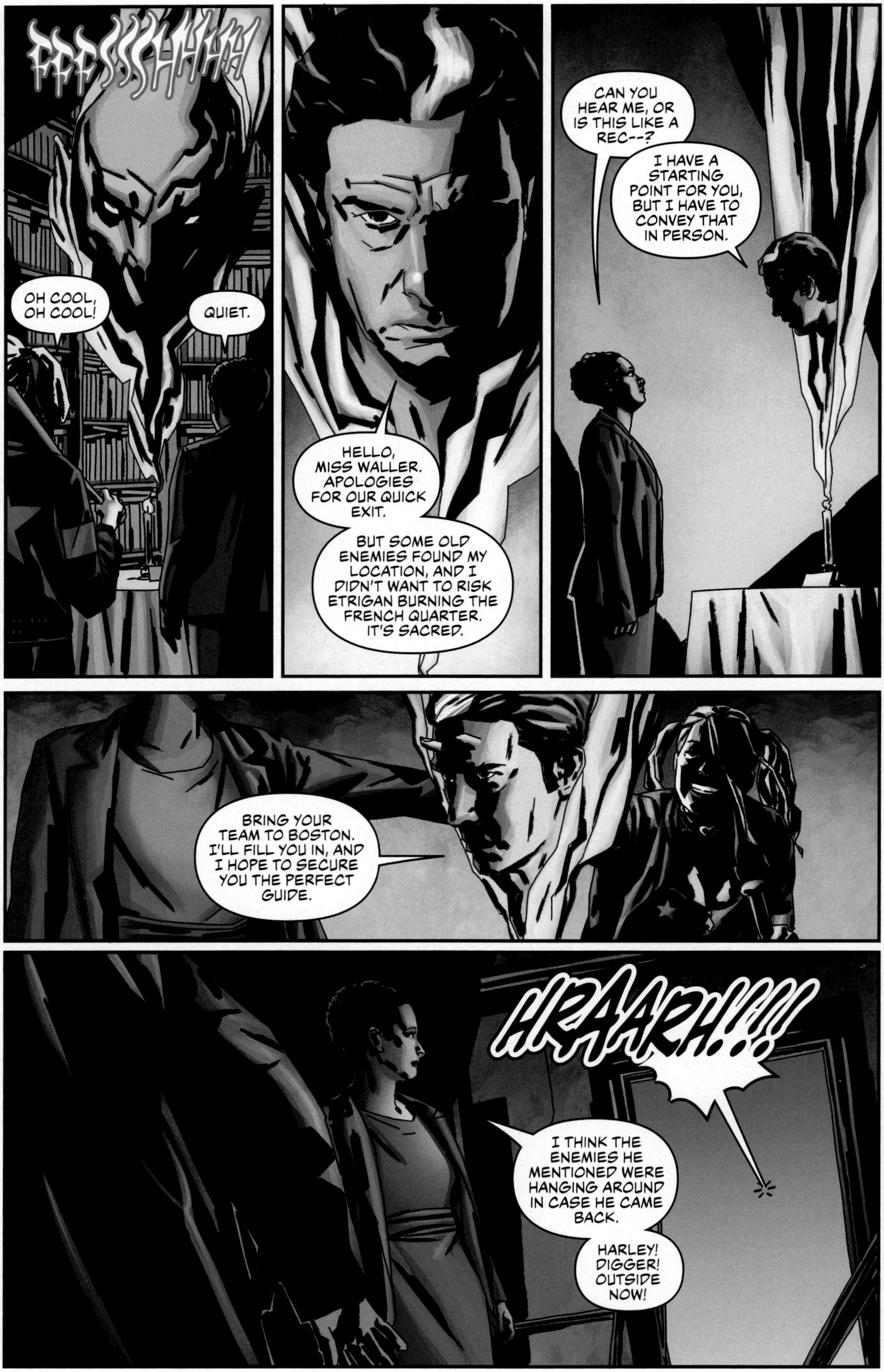

FFFSSSHHHH
OH COOL, OH COOL!
QUIET.
HELLO, MISS WALLER. APOLOGIES FOR OUR QUICK EXIT.
BUT SOME OLD ENEMIES FOUND MY LOCATION, AND I DIDN'T WANT TO RISK ETRIGAN BURNING THE FRENCH QUARTER. IT'S SACRED.
CAN YOU HEAR ME, OR IS THIS LIKE A REC--?
I HAVE A STARTING POINT FOR YOU, BUT I HAVE TO CONVEY THAT IN PERSON.
BRING YOUR TEAM TO BOSTON. I'LL FILL YOU IN, AND I HOPE TO SECURE YOU THE PERFECT GUIDE.
HRAARH!!!
I THINK THE ENEMIES HE MENTIONED WERE HANGING AROUND IN CASE HE CAME BACK.
HARLEY! DIGGER! OUTSIDE NOW!

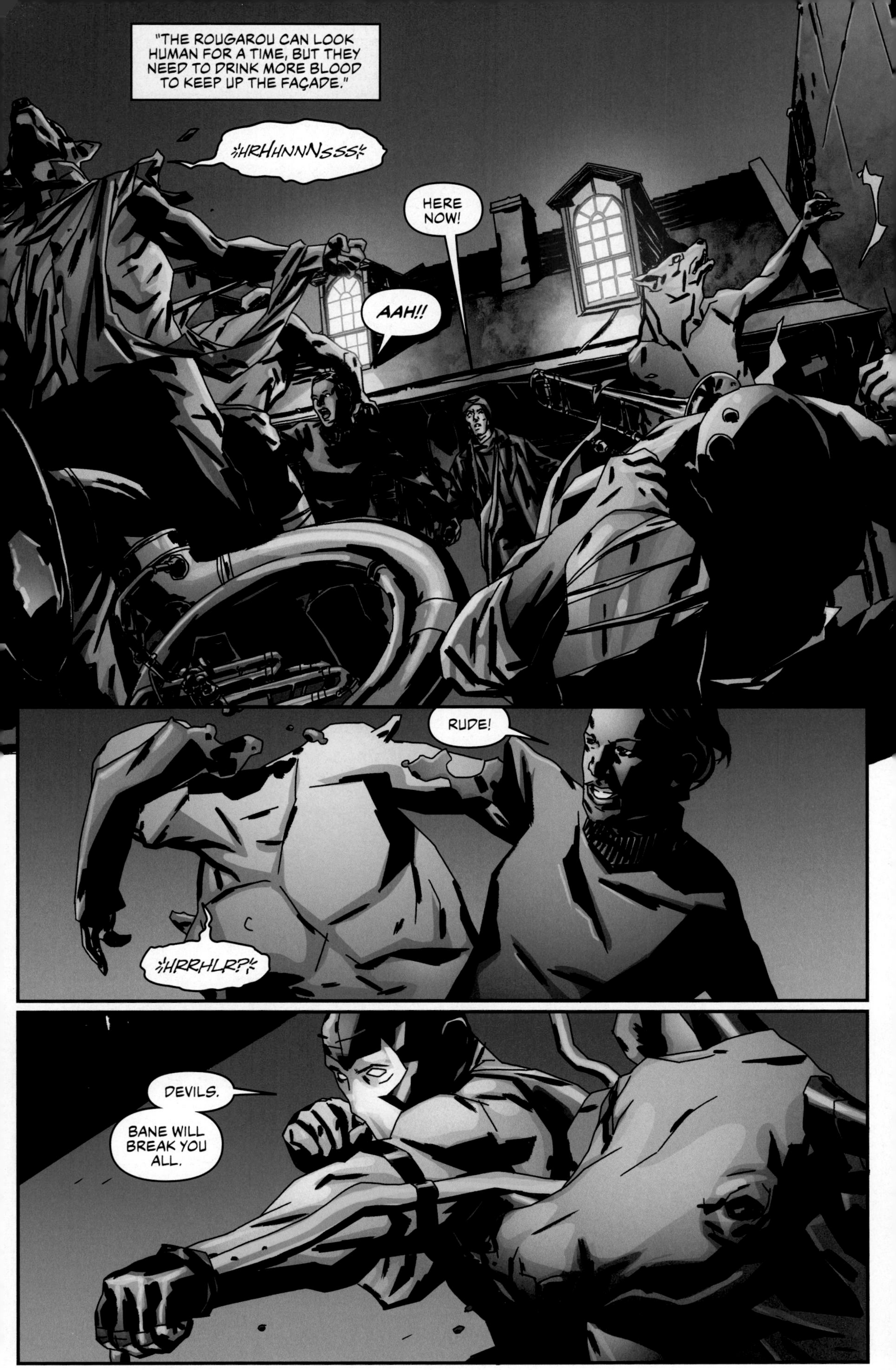
"THE ROUGAROU CAN LOOK HUMAN FOR A TIME, BUT THEY NEED TO DRINK MORE BLOOD TO KEEP UP THE FAÇADE."
HRHHNNNSSS
HERE NOW!
AAH!!
RUDE!
HRRHLR?
DEVILS.
BANE WILL BREAK YOU ALL.

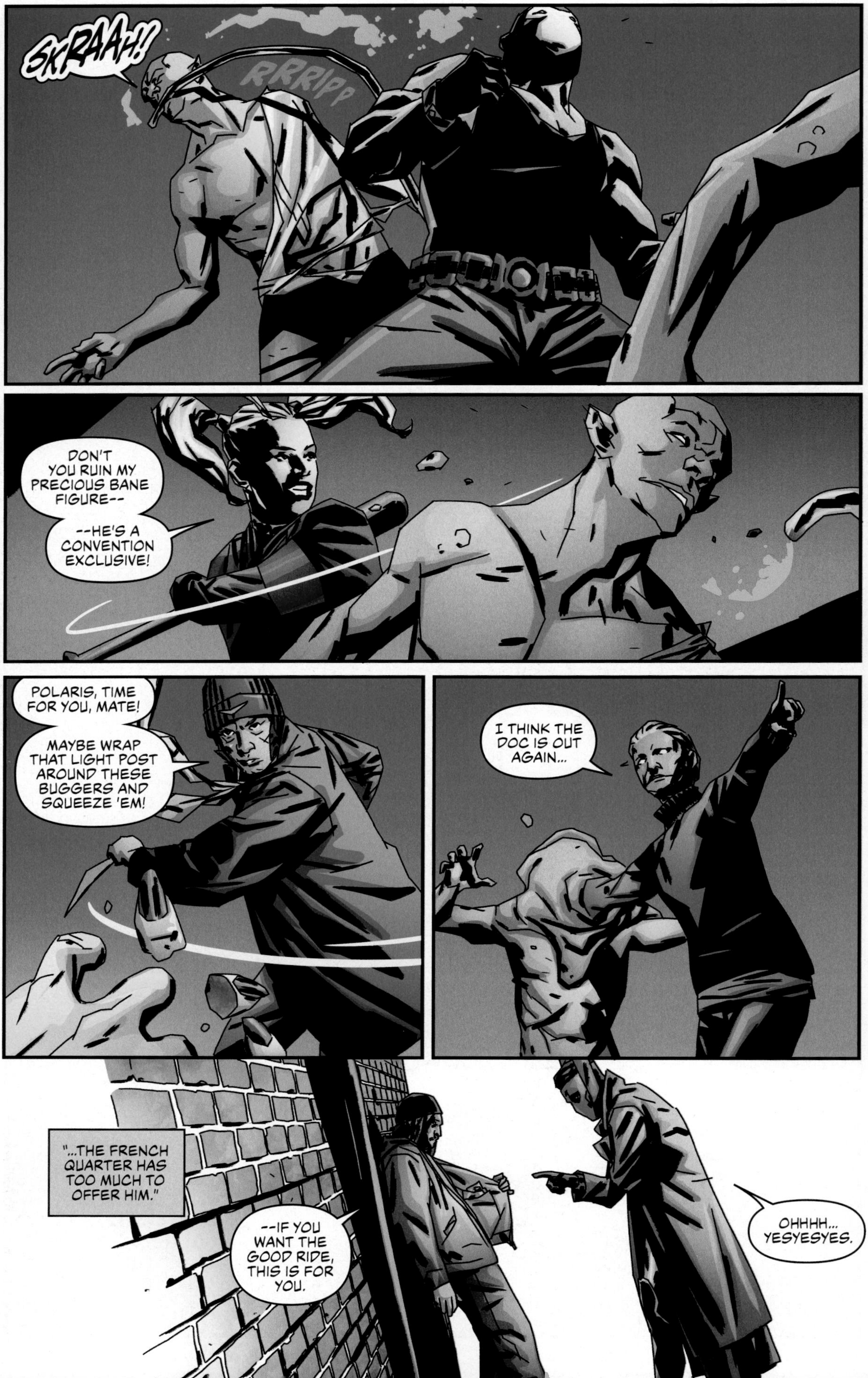
SKRAAH!!
RRRIPP
DON'T YOU RUIN MY PRECIOUS BANE FIGURE--
--HE'S A CONVENTION EXCLUSIVE!
POLARIS, TIME FOR YOU, MATE!
MAYBE WRAP THAT LIGHT POST AROUND THESE BUGGERS AND SQUEEZE 'EM!
I THINK THE DOC IS OUT AGAIN...
"...THE FRENCH QUARTER HAS TOO MUCH TO OFFER HIM."
--IF YOU WANT THE GOOD RIDE, THIS IS FOR YOU.
OHHHH... YESYESYES.

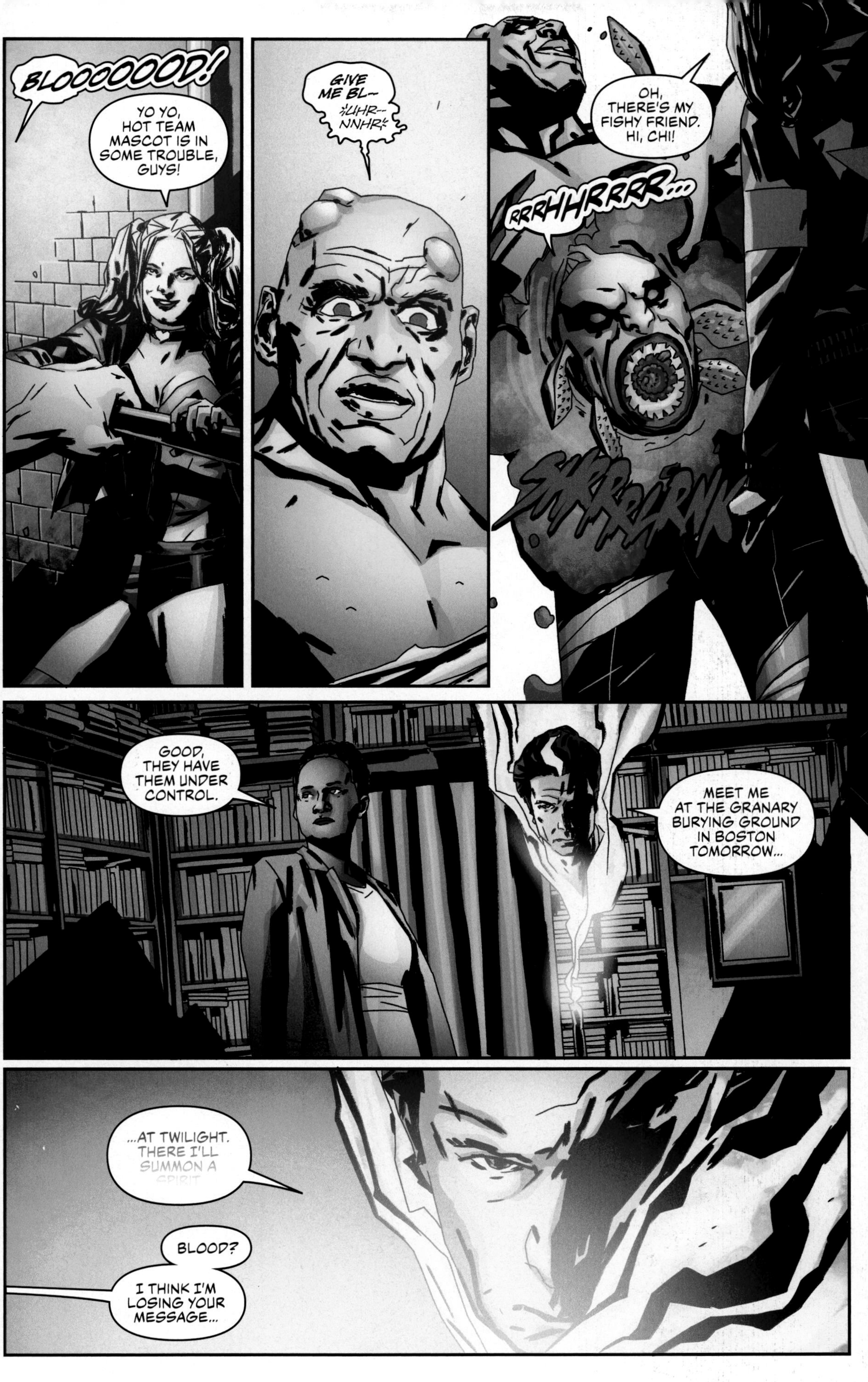
BLOOOOOOD!
YO YO, HOT TEAM MASCOT IS IN SOME TROUBLE, GUYS!
GIVE ME BL--
UHR-- NNHR
OH, THERE'S MY FISHY FRIEND. HI, CHI!
RRRHHRRRR...
GOOD, THEY HAVE THEM UNDER CONTROL.
MEET ME AT THE GRANARY BURYING GROUND IN BOSTON TOMORROW...
...AT TWILIGHT. THERE I'LL SUMMON A
BLOOD?
I THINK I'M LOSING YOUR MESSAGE...

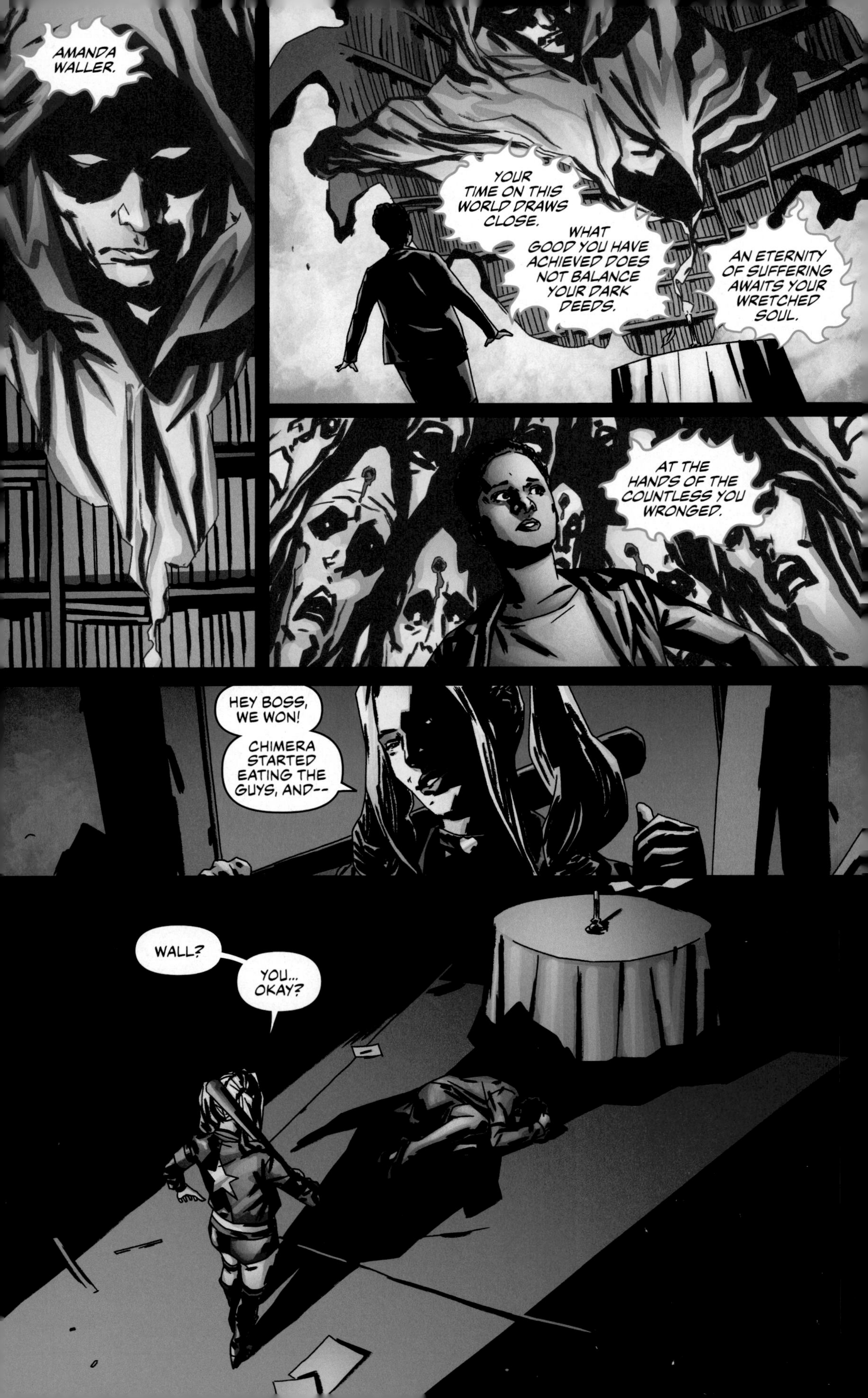
AMANDA WALLER.
YOUR TIME ON THIS WORLD DRAWS CLOSE.
WHAT GOOD YOU HAVE ACHIEVED DOES NOT BALANCE YOUR DARK DEEDS.
AN ETERNITY OF SUFFERING AWAITS YOUR WRETCHED SOUL.
AT THE HANDS OF THE COUNTLESS YOU WRONGED.
HEY BOSS, WE WON!
CHIMERA STARTED EATING THE GUYS, AND--
WALL?
YOU... OKAY?

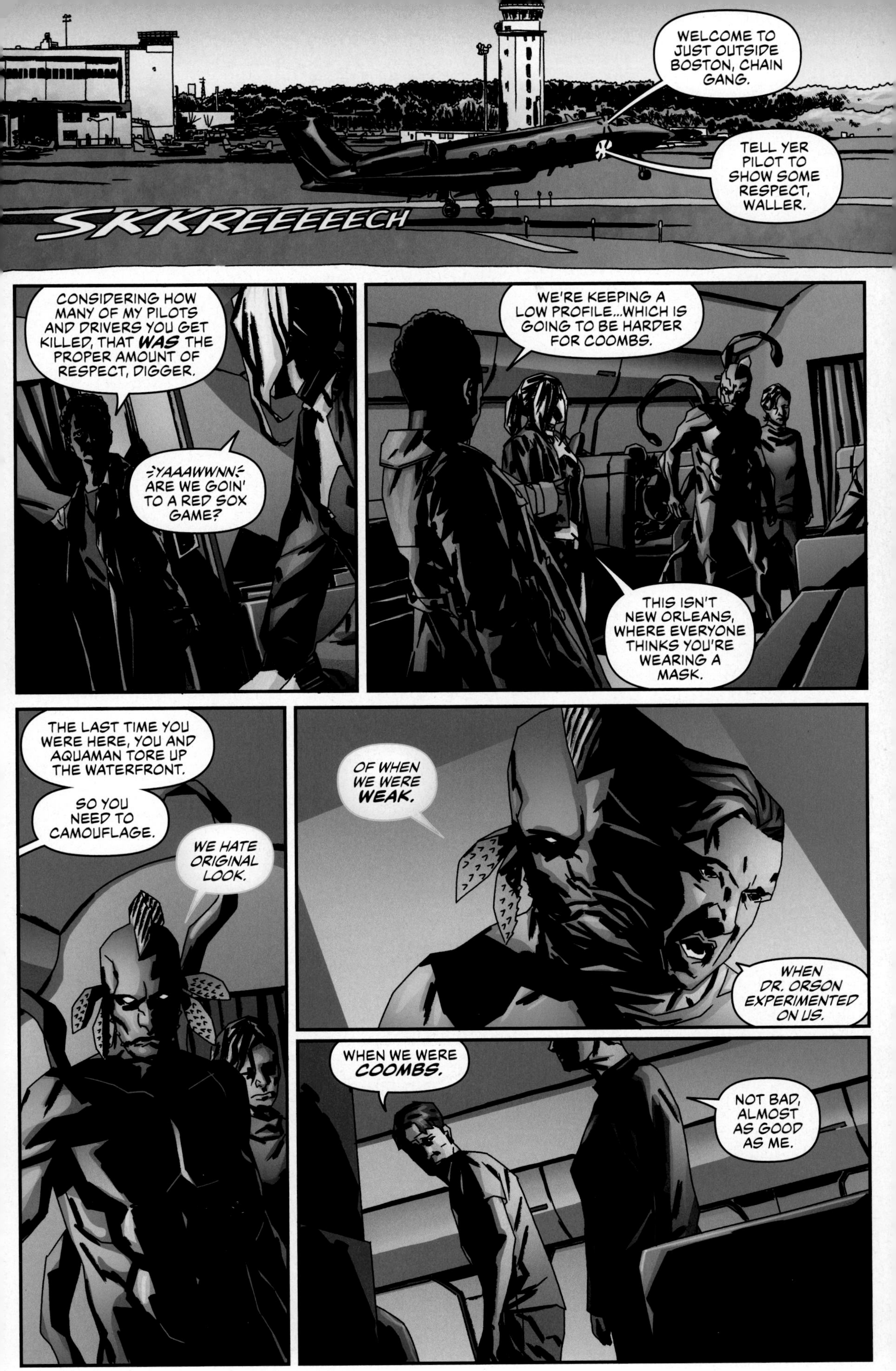
WELCOME TO JUST OUTSIDE BOSTON, CHAIN GANG.
TELL YER PILOT TO SHOW SOME RESPECT, WALLER.
SKKREEEEEECH
CONSIDERING HOW MANY OF MY PILOTS AND DRIVERS YOU GET KILLED, THAT WAS THE PROPER AMOUNT OF RESPECT, DIGGER.
YAAAWWNN ARE WE GOIN' TO A RED SOX GAME?
WE'RE KEEPING A LOW PROFILE...WHICH IS GOING TO BE HARDER FOR COOMBS.
THIS ISN'T NEW ORLEANS, WHERE EVERYONE THINKS YOU'RE WEARING A MASK.
THE LAST TIME YOU WERE HERE, YOU AND AQUAMAN TORE UP THE WATERFRONT.
SO YOU NEED TO CAMOUFLAGE.
WE HATE ORIGINAL LOOK.
OF WHEN WE WERE WEAK.
WHEN DR. ORSON EXPERIMENTED ON US.
WHEN WE WERE COOMBS.
NOT BAD, ALMOST AS GOOD AS ME.

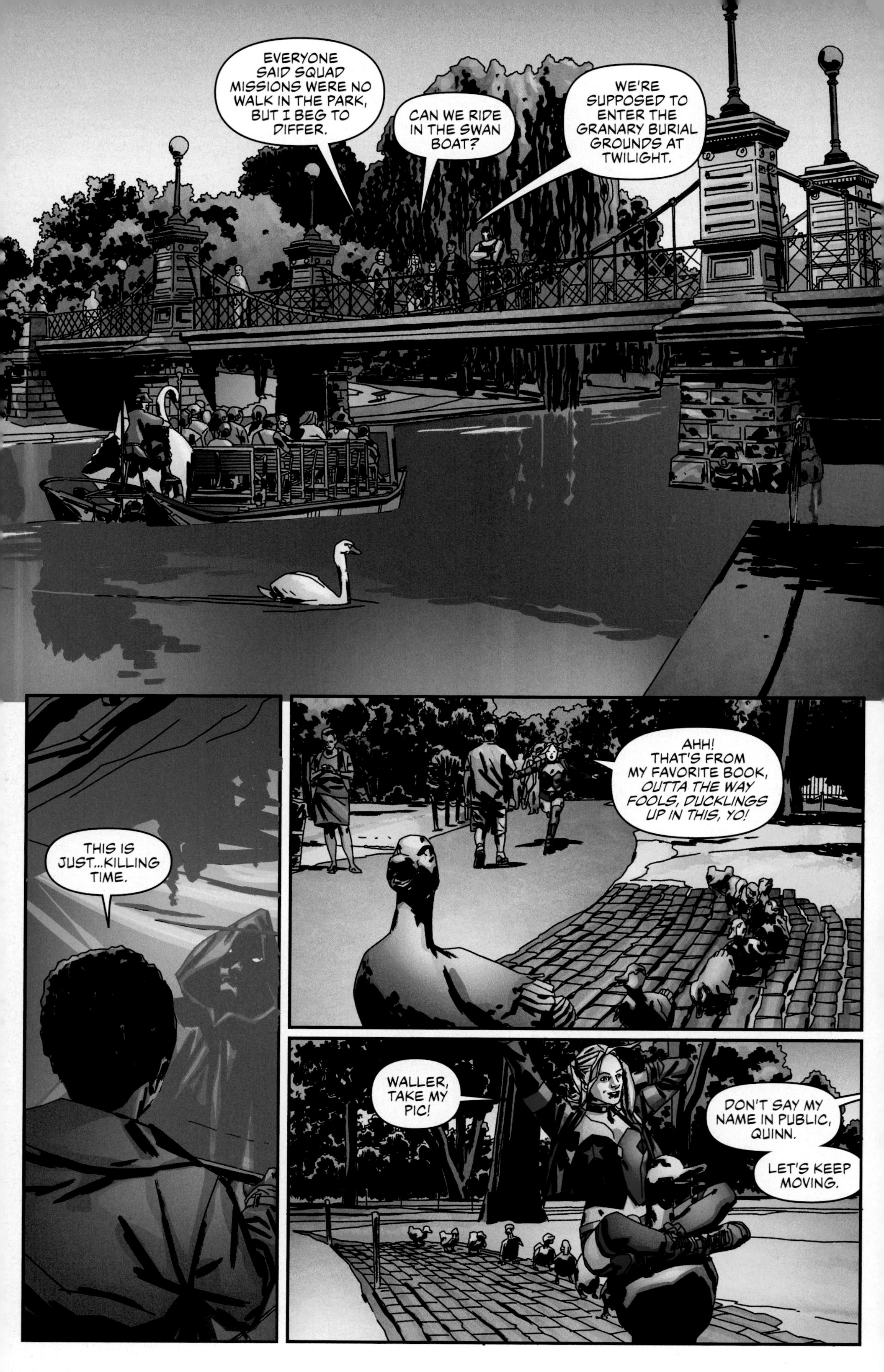
EVERYONE SAID SQUAD MISSIONS WERE NO WALK IN THE PARK, BUT I BEG TO DIFFER.
CAN WE RIDE IN THE SWAN BOAT?
WE'RE SUPPOSED TO ENTER THE GRANARY BURIAL GROUNDS AT TWILIGHT.
THIS IS JUST...KILLING TIME.
AHH! THAT'S FROM MY FAVORITE BOOK, *OUTTA THE WAY FOOLS, DUCKLINGS UP IN THIS, YO!*
WALLER, TAKE MY PIC!
DON'T SAY MY NAME IN PUBLIC, QUINN.
LET'S KEEP MOVING.

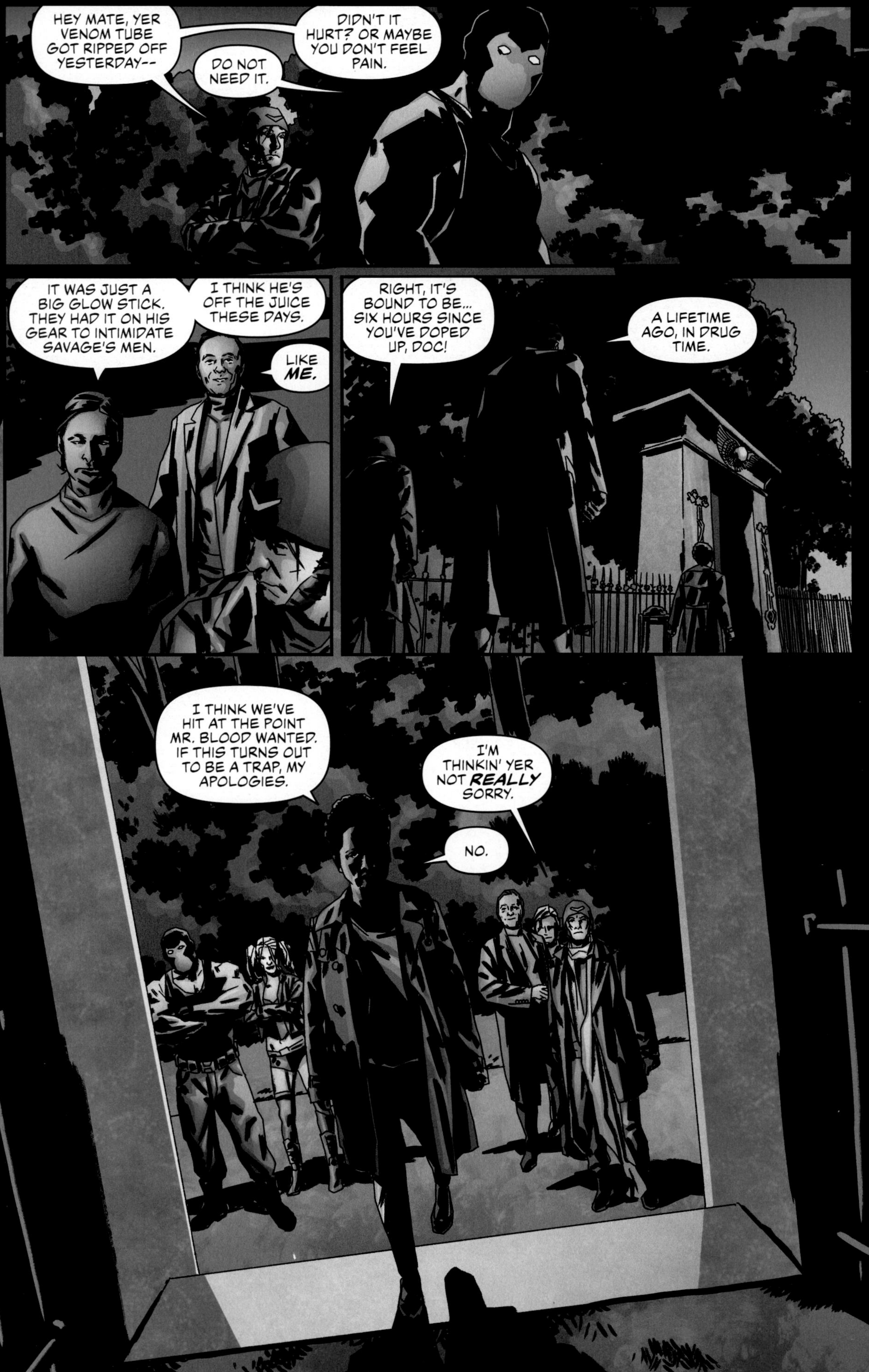
HEY MATE, YER VENOM TUBE GOT RIPPED OFF YESTERDAY--
DIDN'T IT HURT? OR MAYBE YOU DON'T FEEL PAIN.
DO NOT NEED IT.
IT WAS JUST A BIG GLOW STICK. THEY HAD IT ON HIS GEAR TO INTIMIDATE SAVAGE'S MEN.
I THINK HE'S OFF THE JUICE THESE DAYS.
LIKE ME.
RIGHT, IT'S BOUND TO BE... SIX HOURS SINCE YOU'VE DOPED UP, DOC!
A LIFETIME AGO, IN DRUG TIME.
I THINK WE'VE HIT AT THE POINT MR. BLOOD WANTED. IF THIS TURNS OUT TO BE A TRAP, MY APOLOGIES.
I'M THINKIN' YER NOT REALLY SORRY.
NO.

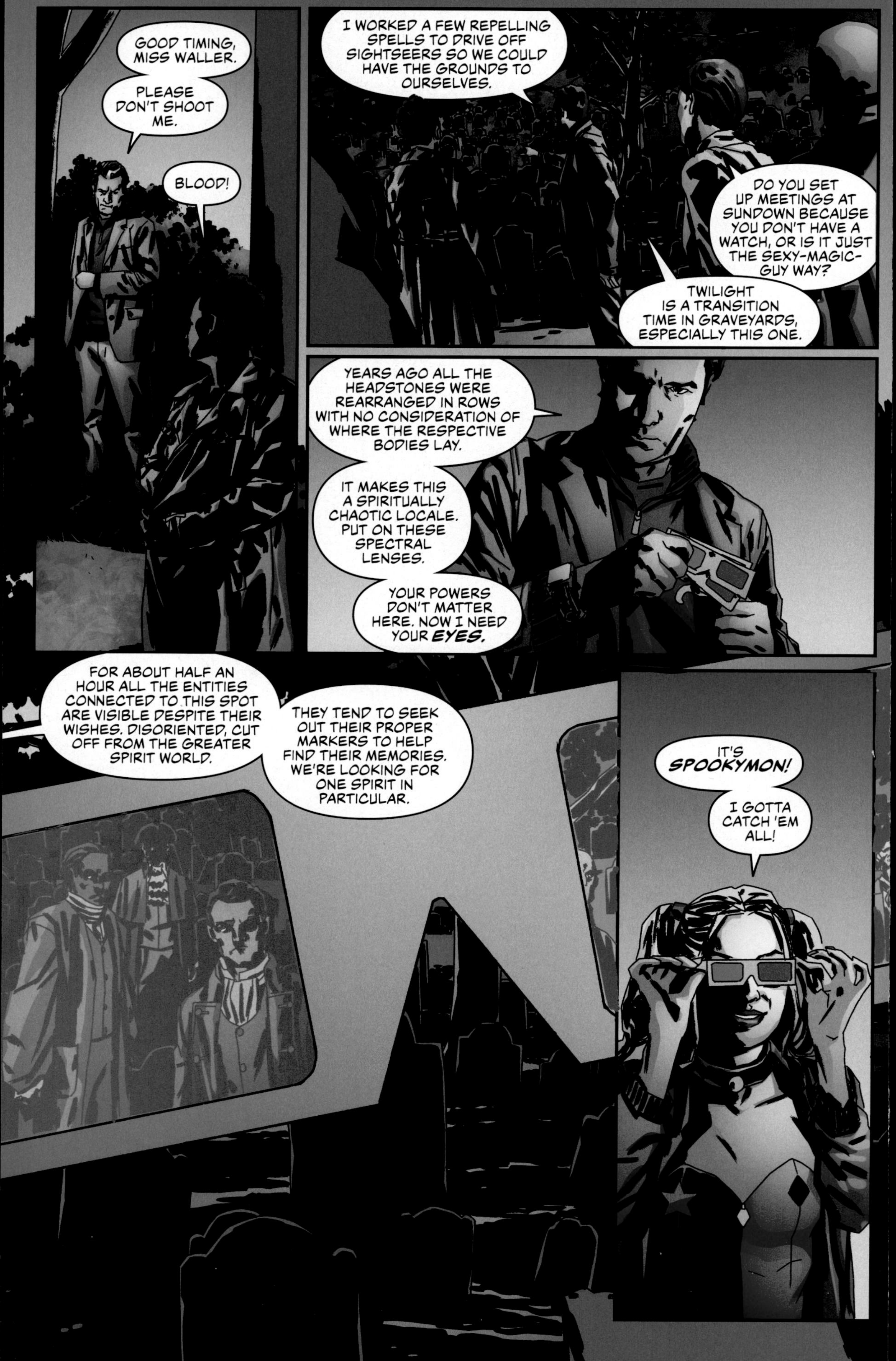
GOOD TIMING, MISS WALLER.
PLEASE DON'T SHOOT ME.
BLOOD!
I WORKED A FEW REPELLING SPELLS TO DRIVE OFF SIGHTSEERS SO WE COULD HAVE THE GROUNDS TO OURSELVES.
DO YOU SET UP MEETINGS AT SUNDOWN BECAUSE YOU DON'T HAVE A WATCH, OR IS IT JUST THE SEXY-MAGIC-GUY WAY?
TWILIGHT IS A TRANSITION TIME IN GRAVEYARDS, ESPECIALLY THIS ONE.
YEARS AGO ALL THE HEADSTONES WERE REARRANGED IN ROWS WITH NO CONSIDERATION OF WHERE THE RESPECTIVE BODIES LAY.
IT MAKES THIS A SPIRITUALLY CHAOTIC LOCALE. PUT ON THESE SPECTRAL LENSES.
YOUR POWERS DON'T MATTER HERE. NOW I NEED YOUR EYES.
FOR ABOUT HALF AN HOUR ALL THE ENTITIES CONNECTED TO THIS SPOT ARE VISIBLE DESPITE THEIR WISHES. DISORIENTED, CUT OFF FROM THE GREATER SPIRIT WORLD.
THEY TEND TO SEEK OUT THEIR PROPER MARKERS TO HELP FIND THEIR MEMORIES. WE'RE LOOKING FOR ONE SPIRIT IN PARTICULAR.
IT'S SPOOKYMON!
I GOTTA CATCH 'EM ALL!

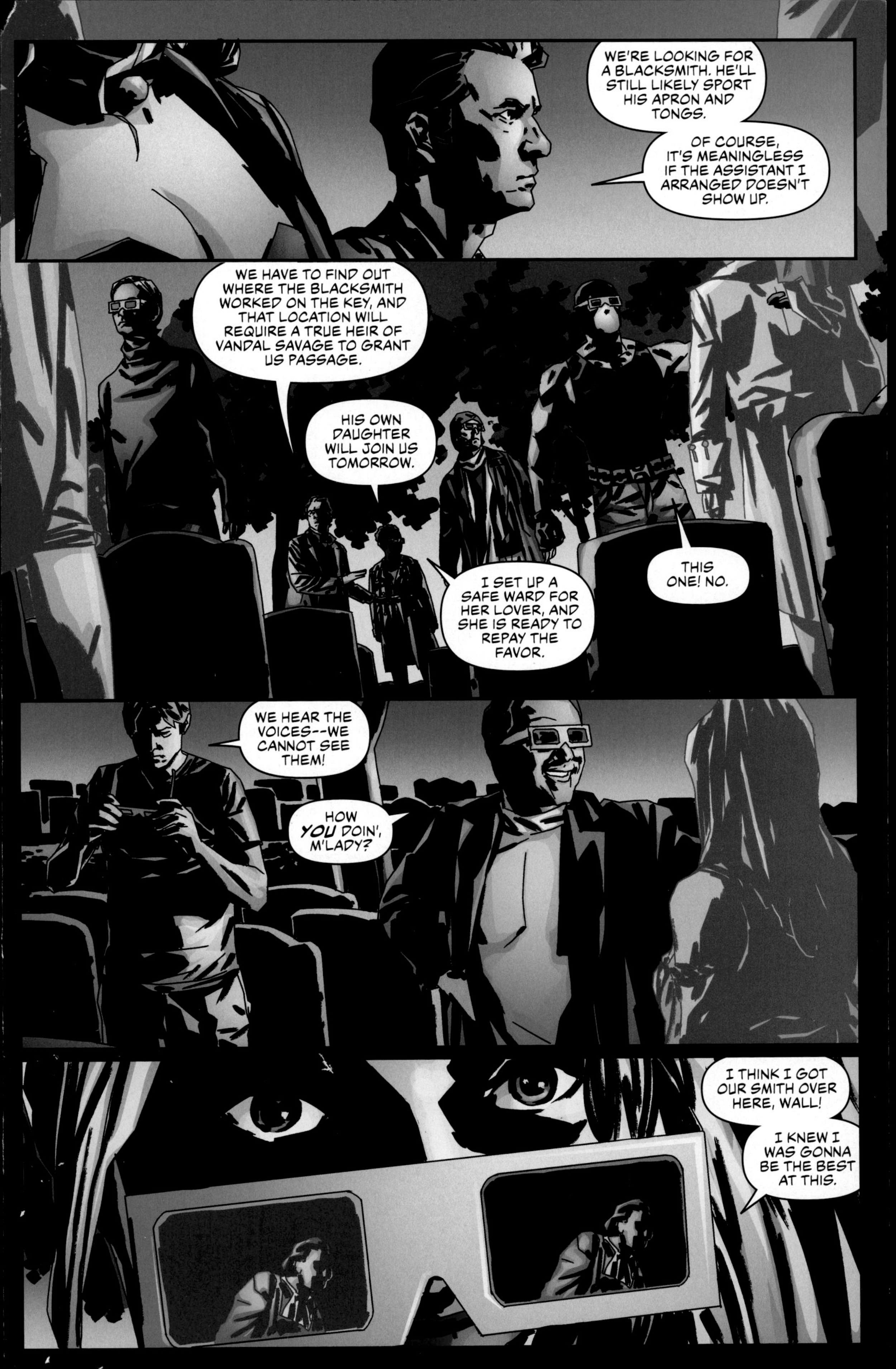
WE'RE LOOKING FOR A BLACKSMITH. HE'LL STILL LIKELY SPORT HIS APRON AND TONGS.
OF COURSE, IT'S MEANINGLESS IF THE ASSISTANT I ARRANGED DOESN'T SHOW UP.
WE HAVE TO FIND OUT WHERE THE BLACKSMITH WORKED ON THE KEY, AND THAT LOCATION WILL REQUIRE A TRUE HEIR OF VANDAL SAVAGE TO GRANT US PASSAGE.
HIS OWN DAUGHTER WILL JOIN US TOMORROW.
I SET UP A SAFE WARD FOR HER LOVER, AND SHE IS READY TO REPAY THE FAVOR.
THIS ONE! NO.
WE HEAR THE VOICES--WE CANNOT SEE THEM!
HOW YOU DOIN', M'LADY?
I THINK I GOT OUR SMITH OVER HERE, WALL!
I KNEW I WAS GONNA BE THE BEST AT THIS.

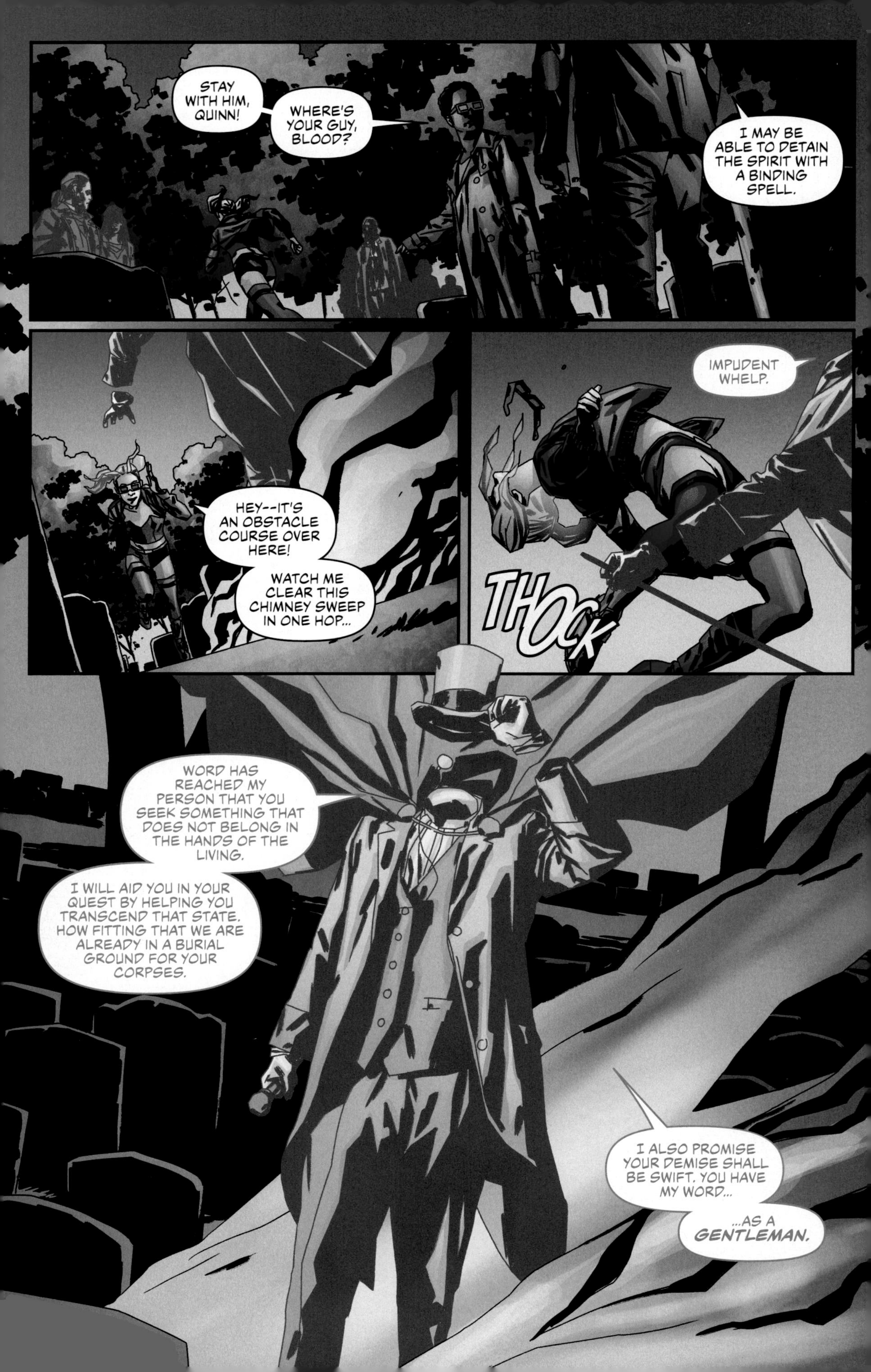
STAY WITH HIM, QUINN!
WHERE'S YOUR GUY, BLOOD?
I MAY BE ABLE TO DETAIN THE SPIRIT WITH A BINDING SPELL.
HEY--IT'S AN OBSTACLE COURSE OVER HERE!
WATCH ME CLEAR THIS CHIMNEY SWEEP IN ONE HOP...
IMPUDENT WHELP.
THOCK
WORD HAS REACHED MY PERSON THAT YOU SEEK SOMETHING THAT DOES NOT BELONG IN THE HANDS OF THE LIVING.
I WILL AID YOU IN YOUR QUEST BY HELPING YOU TRANSCEND THAT STATE. HOW FITTING THAT WE ARE ALREADY IN A BURIAL GROUND FOR YOUR CORPSES.
I ALSO PROMISE YOUR DEMISE SHALL BE SWIFT. YOU HAVE MY WORD...
...AS A GENTLEMAN.

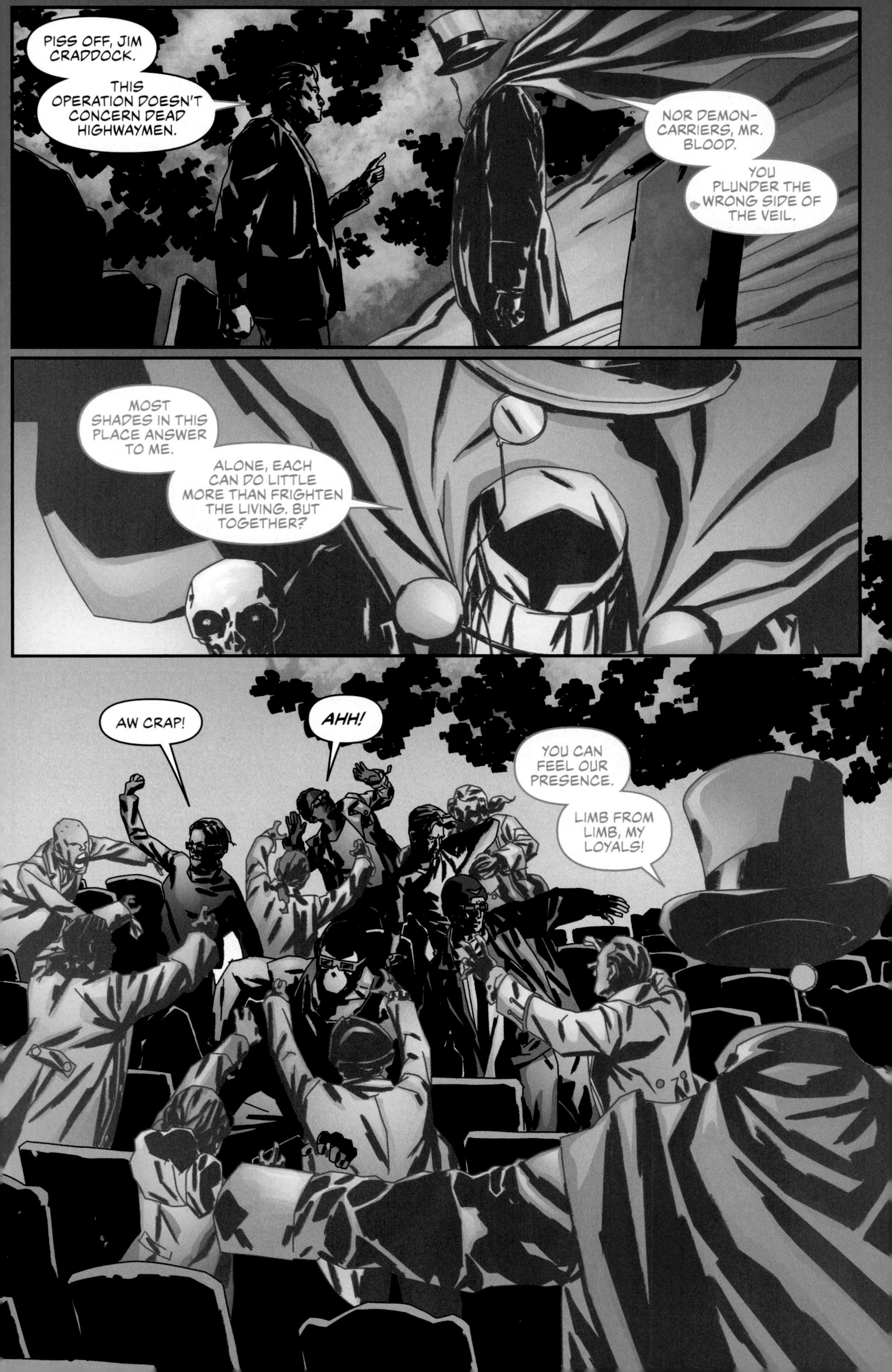
PISS OFF, JIM CRADDOCK.
THIS OPERATION DOESN'T CONCERN DEAD HIGHWAYMEN.
NOR DEMON-CARRIERS, MR. BLOOD.
YOU PLUNDER THE WRONG SIDE OF THE VEIL.
MOST SHADES IN THIS PLACE ANSWER TO ME.
ALONE, EACH CAN DO LITTLE MORE THAN FRIGHTEN THE LIVING. BUT TOGETHER?
AW CRAP!
AHH!
YOU CAN FEEL OUR PRESENCE.
LIMB FROM LIMB, MY LOYALS!

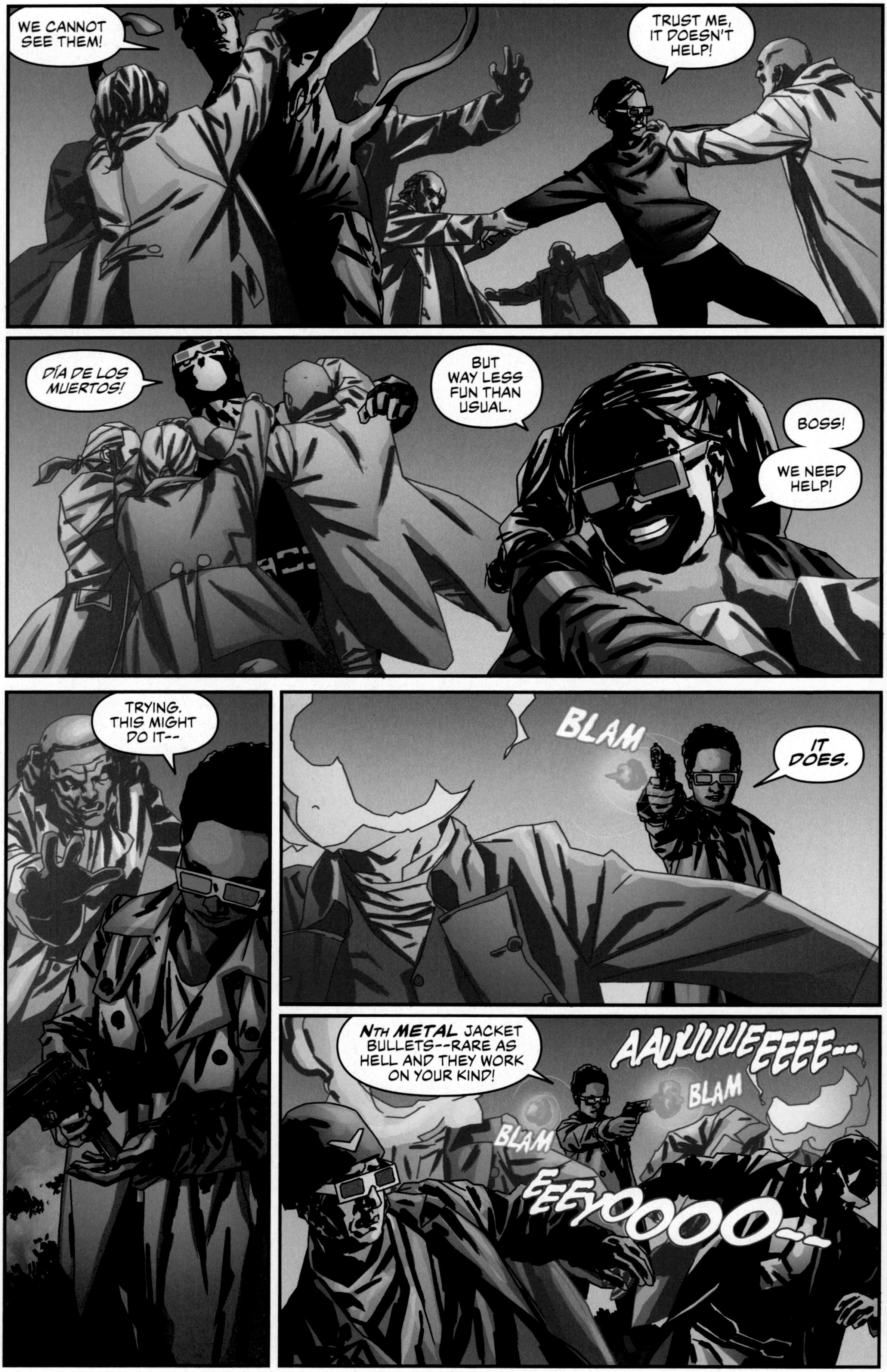
WE CANNOT SEE THEM!
TRUST ME, IT DOESN'T HELP!
DÍA DE LOS MUERTOS!
BUT WAY LESS FUN THAN USUAL.
BOSS!
WE NEED HELP!
TRYING. THIS MIGHT DO IT--
BLAM
IT DOES.
NTH METAL JACKET BULLETS--RARE AS HELL AND THEY WORK ON YOUR KIND!
AAUUUUEEEEE--
BLAM
BLAM
EEEYOOOO--

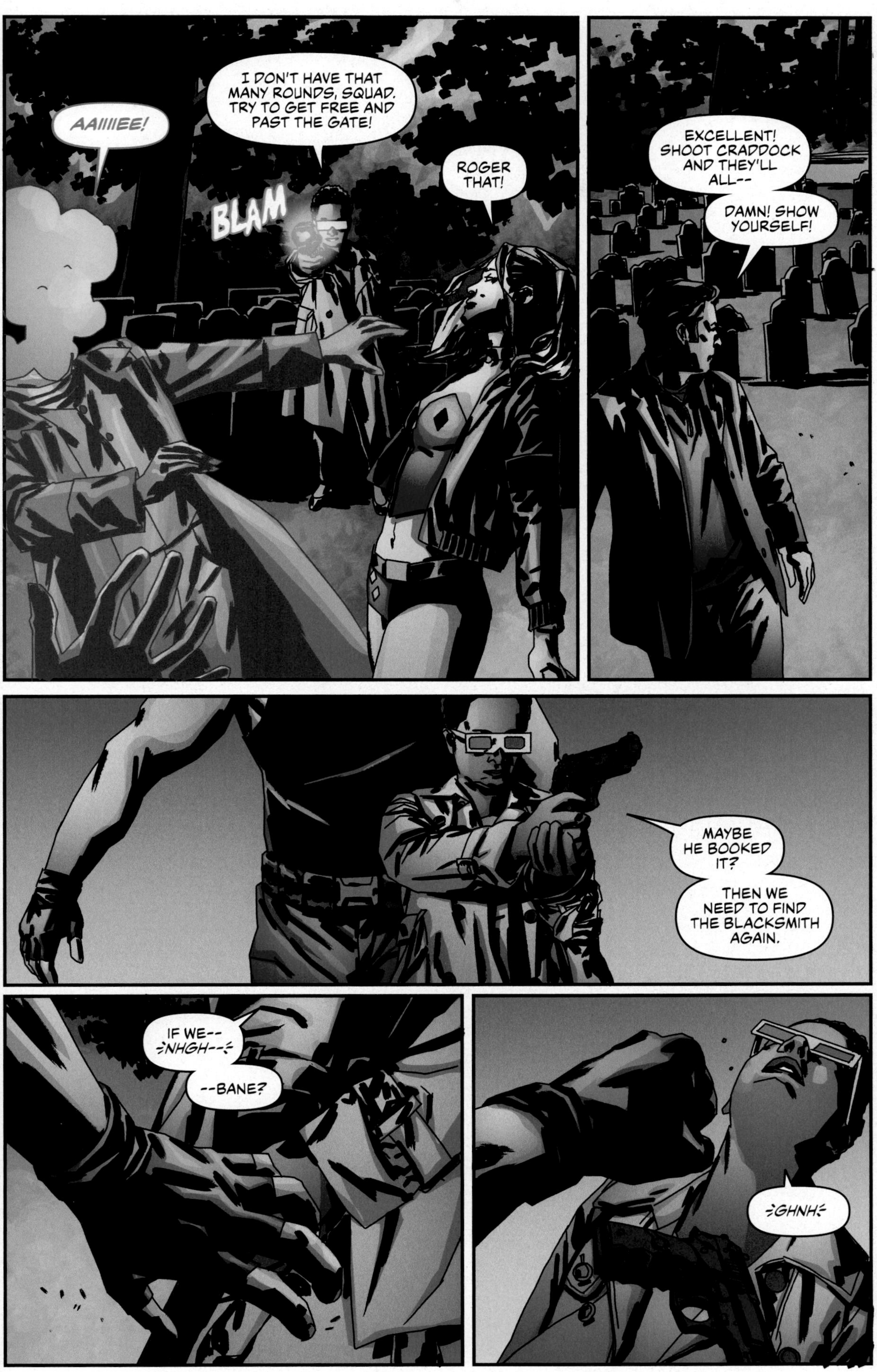
AAIIIIEE!
I DON'T HAVE THAT MANY ROUNDS, SQUAD. TRY TO GET FREE AND PAST THE GATE!
BLAM
ROGER THAT!
EXCELLENT! SHOOT CRADDOCK AND THEY'LL ALL--
DAMN! SHOW YOURSELF!
MAYBE HE BOOKED IT?
THEN WE NEED TO FIND THE BLACKSMITH AGAIN.
IF WE--
NHGH--
--BANE?
GHNH

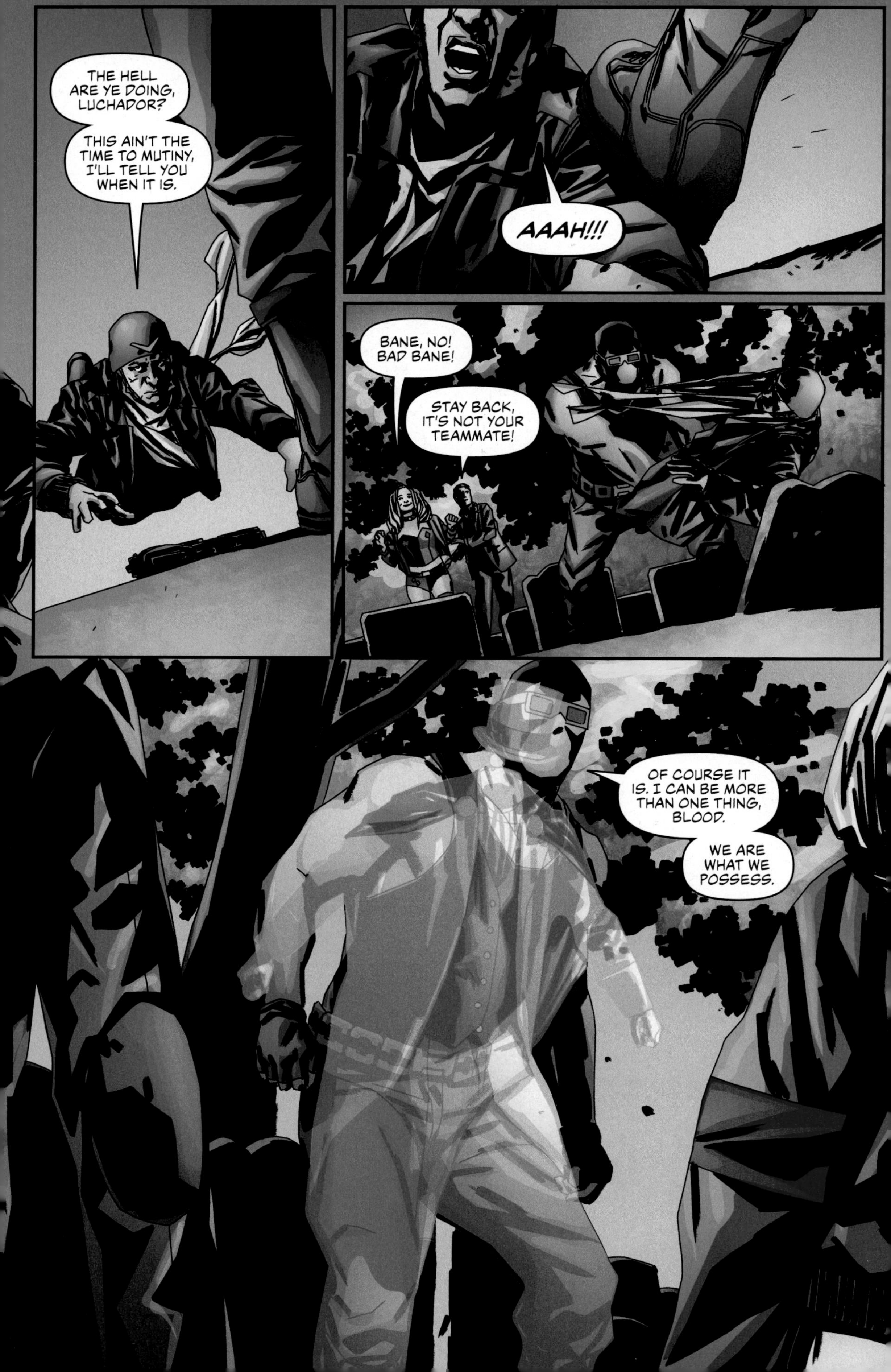
THE HELL ARE YE DOING, LUCHADOR?
THIS AIN'T THE TIME TO MUTINY, I'LL TELL YOU WHEN IT IS.
AAAH!!!
BANE, NO! BAD BANE!
STAY BACK, IT'S NOT YOUR TEAMMATE!
OF COURSE IT IS. I CAN BE MORE THAN ONE THING, BLOOD.
WE ARE WHAT WE POSSESS.

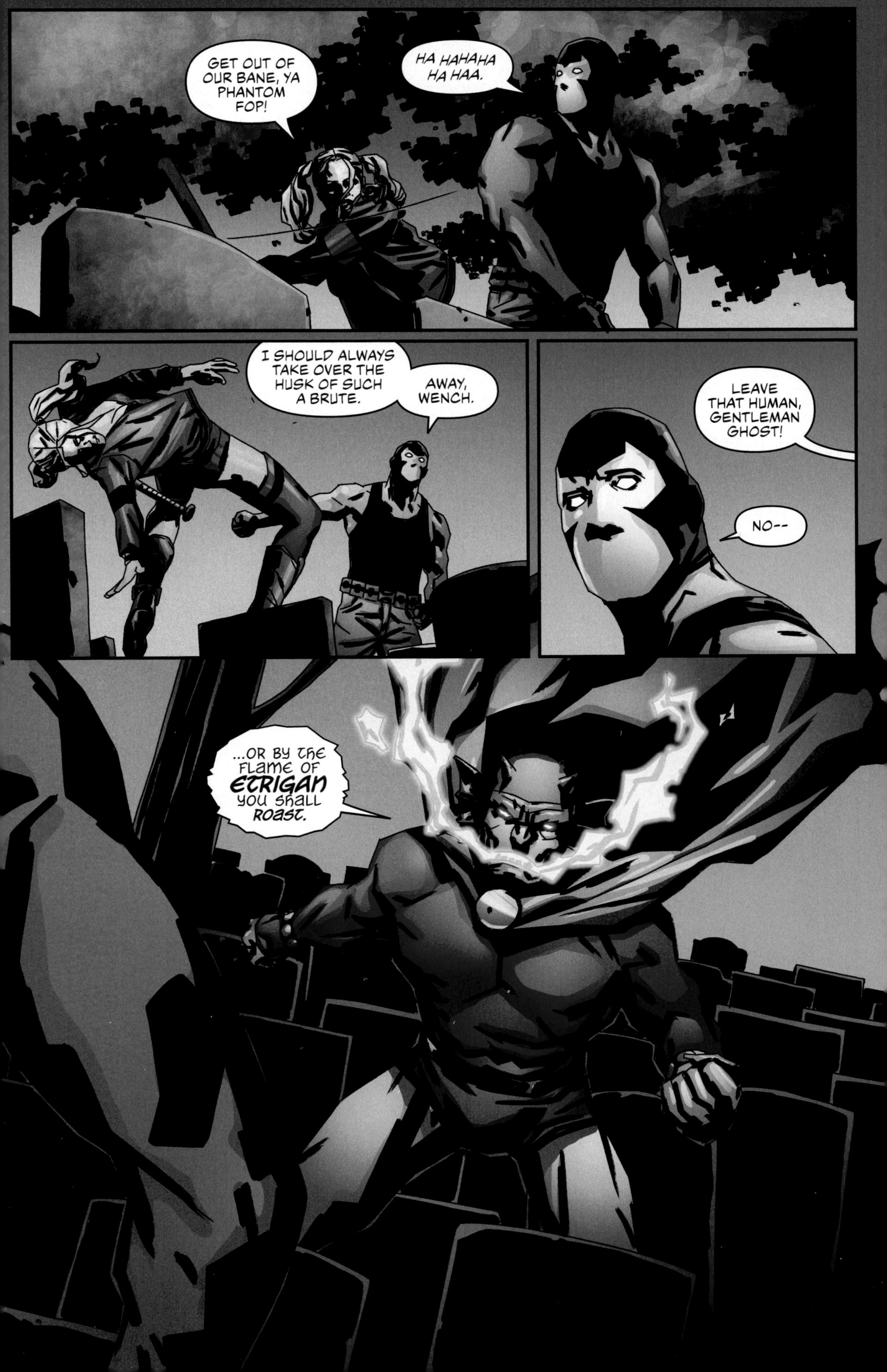
GET OUT OF OUR BANE, YA PHANTOM FOP!
HA HAHAHA HA HAA.
I SHOULD ALWAYS TAKE OVER THE HUSK OF SUCH A BRUTE.
AWAY, WENCH.
LEAVE THAT HUMAN, GENTLEMAN GHOST!
NO--
...OR BY THE FLAME OF ETRIGAN YOU SHALL ROAST.

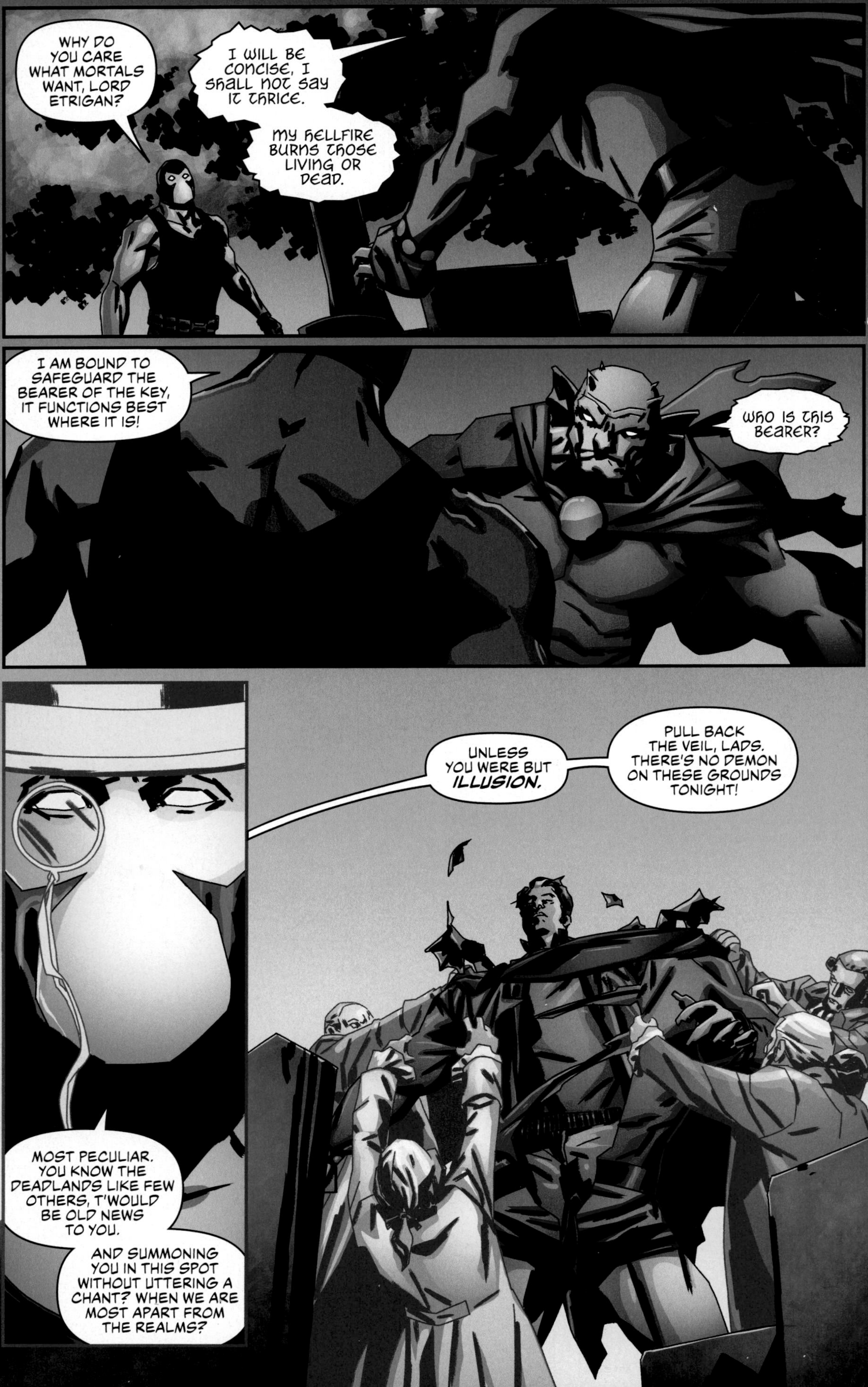
WHY DO YOU CARE WHAT MORTALS WANT, LORD ETRIGAN?
I WILL BE CONCISE, I SHALL NOT SAY IT THRICE.
MY HELLFIRE BURNS THOSE LIVING OR DEAD.
I AM BOUND TO SAFEGUARD THE BEARER OF THE KEY, IT FUNCTIONS BEST WHERE IT IS!
WHO IS THIS BEARER?
UNLESS YOU WERE BUT ILLUSION.
PULL BACK THE VEIL, LADS. THERE'S NO DEMON ON THESE GROUNDS TONIGHT!
MOST PECULIAR. YOU KNOW THE DEADLANDS LIKE FEW OTHERS, T'WOULD BE OLD NEWS TO YOU.
AND SUMMONING YOU IN THIS SPOT WITHOUT UTTERING A CHANT? WHEN WE ARE MOST APART FROM THE REALMS?

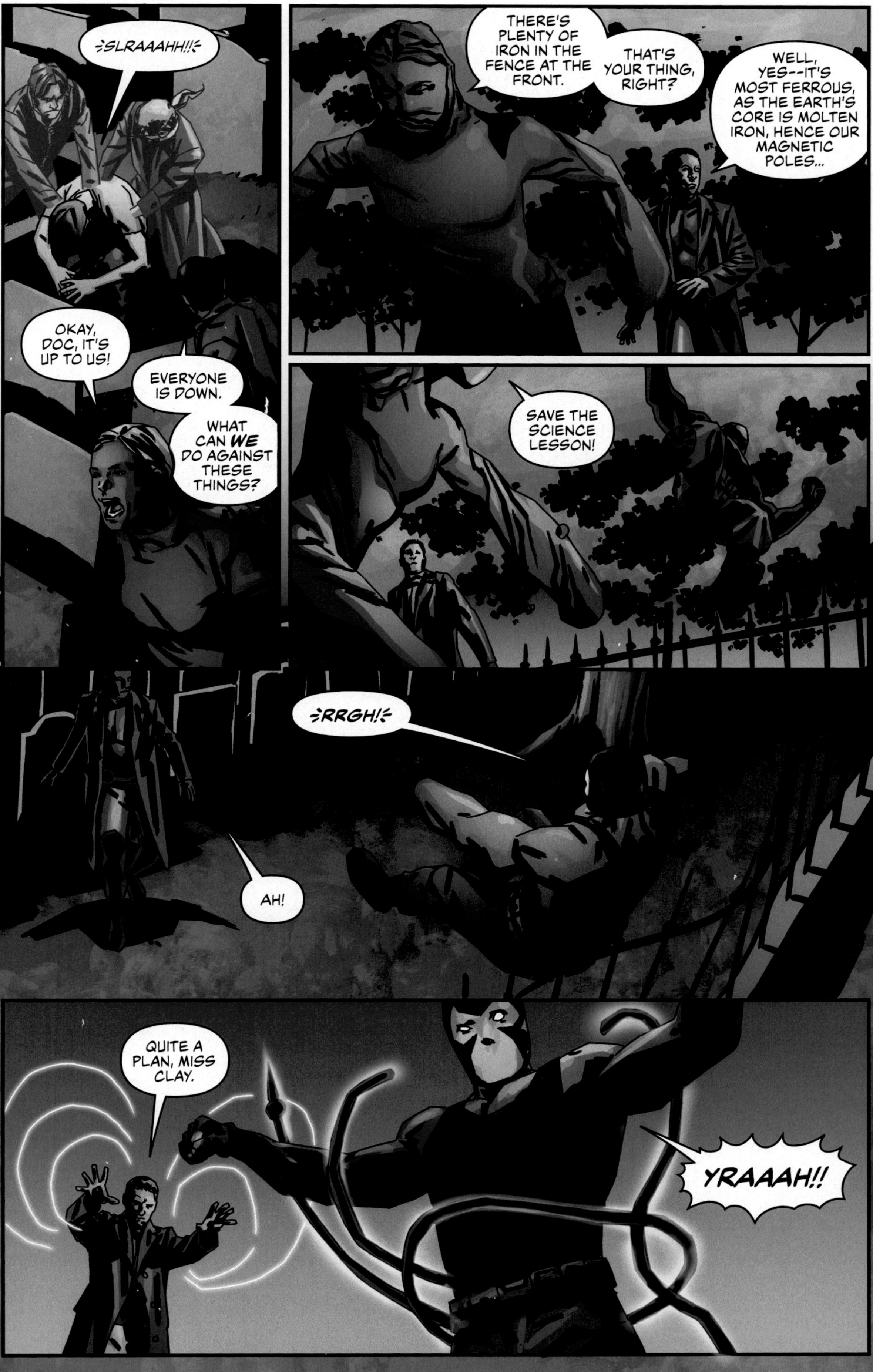

SLRAAAHH!!
OKAY, DOC, IT'S UP TO US!
EVERYONE IS DOWN.
WHAT CAN WE DO AGAINST THESE THINGS?
THERE'S PLENTY OF IRON IN THE FENCE AT THE FRONT.
THAT'S YOUR THING, RIGHT?
WELL, YES--IT'S MOST FERROUS, AS THE EARTH'S CORE IS MOLTEN IRON, HENCE OUR MAGNETIC POLES...
SAVE THE SCIENCE LESSON!
RRGH!
AH!
QUITE A PLAN, MISS CLAY.
YRAAAH!!

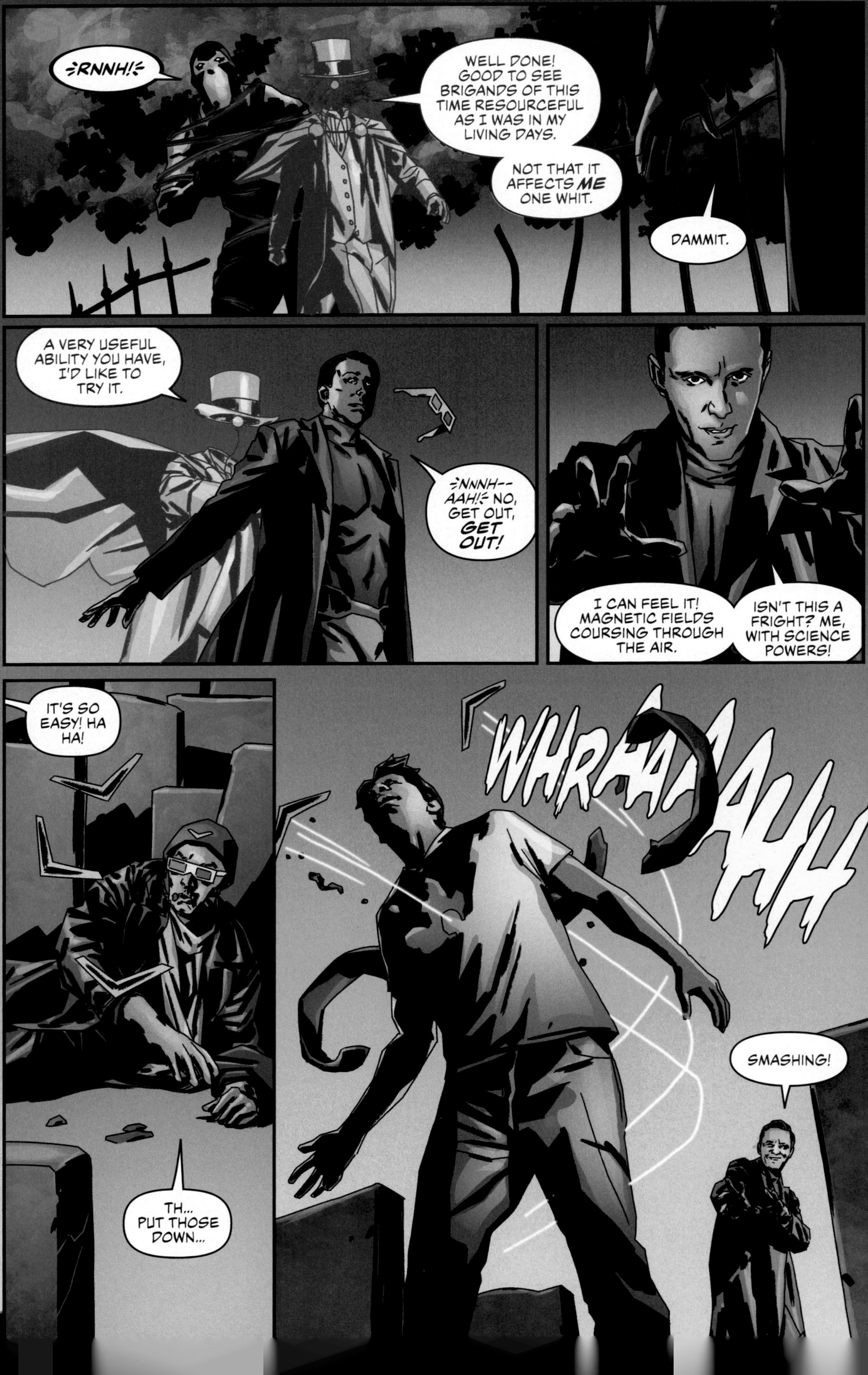
RNNH!
WELL DONE! GOOD TO SEE BRIGANDS OF THIS TIME RESOURCEFUL AS I WAS IN MY LIVING DAYS.
NOT THAT IT AFFECTS ME ONE WHIT.
DAMMIT.
A VERY USEFUL ABILITY YOU HAVE, I'D LIKE TO TRY IT.
NNNH-- AAH! NO, GET OUT, GET OUT!
I CAN FEEL IT! MAGNETIC FIELDS COURSING THROUGH THE AIR.
ISN'T THIS A FRIGHT? ME, WITH SCIENCE POWERS!
IT'S SO EASY! HA HA!
WHRAAAAAHH
TH... PUT THOSE DOWN...
SMASHING!

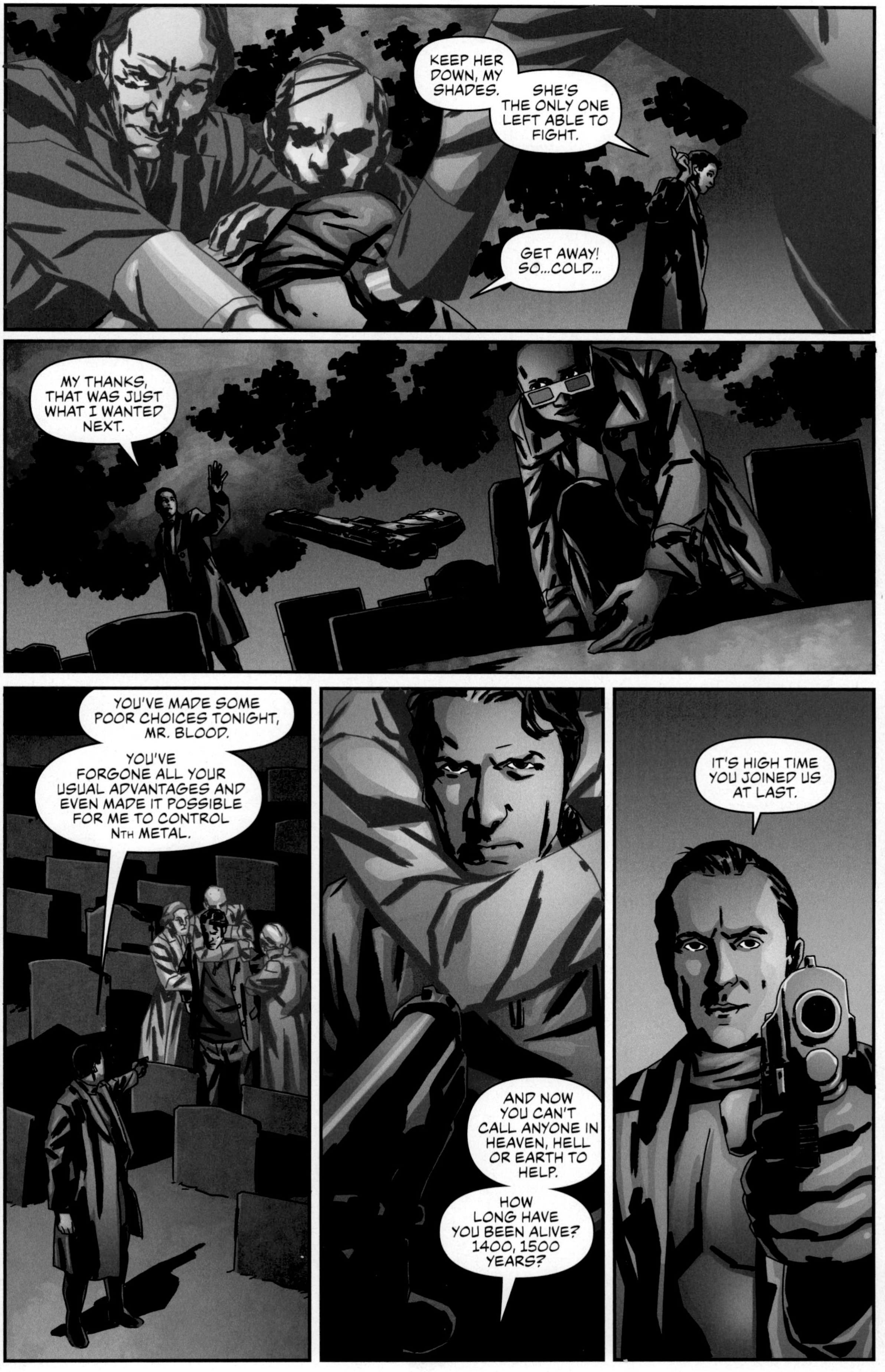

KEEP HER DOWN, MY SHADES.
SHE'S THE ONLY ONE LEFT ABLE TO FIGHT.
GET AWAY! SO...COLD...
MY THANKS, THAT WAS JUST WHAT I WANTED NEXT.
YOU'VE MADE SOME POOR CHOICES TONIGHT, MR. BLOOD.
YOU'VE FORGONE ALL YOUR USUAL ADVANTAGES AND EVEN MADE IT POSSIBLE FOR ME TO CONTROL NTH METAL.
AND NOW YOU CAN'T CALL ANYONE IN HEAVEN, HELL OR EARTH TO HELP.
HOW LONG HAVE YOU BEEN ALIVE? 1400, 1500 YEARS?
IT'S HIGH TIME YOU JOINED US AT LAST.

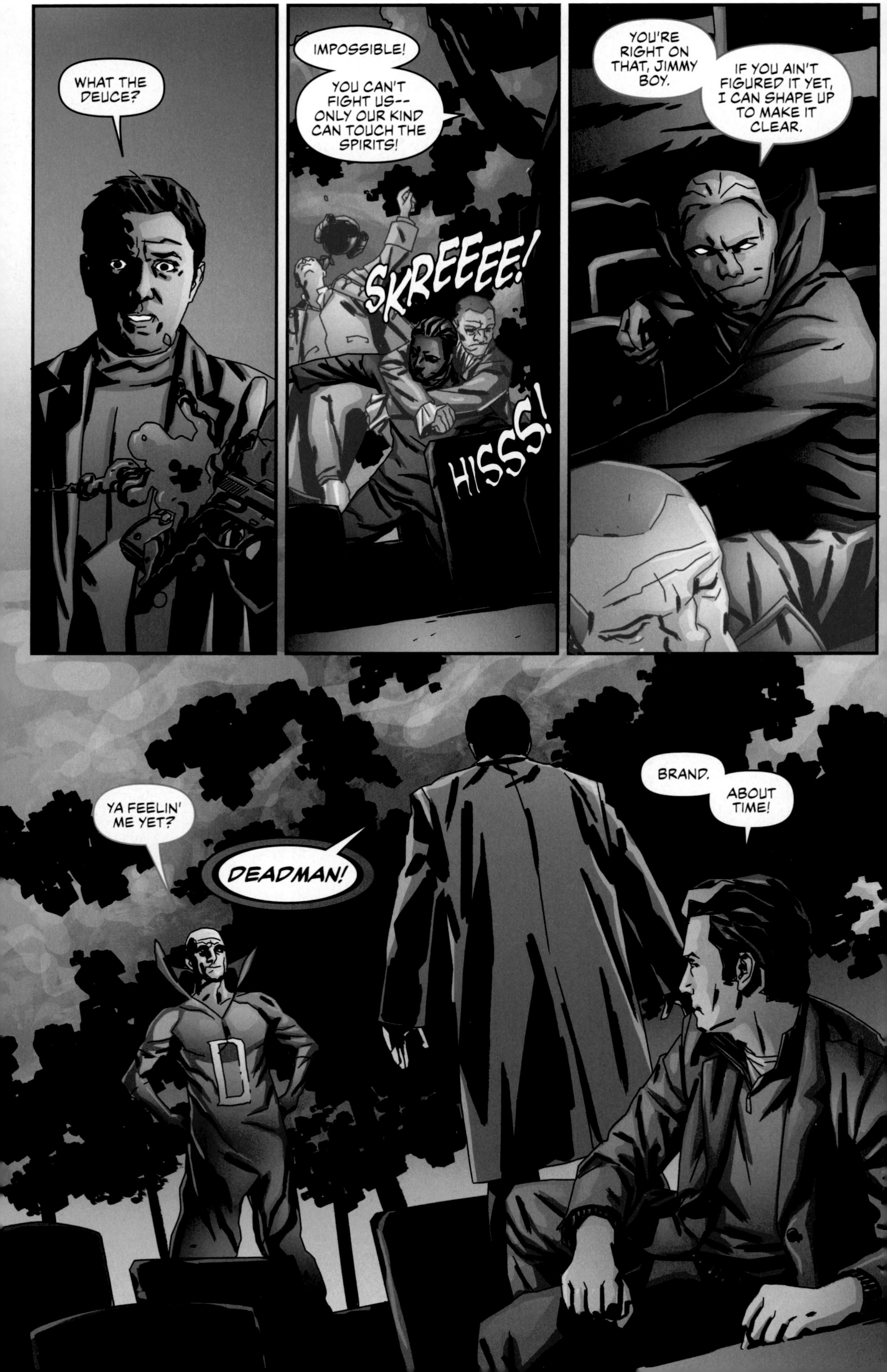
WHAT THE DEUCE?
IMPOSSIBLE!
YOU CAN'T FIGHT US-- ONLY OUR KIND CAN TOUCH THE SPIRITS!
SKREEEEE!
HISSS!
YOU'RE RIGHT ON THAT, JIMMY BOY.
IF YOU AIN'T FIGURED IT YET, I CAN SHAPE UP TO MAKE IT CLEAR.
YA FEELIN' ME YET?
DEADMAN!
BRAND.
ABOUT TIME!

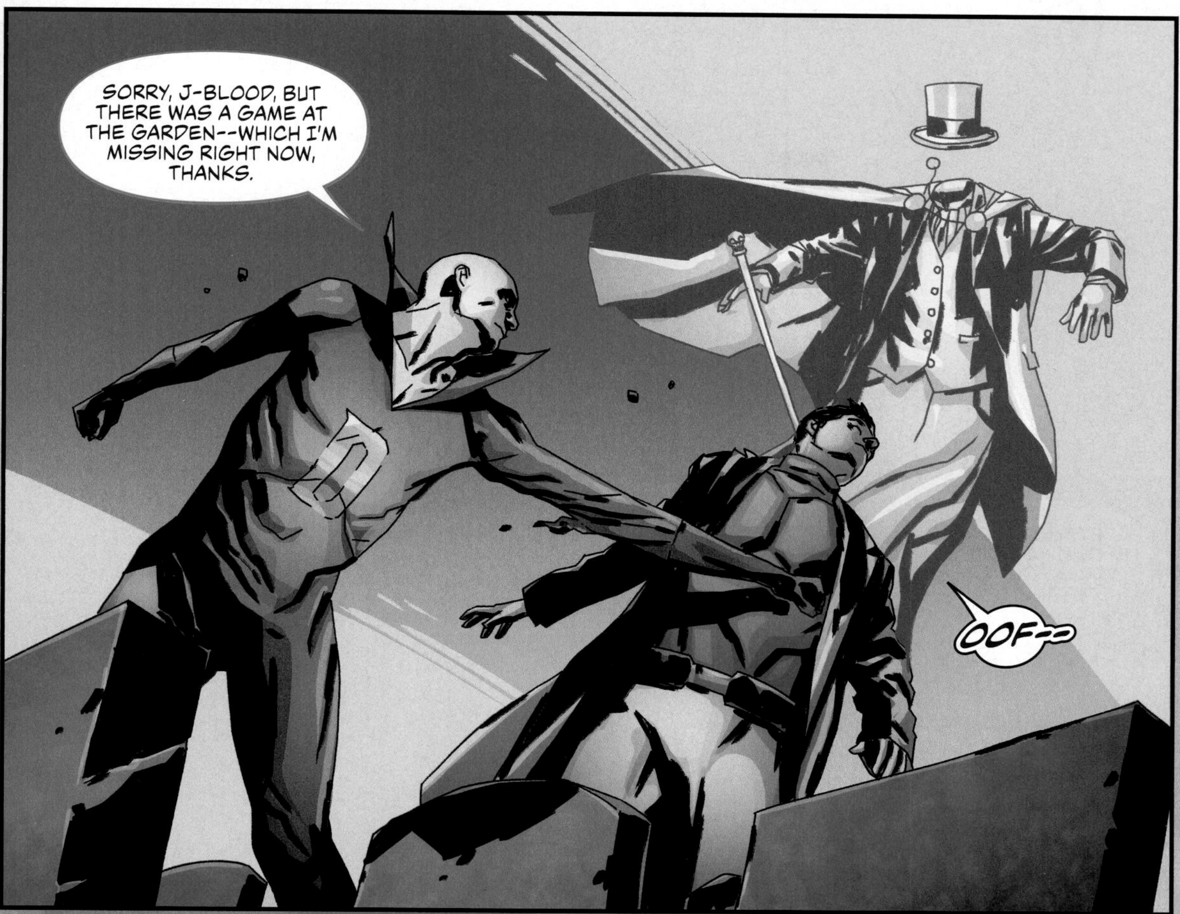
SORRY, J-BLOOD, BUT THERE WAS A GAME AT THE GARDEN--WHICH I'M MISSING RIGHT NOW, THANKS.
OOF--

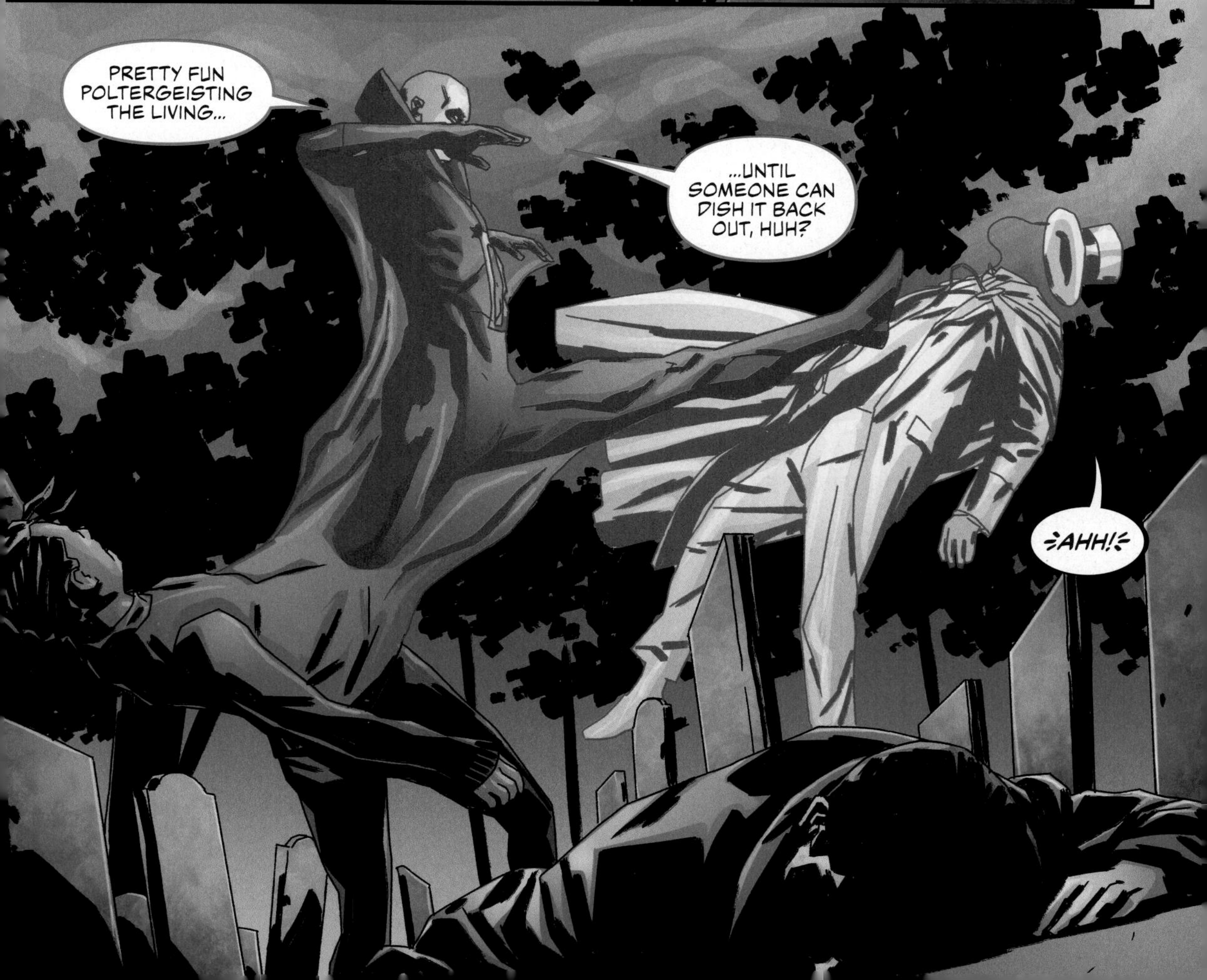
PRETTY FUN POLTERGEISTING THE LIVING...
...UNTIL SOMEONE CAN DISH IT BACK OUT, HUH?
AHH!

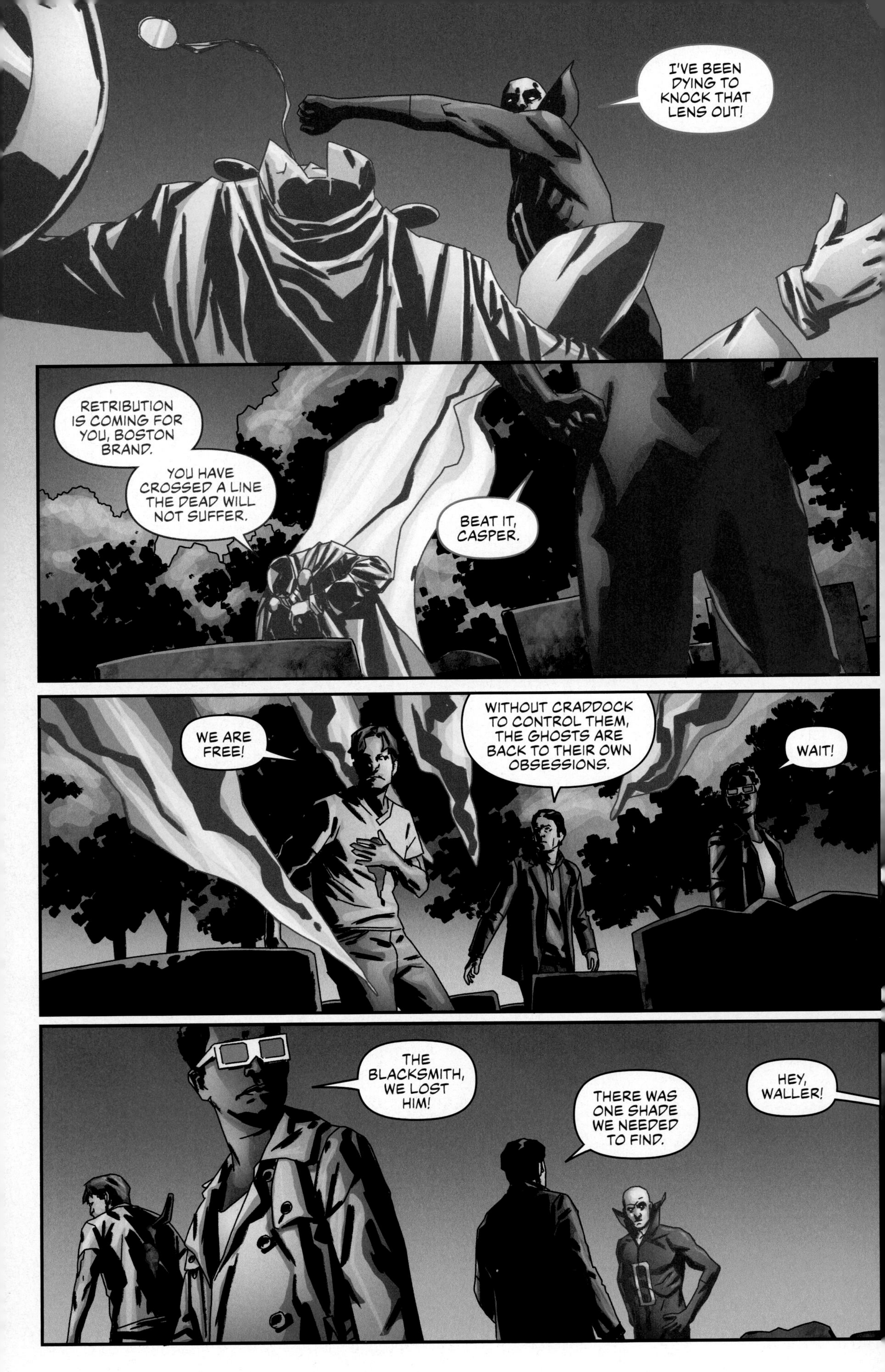
I'VE BEEN DYING TO KNOCK THAT LENS OUT!
RETRIBUTION IS COMING FOR YOU, BOSTON BRAND.
YOU HAVE CROSSED A LINE THE DEAD WILL NOT SUFFER.
BEAT IT, CASPER.
WE ARE FREE!
WITHOUT CRADDOCK TO CONTROL THEM, THE GHOSTS ARE BACK TO THEIR OWN OBSESSIONS.
WAIT!
THE BLACKSMITH, WE LOST HIM!
THERE WAS ONE SHADE WE NEEDED TO FIND.
HEY, WALLER!

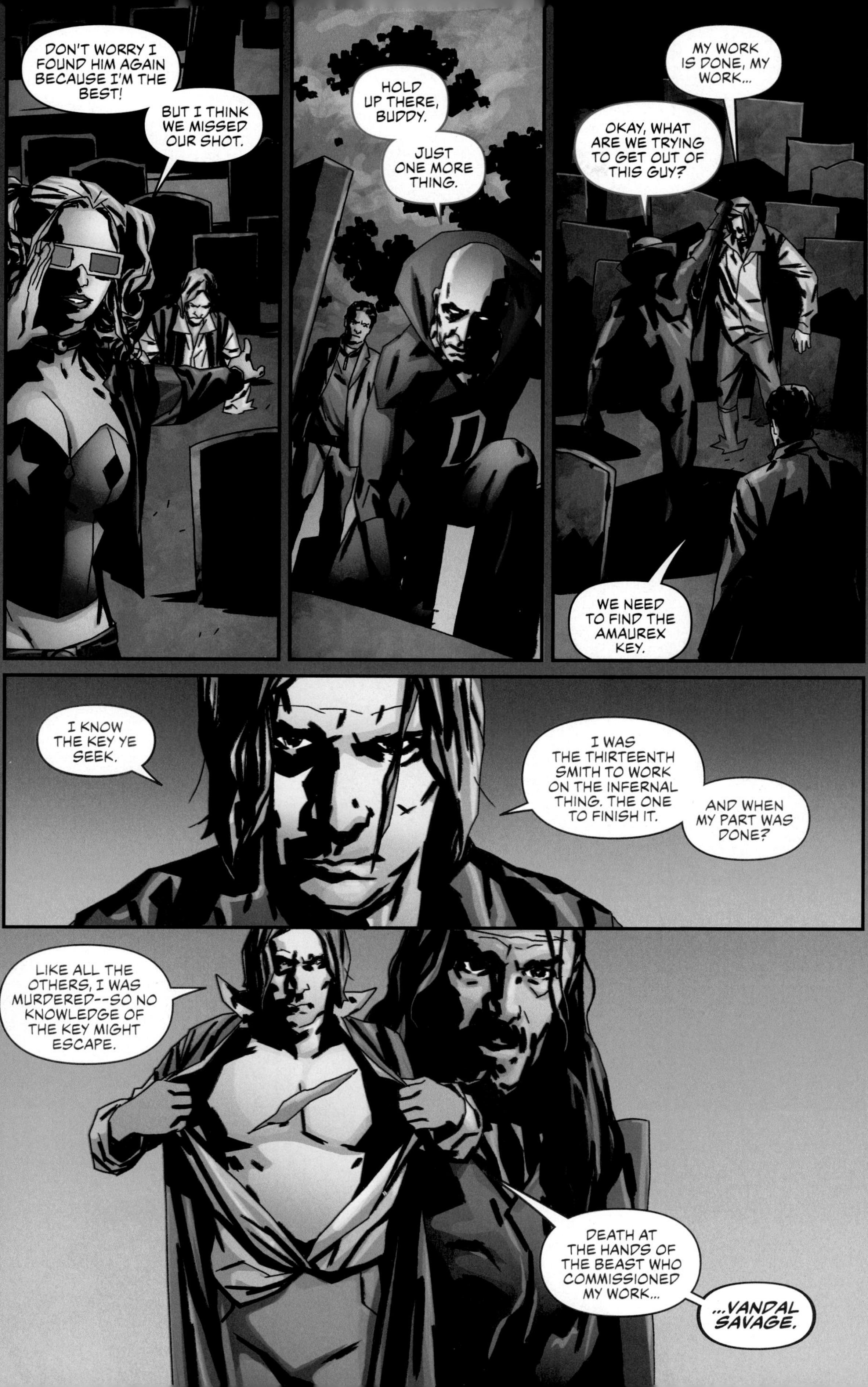
DON'T WORRY I FOUND HIM AGAIN BECAUSE I'M THE BEST!
BUT I THINK WE MISSED OUR SHOT.
HOLD UP THERE, BUDDY.
JUST ONE MORE THING.
MY WORK IS DONE, MY WORK...
OKAY, WHAT ARE WE TRYING TO GET OUT OF THIS GUY?
WE NEED TO FIND THE AMAUREX KEY.
I KNOW THE KEY YE SEEK.
I WAS THE THIRTEENTH SMITH TO WORK ON THE INFERNAL THING. THE ONE TO FINISH IT.
AND WHEN MY PART WAS DONE?
LIKE ALL THE OTHERS, I WAS MURDERED--SO NO KNOWLEDGE OF THE KEY MIGHT ESCAPE.
DEATH AT THE HANDS OF THE BEAST WHO COMMISSIONED MY WORK...
...VANDAL SAVAGE.

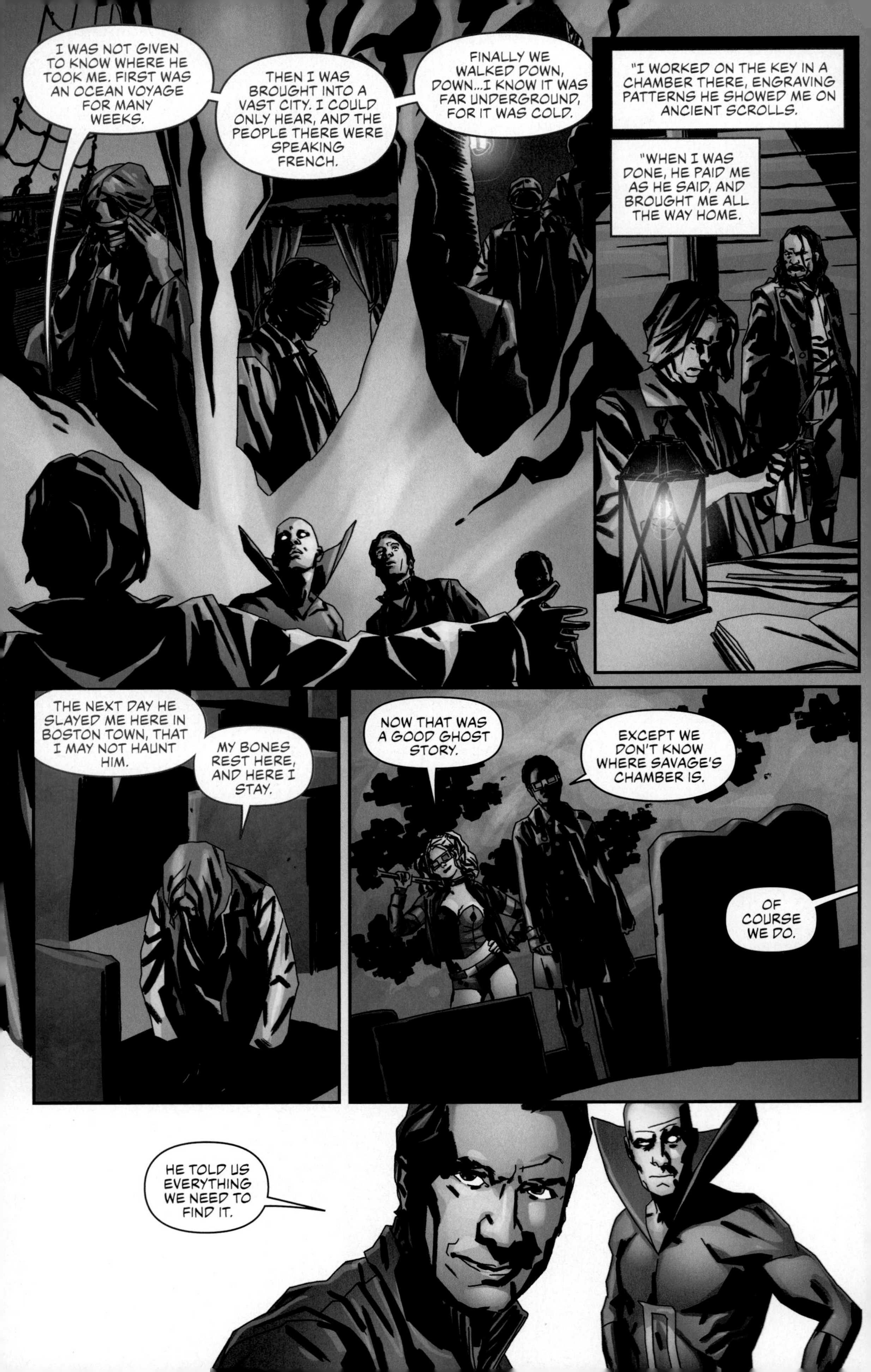
I WAS NOT GIVEN TO KNOW WHERE HE TOOK ME. FIRST WAS AN OCEAN VOYAGE FOR MANY WEEKS.
THEN I WAS BROUGHT INTO A VAST CITY. I COULD ONLY HEAR, AND THE PEOPLE THERE WERE SPEAKING FRENCH.
FINALLY WE WALKED DOWN, DOWN...I KNOW IT WAS FAR UNDERGROUND, FOR IT WAS COLD.
"I WORKED ON THE KEY IN A CHAMBER THERE, ENGRAVING PATTERNS HE SHOWED ME ON ANCIENT SCROLLS.
"WHEN I WAS DONE, HE PAID ME AS HE SAID, AND BROUGHT ME ALL THE WAY HOME.
THE NEXT DAY HE SLAYED ME HERE IN BOSTON TOWN, THAT I MAY NOT HAUNT HIM.
MY BONES REST HERE, AND HERE I STAY.
NOW THAT WAS A GOOD GHOST STORY.
EXCEPT WE DON'T KNOW WHERE SAVAGE'S CHAMBER IS.
OF COURSE WE DO.
HE TOLD US EVERYTHING WE NEED TO FIND IT.

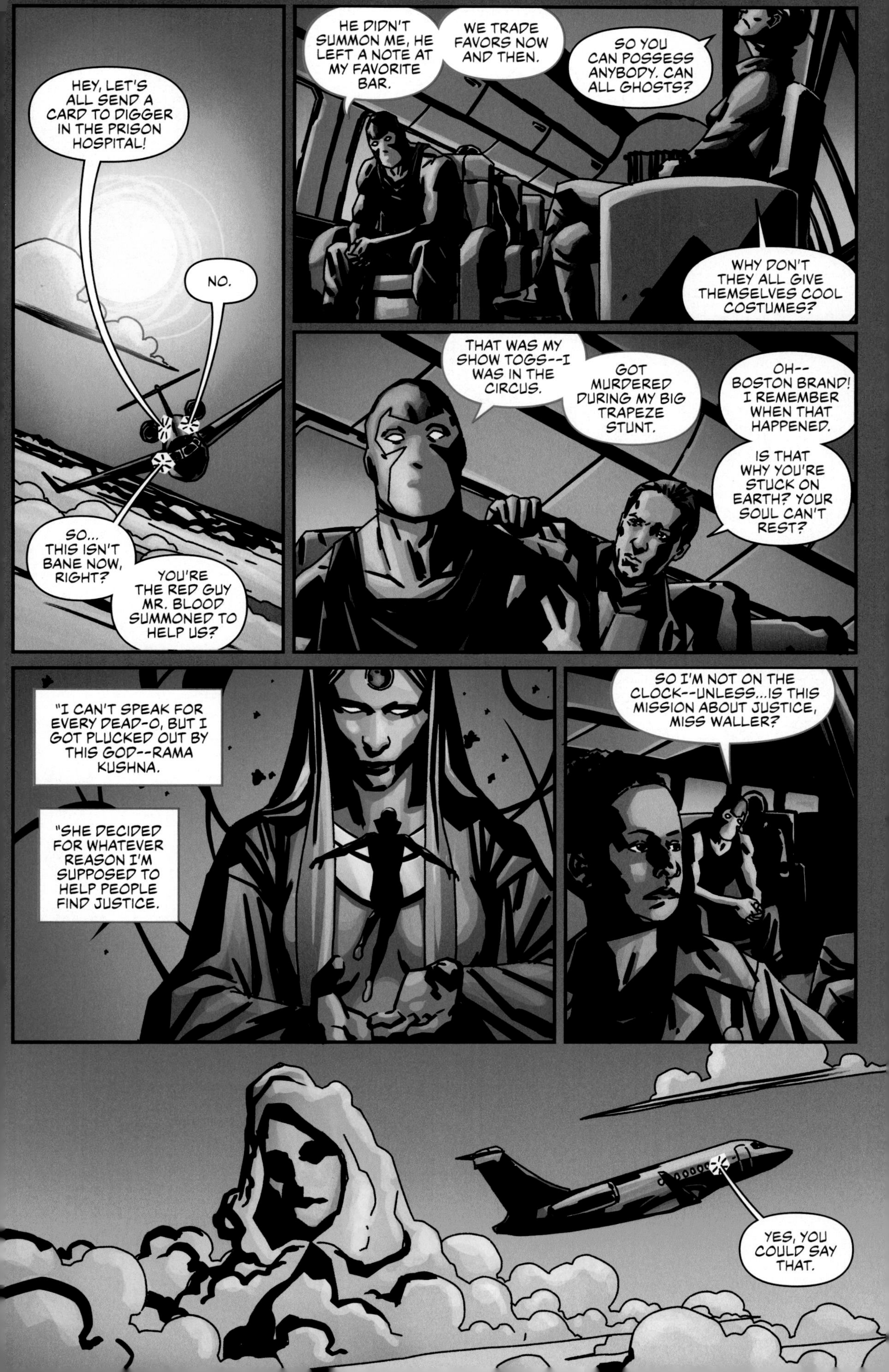
HEY, LET'S ALL SEND A CARD TO DIGGER IN THE PRISON HOSPITAL!
NO.
SO... THIS ISN'T BANE NOW, RIGHT?
YOU'RE THE RED GUY MR. BLOOD SUMMONED TO HELP US?
HE DIDN'T SUMMON ME, HE LEFT A NOTE AT MY FAVORITE BAR.
WE TRADE FAVORS NOW AND THEN.
SO YOU CAN POSSESS ANYBODY. CAN ALL GHOSTS?
WHY DON'T THEY ALL GIVE THEMSELVES COOL COSTUMES?
THAT WAS MY SHOW TOGS--I WAS IN THE CIRCUS.
GOT MURDERED DURING MY BIG TRAPEZE STUNT.
OH-- BOSTON BRAND! I REMEMBER WHEN THAT HAPPENED.
IS THAT WHY YOU'RE STUCK ON EARTH? YOUR SOUL CAN'T REST?
"I CAN'T SPEAK FOR EVERY DEAD-O, BUT I GOT PLUCKED OUT BY THIS GOD--RAMA KUSHNA.
"SHE DECIDED FOR WHATEVER REASON I'M SUPPOSED TO HELP PEOPLE FIND JUSTICE.
SO I'M NOT ON THE CLOCK--UNLESS...IS THIS MISSION ABOUT JUSTICE, MISS WALLER?
YES, YOU COULD SAY THAT.

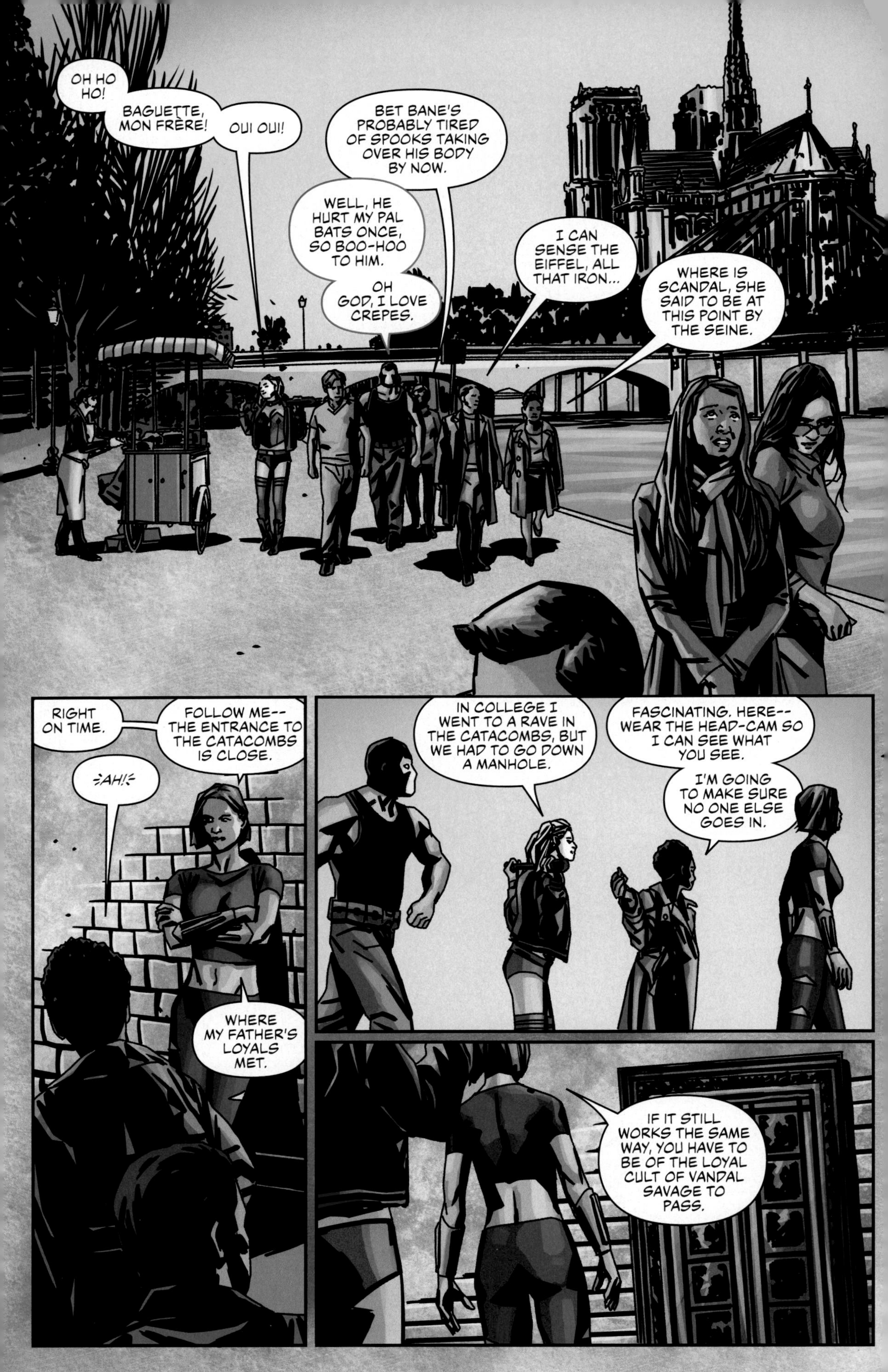
OH HO HO!
BAGUETTE, MON FRÈRE!
OUI OUI!
BET BANE'S PROBABLY TIRED OF SPOOKS TAKING OVER HIS BODY BY NOW.
WELL, HE HURT MY PAL BATS ONCE, SO BOO-HOO TO HIM.
OH GOD, I LOVE CREPES.
I CAN SENSE THE EIFFEL, ALL THAT IRON...
WHERE IS SCANDAL, SHE SAID TO BE AT THIS POINT BY THE SEINE.
RIGHT ON TIME.
FOLLOW ME-- THE ENTRANCE TO THE CATACOMBS IS CLOSE.
AH!
WHERE MY FATHER'S LOYALS MET.
IN COLLEGE I WENT TO A RAVE IN THE CATACOMBS, BUT WE HAD TO GO DOWN A MANHOLE.
FASCINATING. HERE-- WEAR THE HEAD-CAM SO I CAN SEE WHAT YOU SEE.
I'M GOING TO MAKE SURE NO ONE ELSE GOES IN.
IF IT STILL WORKS THE SAME WAY, YOU HAVE TO BE OF THE LOYAL CULT OF VANDAL SAVAGE TO PASS.

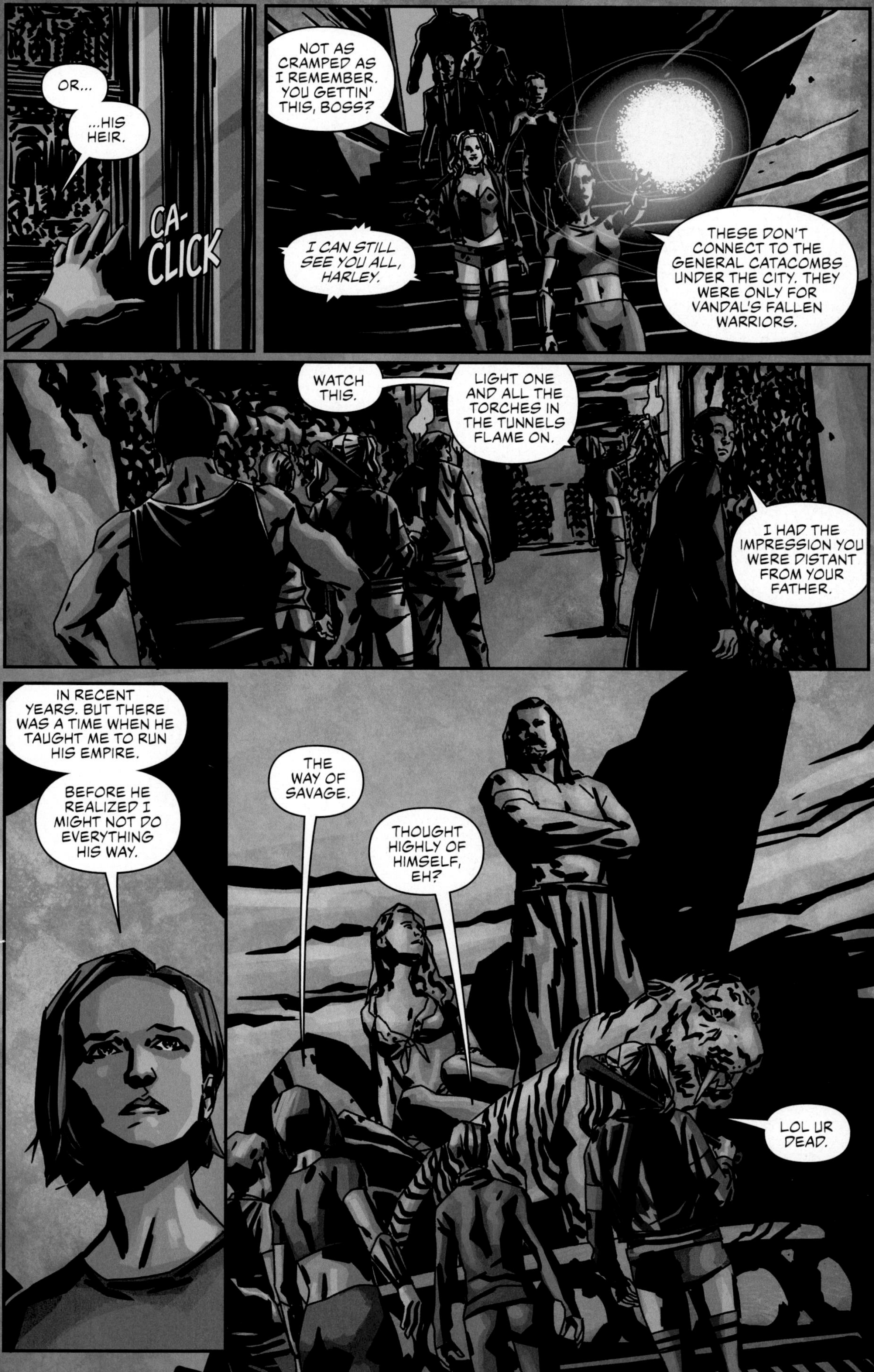
OR...
...HIS HEIR.
CA-CLICK
NOT AS CRAMPED AS I REMEMBER. YOU GETTIN' THIS, BOSS?
I CAN STILL SEE YOU ALL, HARLEY.
THESE DON'T CONNECT TO THE GENERAL CATACOMBS UNDER THE CITY. THEY WERE ONLY FOR VANDAL'S FALLEN WARRIORS.
WATCH THIS.
LIGHT ONE AND ALL THE TORCHES IN THE TUNNELS FLAME ON.
I HAD THE IMPRESSION YOU WERE DISTANT FROM YOUR FATHER.
IN RECENT YEARS. BUT THERE WAS A TIME WHEN HE TAUGHT ME TO RUN HIS EMPIRE.
BEFORE HE REALIZED I MIGHT NOT DO EVERYTHING HIS WAY.
THE WAY OF SAVAGE.
THOUGHT HIGHLY OF HIMSELF, EH?
LOL UR DEAD.

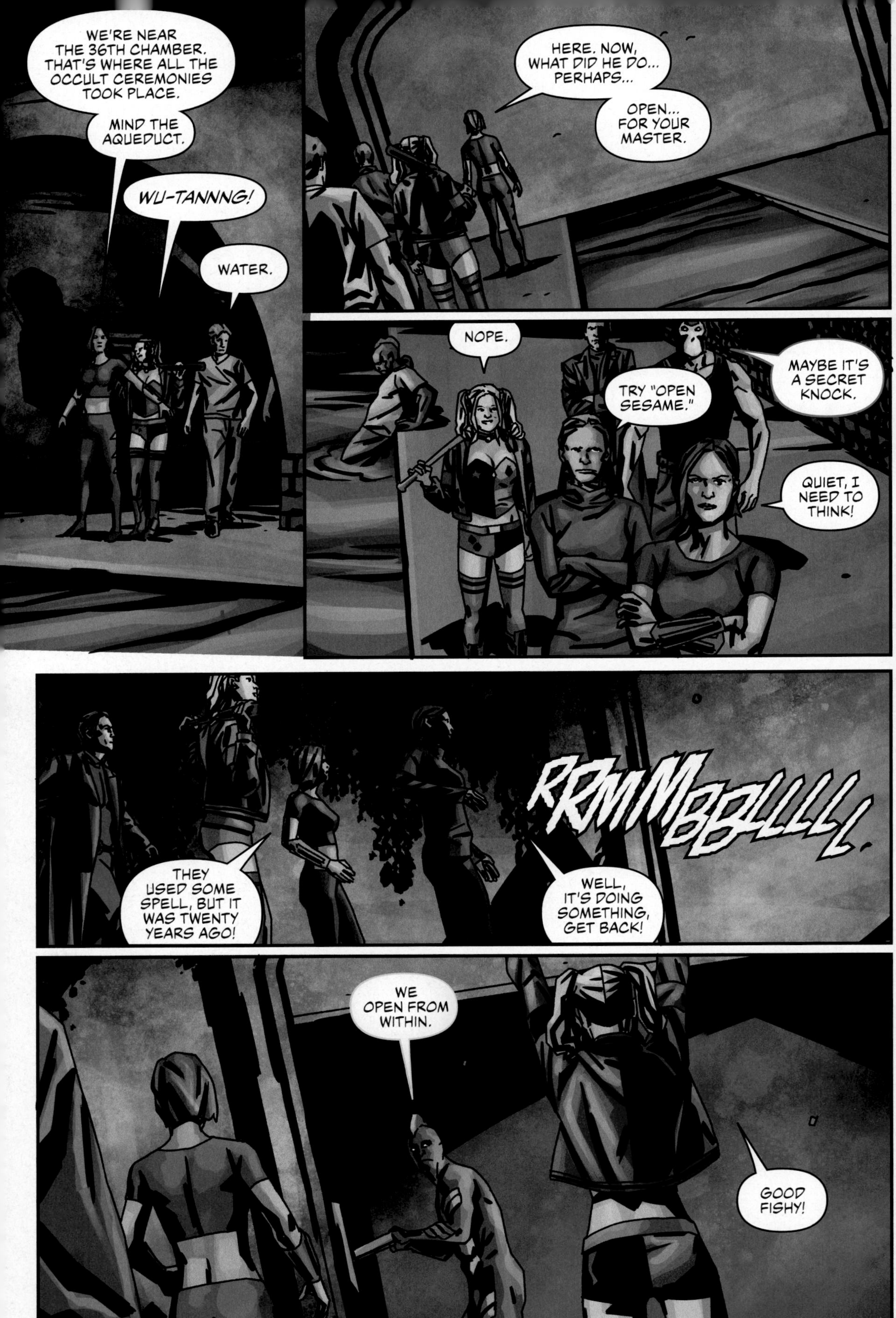

WE'RE NEAR THE 36TH CHAMBER. THAT'S WHERE ALL THE OCCULT CEREMONIES TOOK PLACE.
MIND THE AQUEDUCT.
WU-TANNNG!
WATER.
HERE. NOW, WHAT DID HE DO... PERHAPS...
OPEN... FOR YOUR MASTER.
NOPE.
TRY "OPEN SESAME."
MAYBE IT'S A SECRET KNOCK.
QUIET, I NEED TO THINK!
RRMMBBLLLLL.
THEY USED SOME SPELL, BUT IT WAS TWENTY YEARS AGO!
WELL, IT'S DOING SOMETHING, GET BACK!
WE OPEN FROM WITHIN.
GOOD FISHY!

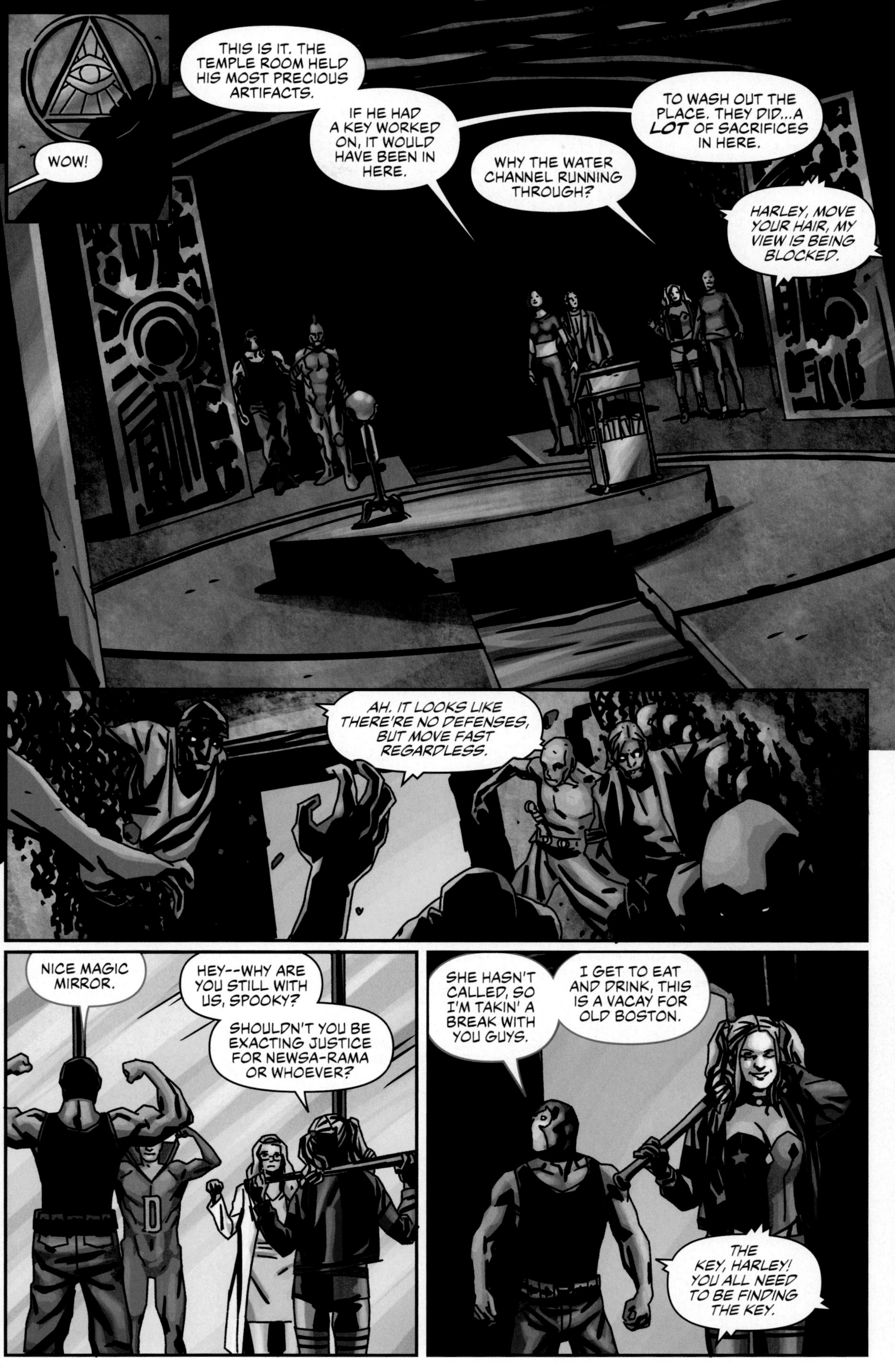
WOW!
THIS IS IT. THE TEMPLE ROOM HELD HIS MOST PRECIOUS ARTIFACTS.
IF HE HAD A KEY WORKED ON, IT WOULD HAVE BEEN IN HERE.
WHY THE WATER CHANNEL RUNNING THROUGH?
TO WASH OUT THE PLACE. THEY DID...A LOT OF SACRIFICES IN HERE.
HARLEY, MOVE YOUR HAIR, MY VIEW IS BEING BLOCKED.
AH. IT LOOKS LIKE THERE'RE NO DEFENSES, BUT MOVE FAST REGARDLESS.
NICE MAGIC MIRROR.
HEY--WHY ARE YOU STILL WITH US, SPOOKY?
SHOULDN'T YOU BE EXACTING JUSTICE FOR NEWSA-RAMA OR WHOEVER?
SHE HASN'T CALLED, SO I'M TAKIN' A BREAK WITH YOU GUYS.
I GET TO EAT AND DRINK, THIS IS A VACAY FOR OLD BOSTON.
THE KEY, HARLEY! YOU ALL NEED TO BE FINDING THE KEY.

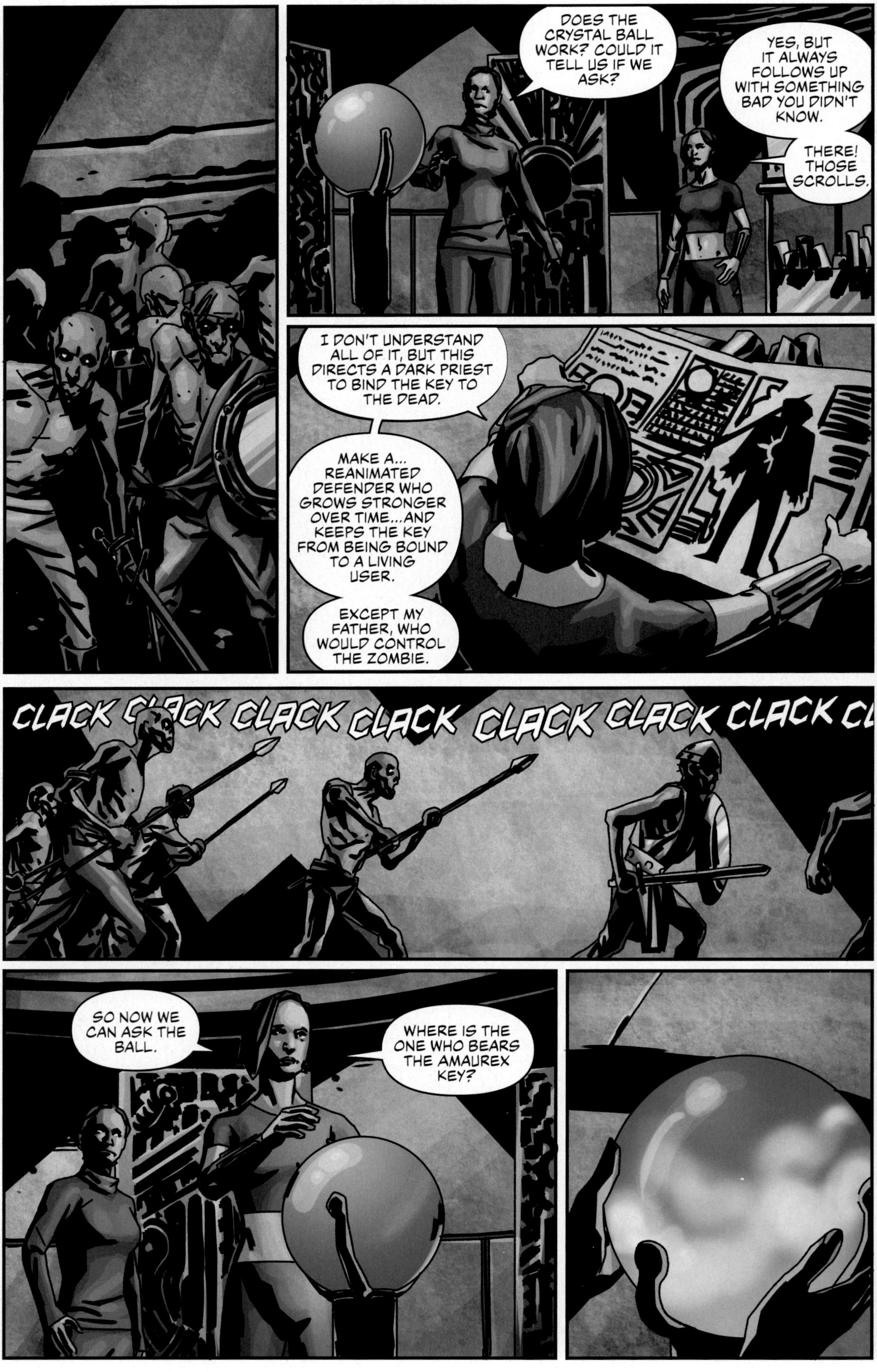
DOES THE CRYSTAL BALL WORK? COULD IT TELL US IF WE ASK?
YES, BUT IT ALWAYS FOLLOWS UP WITH SOMETHING BAD YOU DIDN'T KNOW.
THERE! THOSE SCROLLS.
I DON'T UNDERSTAND ALL OF IT, BUT THIS DIRECTS A DARK PRIEST TO BIND THE KEY TO THE DEAD.
MAKE A... REANIMATED DEFENDER WHO GROWS STRONGER OVER TIME...AND KEEPS THE KEY FROM BEING BOUND TO A LIVING USER.
EXCEPT MY FATHER, WHO WOULD CONTROL THE ZOMBIE.
CLACK CLACK CLACK CLACK CLACK CLACK CLACK
SO NOW WE CAN ASK THE BALL.
WHERE IS THE ONE WHO BEARS THE AMAUREX KEY?

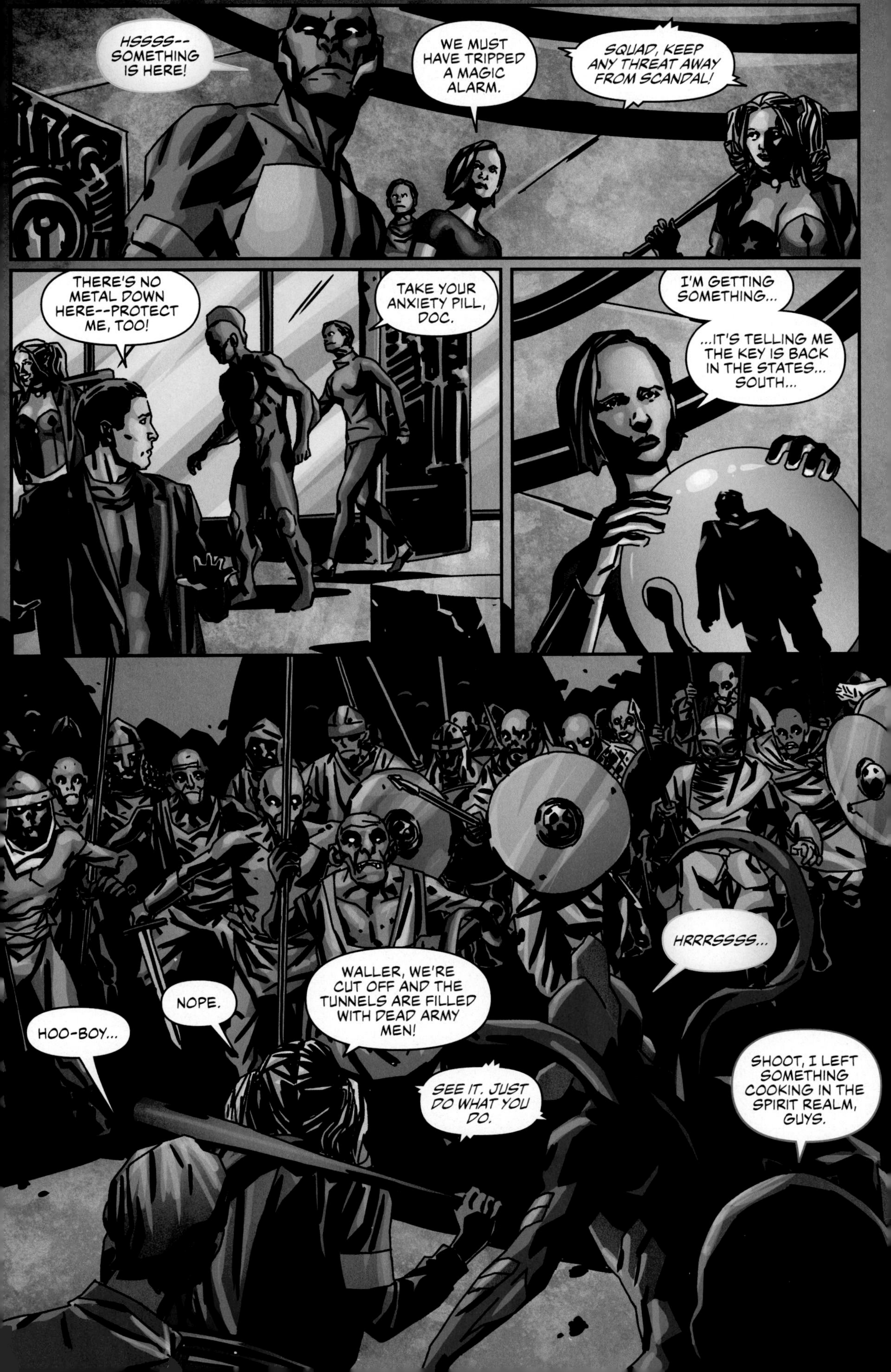
HSSSS-- SOMETHING IS HERE!
WE MUST HAVE TRIPPED A MAGIC ALARM.
SQUAD, KEEP ANY THREAT AWAY FROM SCANDAL!
THERE'S NO METAL DOWN HERE--PROTECT ME, TOO!
TAKE YOUR ANXIETY PILL, DOC.
I'M GETTING SOMETHING...
...IT'S TELLING ME THE KEY IS BACK IN THE STATES... SOUTH...
HRRRSSSS...
WALLER, WE'RE CUT OFF AND THE TUNNELS ARE FILLED WITH DEAD ARMY MEN!
NOPE.
HOO-BOY...
SEE IT. JUST DO WHAT YOU DO.
SHOOT, I LEFT SOMETHING COOKING IN THE SPIRIT REALM, GUYS.

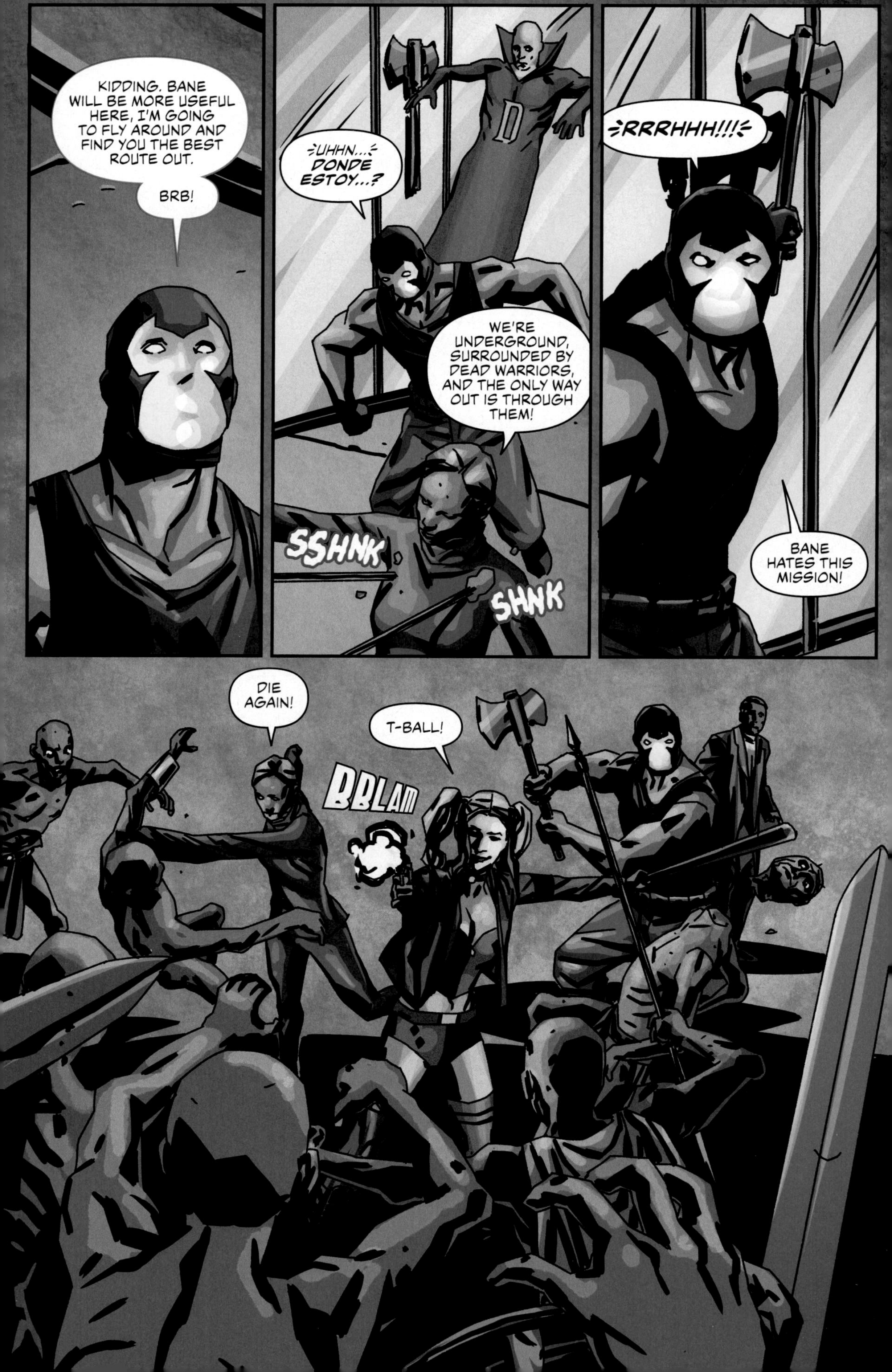
KIDDING. BANE WILL BE MORE USEFUL HERE, I'M GOING TO FLY AROUND AND FIND YOU THE BEST ROUTE OUT.
BRB!
UHHN... DONDE ESTOY...?
WE'RE UNDERGROUND, SURROUNDED BY DEAD WARRIORS, AND THE ONLY WAY OUT IS THROUGH THEM!
SSHNK
SHNK
RRRHHH!!!
BANE HATES THIS MISSION!
DIE AGAIN!
T-BALL!
BBLAM

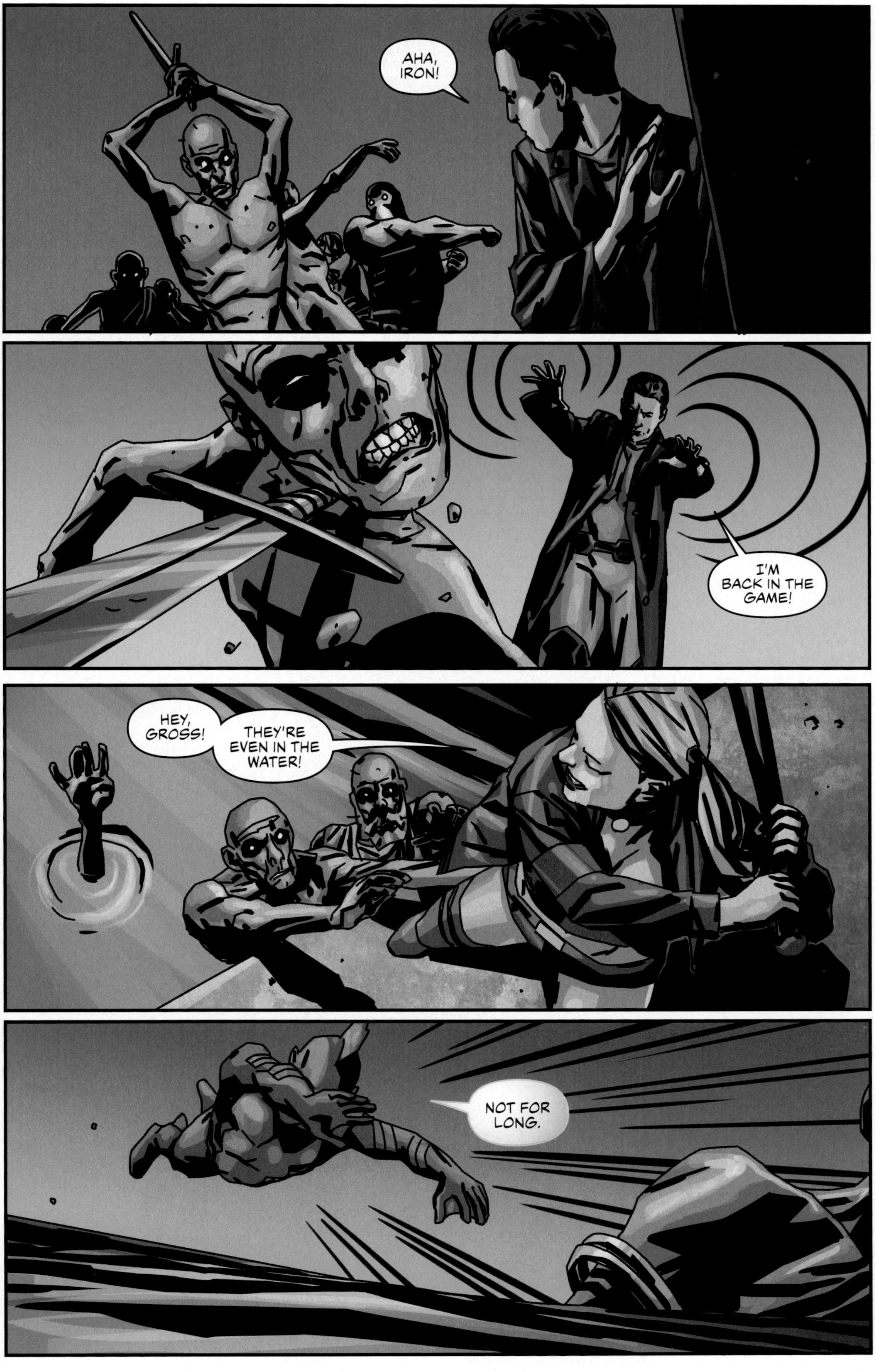
AHA, IRON!
I'M BACK IN THE GAME!
HEY, GROSS!
THEY'RE EVEN IN THE WATER!
NOT FOR LONG.

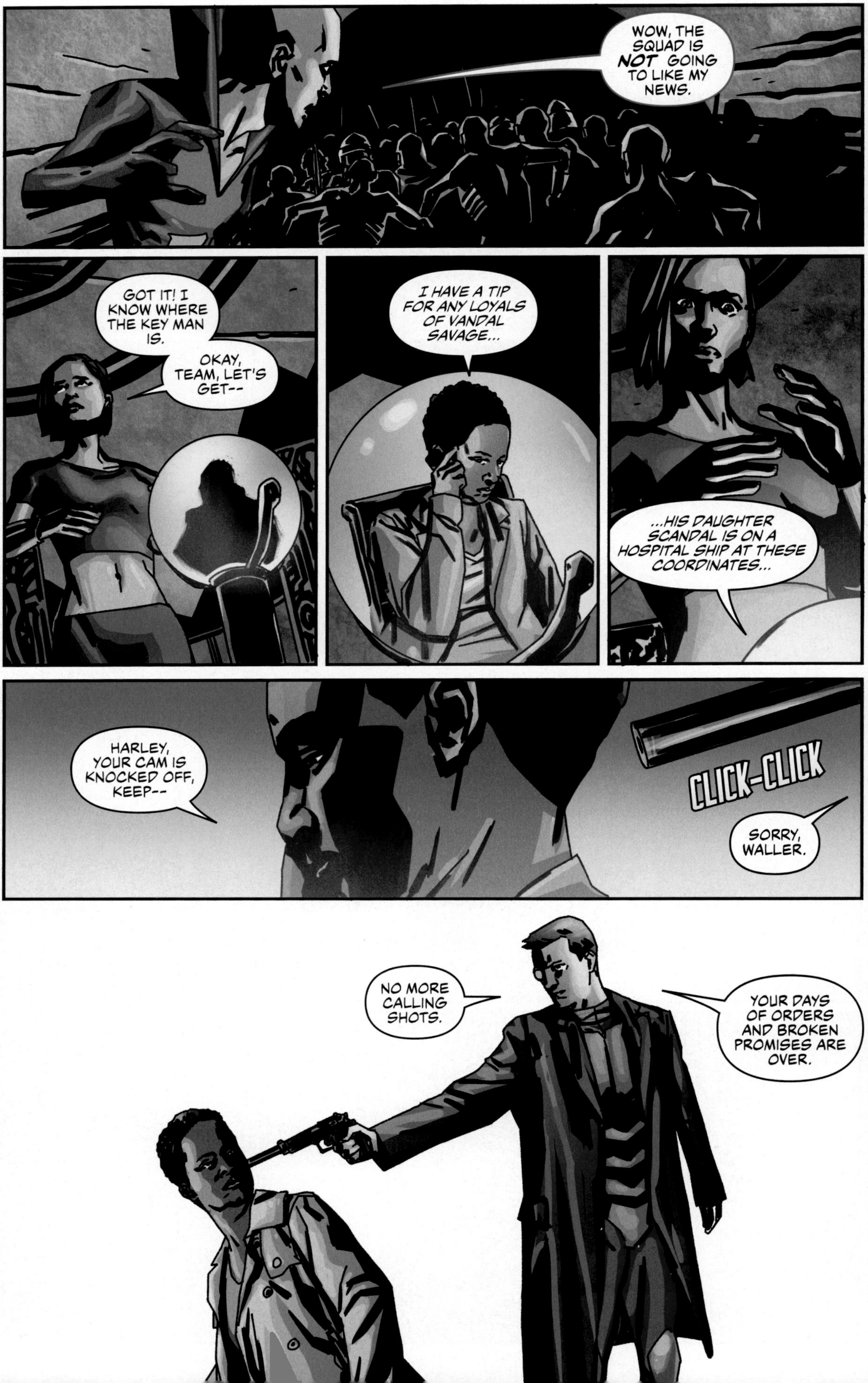
WOW, THE SQUAD IS NOT GOING TO LIKE MY NEWS.
GOT IT! I KNOW WHERE THE KEY MAN IS.
OKAY, TEAM, LET'S GET--
I HAVE A TIP FOR ANY LOYALS OF VANDAL SAVAGE...
...HIS DAUGHTER SCANDAL IS ON A HOSPITAL SHIP AT THESE COORDINATES...
HARLEY, YOUR CAM IS KNOCKED OFF, KEEP--
CLICK-CLICK
SORRY, WALLER.
NO MORE CALLING SHOTS.
YOUR DAYS OF ORDERS AND BROKEN PROMISES ARE OVER.

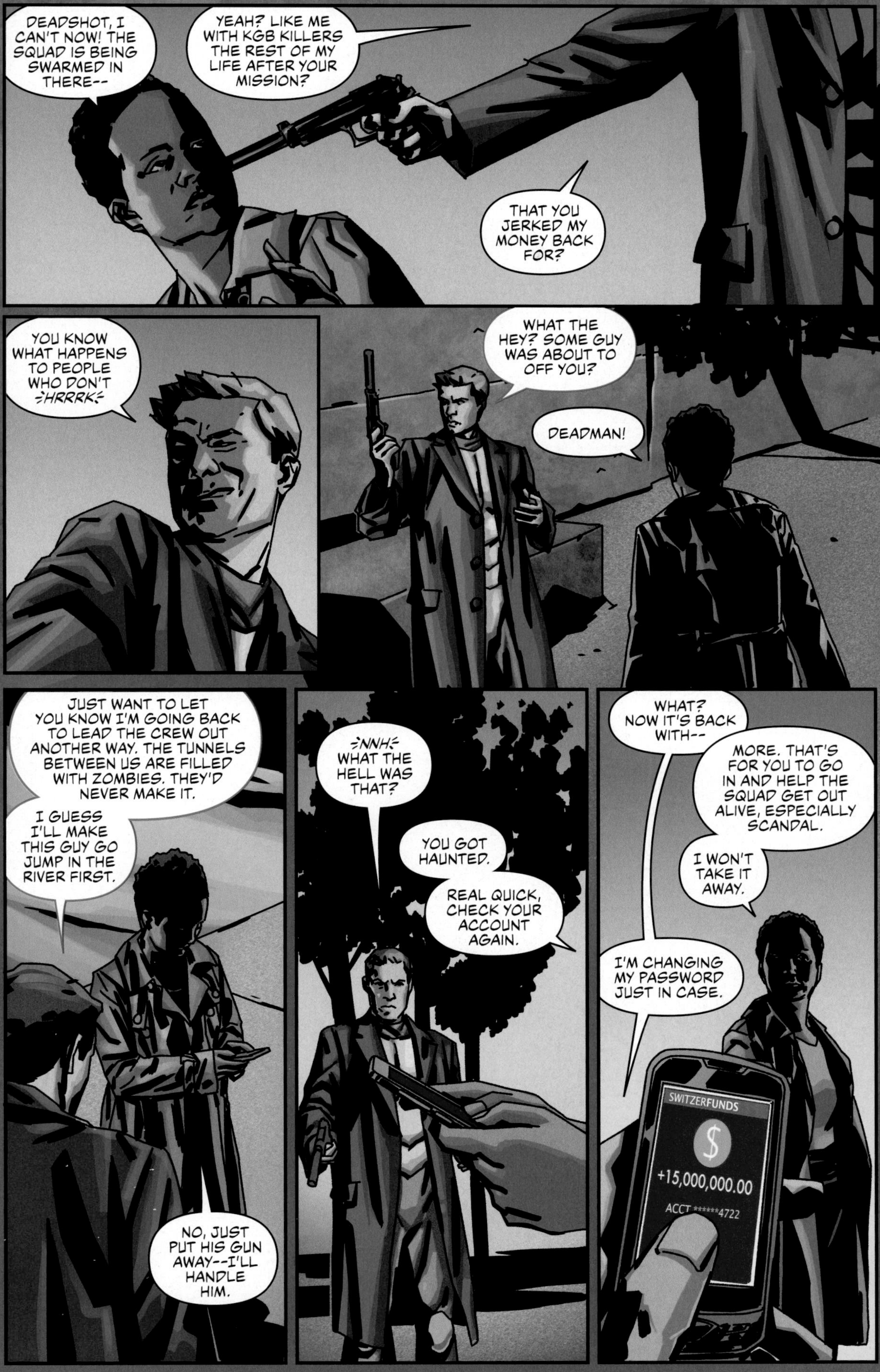
DEADSHOT, I CAN'T NOW! THE SQUAD IS BEING SWARMED IN THERE--
YEAH? LIKE ME WITH KGB KILLERS THE REST OF MY LIFE AFTER YOUR MISSION?
THAT YOU JERKED MY MONEY BACK FOR?
YOU KNOW WHAT HAPPENS TO PEOPLE WHO DON'T ≈HRRRK≈
WHAT THE HEY? SOME GUY WAS ABOUT TO OFF YOU?
DEADMAN!
JUST WANT TO LET YOU KNOW I'M GOING BACK TO LEAD THE CREW OUT ANOTHER WAY. THE TUNNELS BETWEEN US ARE FILLED WITH ZOMBIES. THEY'D NEVER MAKE IT.
I GUESS I'LL MAKE THIS GUY GO JUMP IN THE RIVER FIRST.
NO, JUST PUT HIS GUN AWAY--I'LL HANDLE HIM.
≈NNH≈ WHAT THE HELL WAS THAT?
YOU GOT HAUNTED.
REAL QUICK, CHECK YOUR ACCOUNT AGAIN.
WHAT? NOW IT'S BACK WITH--
MORE. THAT'S FOR YOU TO GO IN AND HELP THE SQUAD GET OUT ALIVE, ESPECIALLY SCANDAL.
I WON'T TAKE IT AWAY.
I'M CHANGING MY PASSWORD JUST IN CASE.
SWITZERFUNDS
$
+15,000,000.00
ACCT *****4722

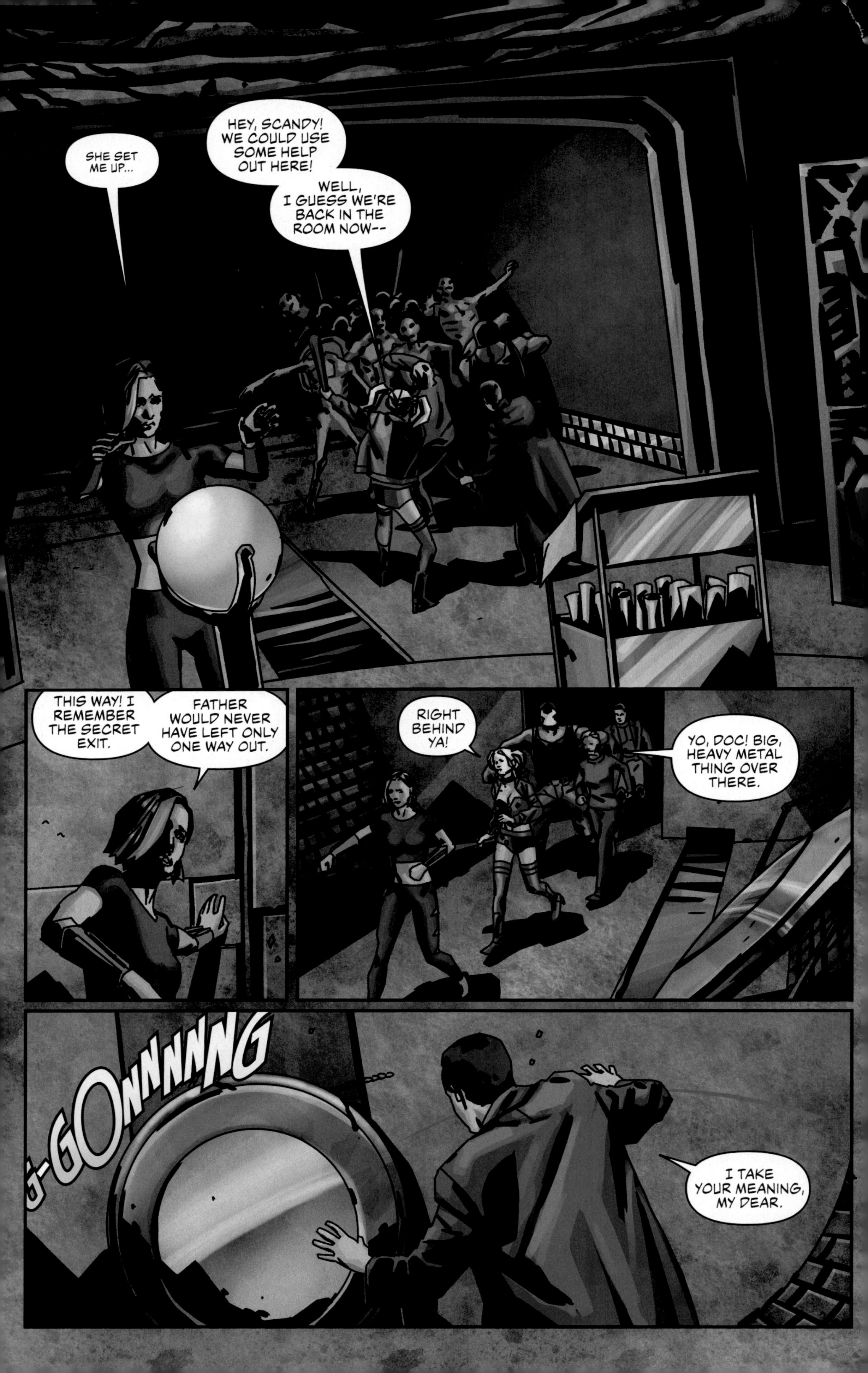

SHE SET ME UP...
HEY, SCANDY! WE COULD USE SOME HELP OUT HERE!
WELL, I GUESS WE'RE BACK IN THE ROOM NOW--
THIS WAY! I REMEMBER THE SECRET EXIT.
FATHER WOULD NEVER HAVE LEFT ONLY ONE WAY OUT.
RIGHT BEHIND YA!
YO, DOC! BIG, HEAVY METAL THING OVER THERE.
G-GONNNNNG
I TAKE YOUR MEANING, MY DEAR.

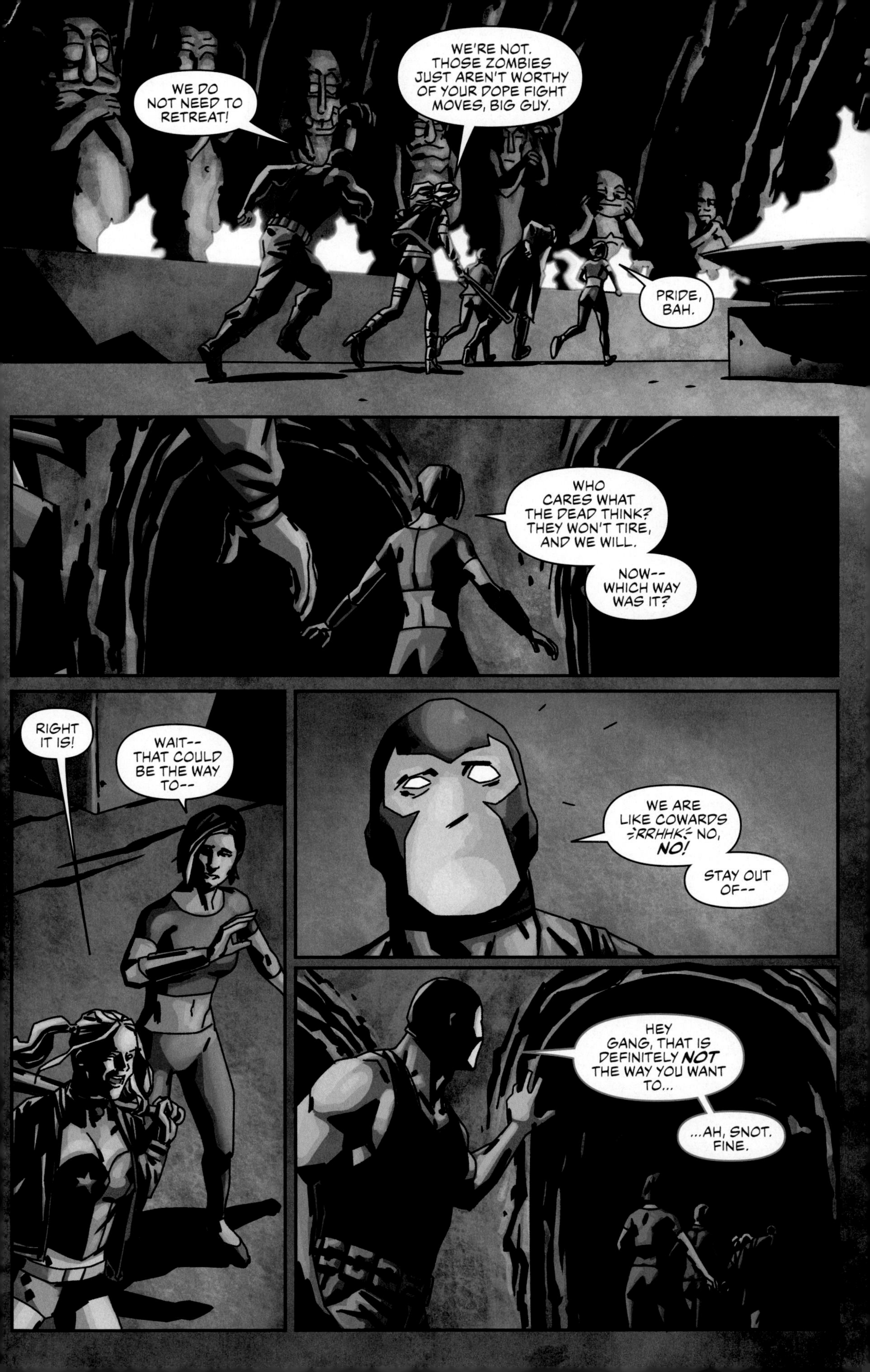
WE DO NOT NEED TO RETREAT!
WE'RE NOT. THOSE ZOMBIES JUST AREN'T WORTHY OF YOUR DOPE FIGHT MOVES, BIG GUY.
PRIDE, BAH.
WHO CARES WHAT THE DEAD THINK? THEY WON'T TIRE, AND WE WILL.
NOW-- WHICH WAY WAS IT?
RIGHT IT IS!
WAIT-- THAT COULD BE THE WAY TO--
WE ARE LIKE COWARDS -RRHHK- NO, NO!
STAY OUT OF--
HEY GANG, THAT IS DEFINITELY NOT THE WAY YOU WANT TO...
...AH, SNOT. FINE.

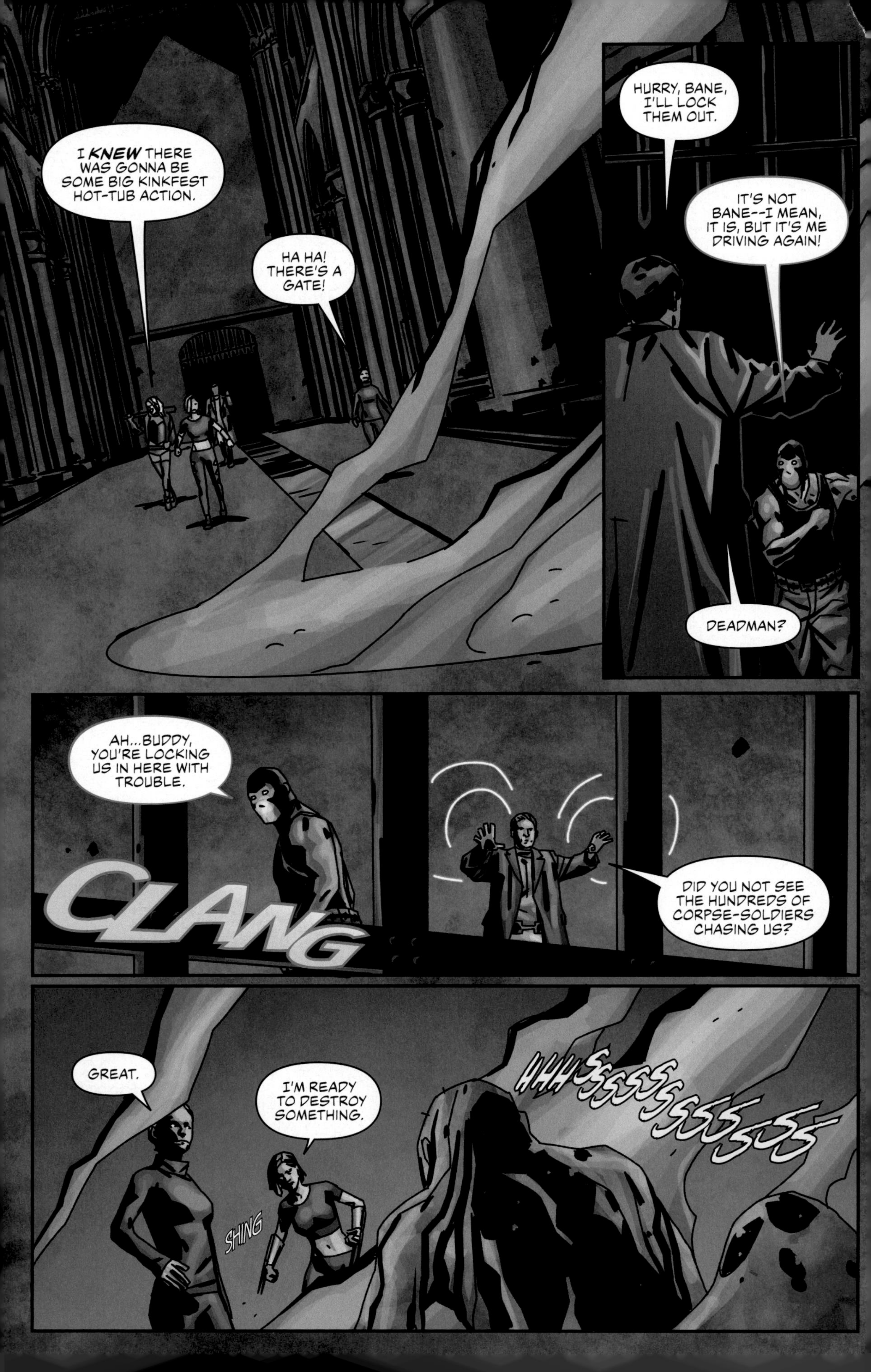
I KNEW THERE WAS GONNA BE SOME BIG KINKFEST HOT-TUB ACTION.
HA HA! THERE'S A GATE!
HURRY, BANE, I'LL LOCK THEM OUT.
IT'S NOT BANE--I MEAN, IT IS, BUT IT'S ME DRIVING AGAIN!
DEADMAN?
AH...BUDDY, YOU'RE LOCKING US IN HERE WITH TROUBLE.
CLANG
DID YOU NOT SEE THE HUNDREDS OF CORPSE-SOLDIERS CHASING US?
GREAT.
I'M READY TO DESTROY SOMETHING.
SHING
HHHSSSSSSSSSSSSSS

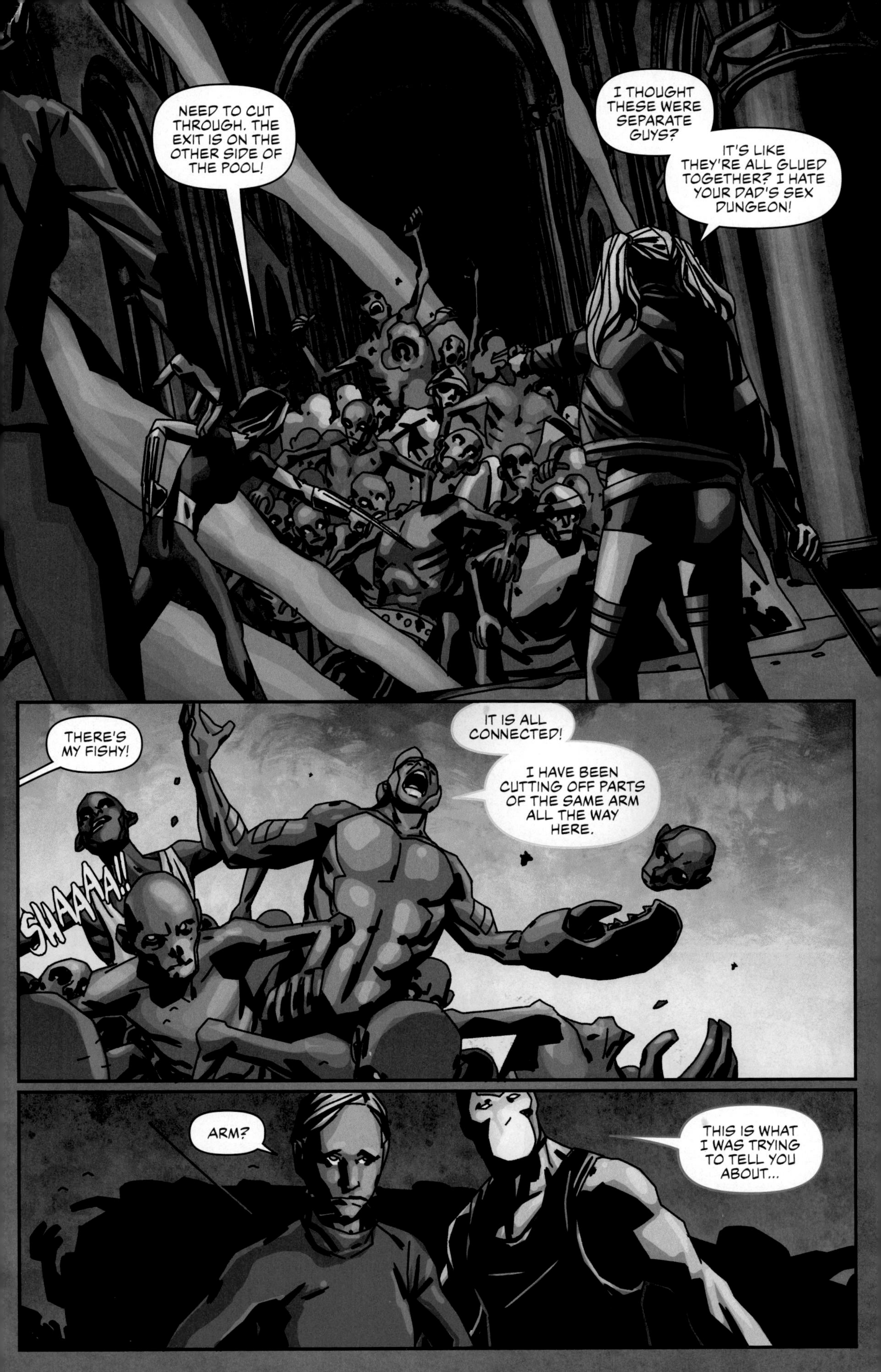
NEED TO CUT THROUGH. THE EXIT IS ON THE OTHER SIDE OF THE POOL!
I THOUGHT THESE WERE SEPARATE GUYS?
IT'S LIKE THEY'RE ALL GLUED TOGETHER? I HATE YOUR DAD'S SEX DUNGEON!
THERE'S MY FISHY!
IT IS ALL CONNECTED!
I HAVE BEEN CUTTING OFF PARTS OF THE SAME ARM ALL THE WAY HERE.
SHAAAA!!
ARM?
THIS IS WHAT I WAS TRYING TO TELL YOU ABOUT...

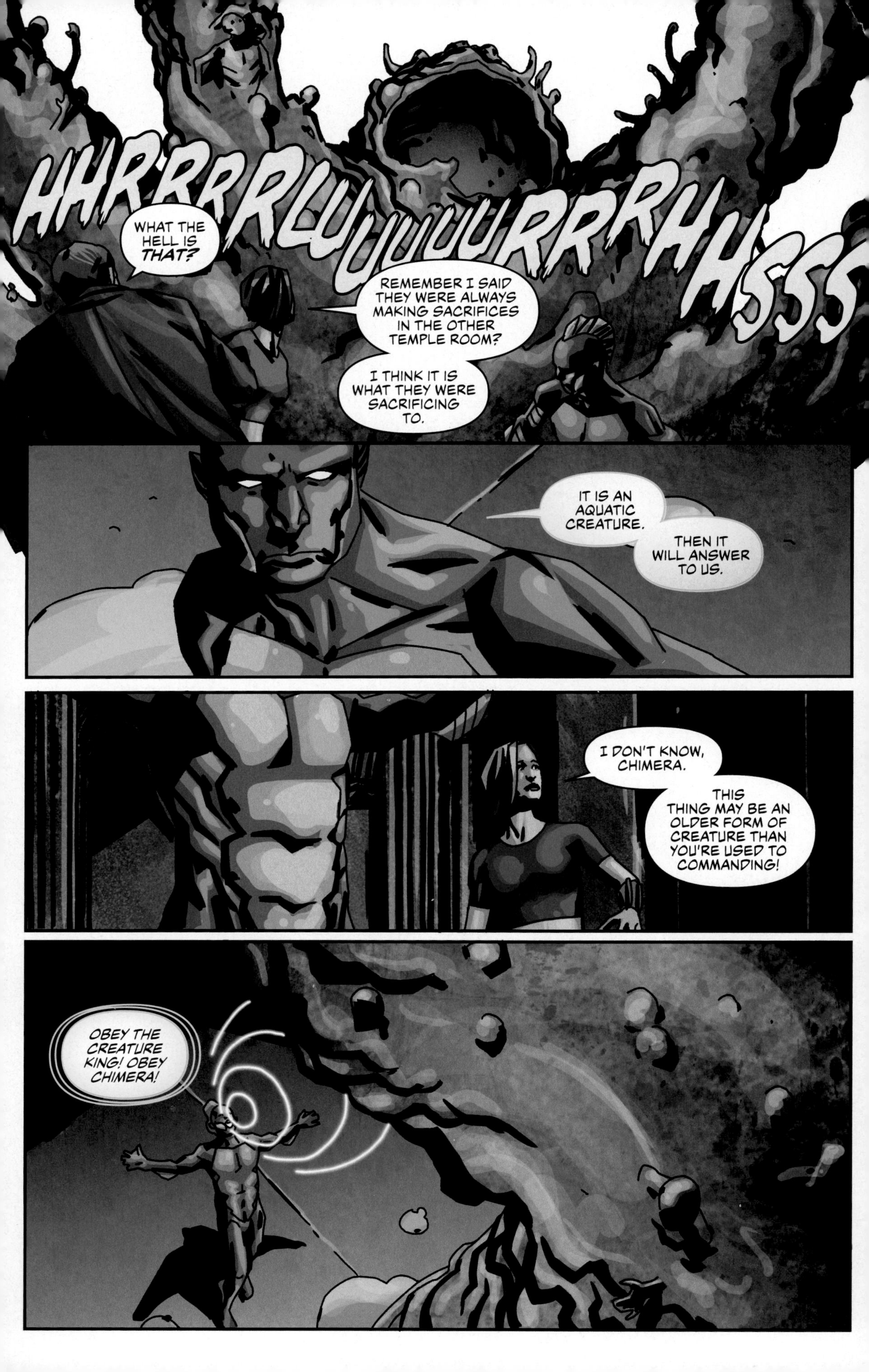
HHRRRRLUUUUUURRRRHHSSS
WHAT THE HELL IS *THAT?*
REMEMBER I SAID THEY WERE ALWAYS MAKING SACRIFICES IN THE OTHER TEMPLE ROOM?
I THINK IT IS WHAT THEY WERE SACRIFICING TO.
IT IS AN AQUATIC CREATURE.
THEN IT WILL ANSWER TO US.
I DON'T KNOW, CHIMERA.
THIS THING MAY BE AN OLDER FORM OF CREATURE THAN YOU'RE USED TO COMMANDING!
OBEY THE CREATURE KING! OBEY CHIMERA!

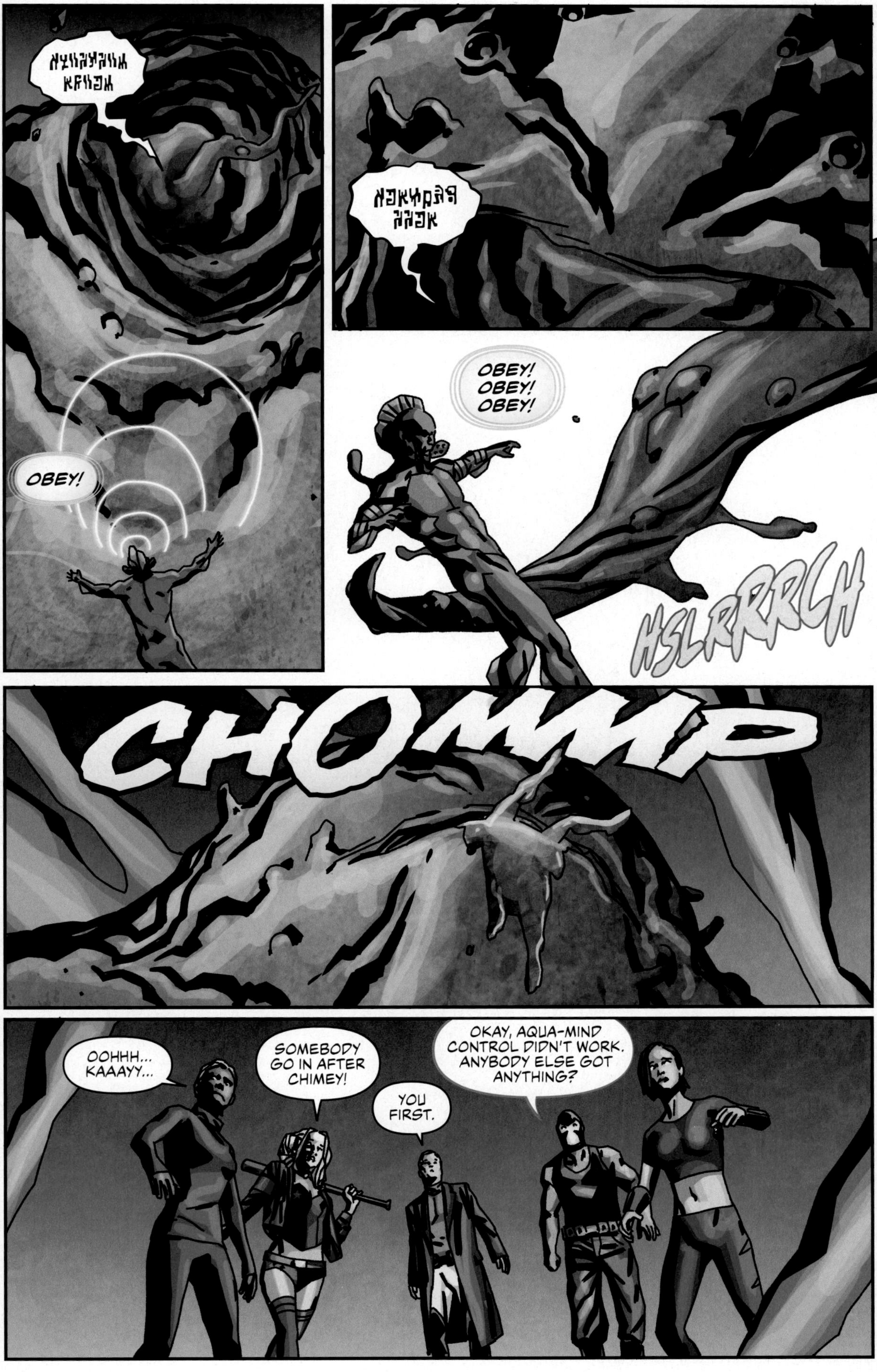
OBEY!
OBEY! OBEY! OBEY!
HSLRRRCH
CHOMMP
OOHHH... KAAAYY...
SOMEBODY GO IN AFTER CHIMEY!
YOU FIRST.
OKAY, AQUA-MIND CONTROL DIDN'T WORK. ANYBODY ELSE GOT ANYTHING?

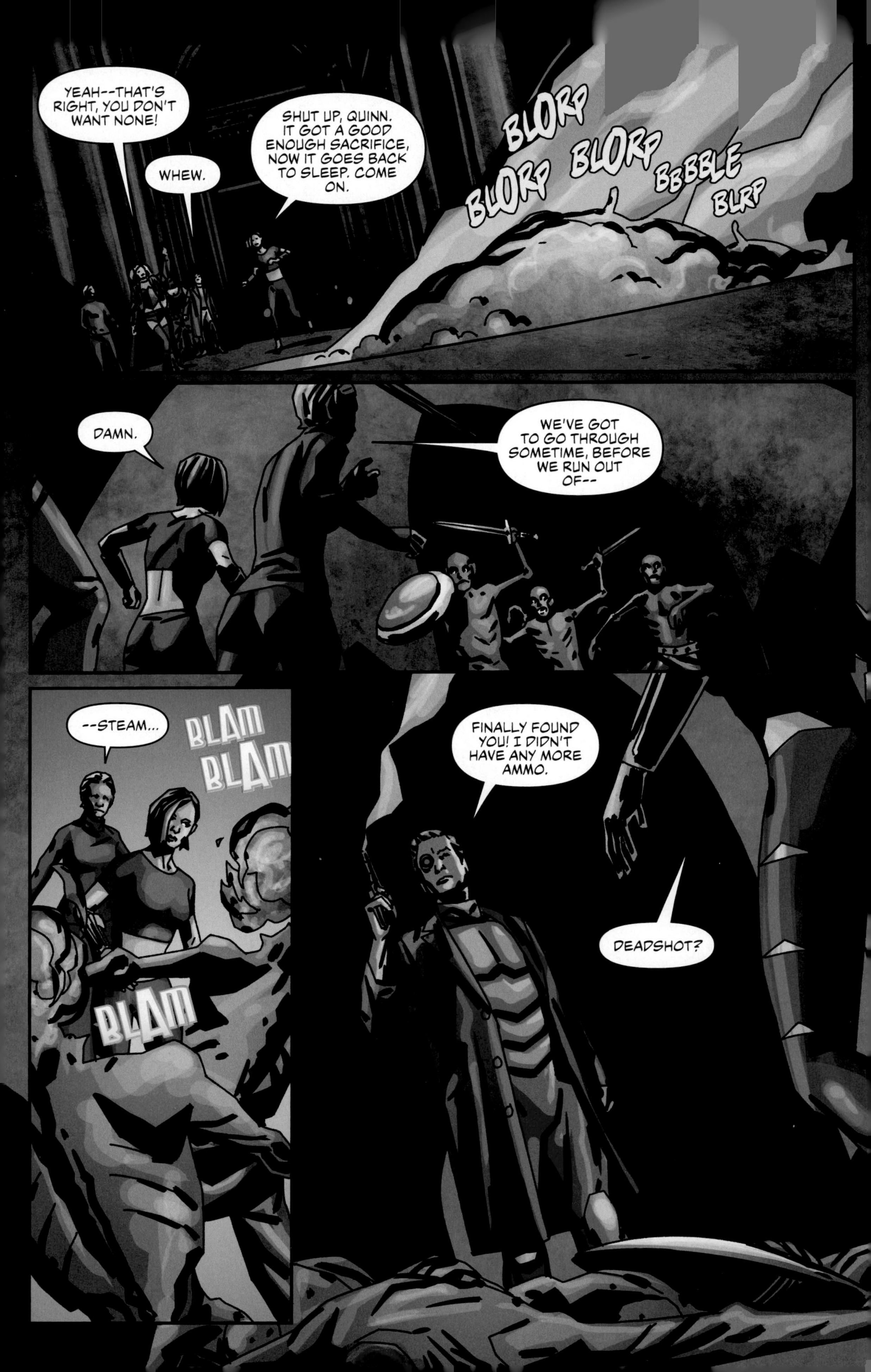
YEAH--THAT'S RIGHT, YOU DON'T WANT NONE!
WHEW.
SHUT UP, QUINN. IT GOT A GOOD ENOUGH SACRIFICE, NOW IT GOES BACK TO SLEEP. COME ON.
BLORP
BLORP BLORP
BBBBLE
BLRP
DAMN.
WE'VE GOT TO GO THROUGH SOMETIME, BEFORE WE RUN OUT OF--
--STEAM...
BLAM
BLAM
BLAM
FINALLY FOUND YOU! I DIDN'T HAVE ANY MORE AMMO.
DEADSHOT?

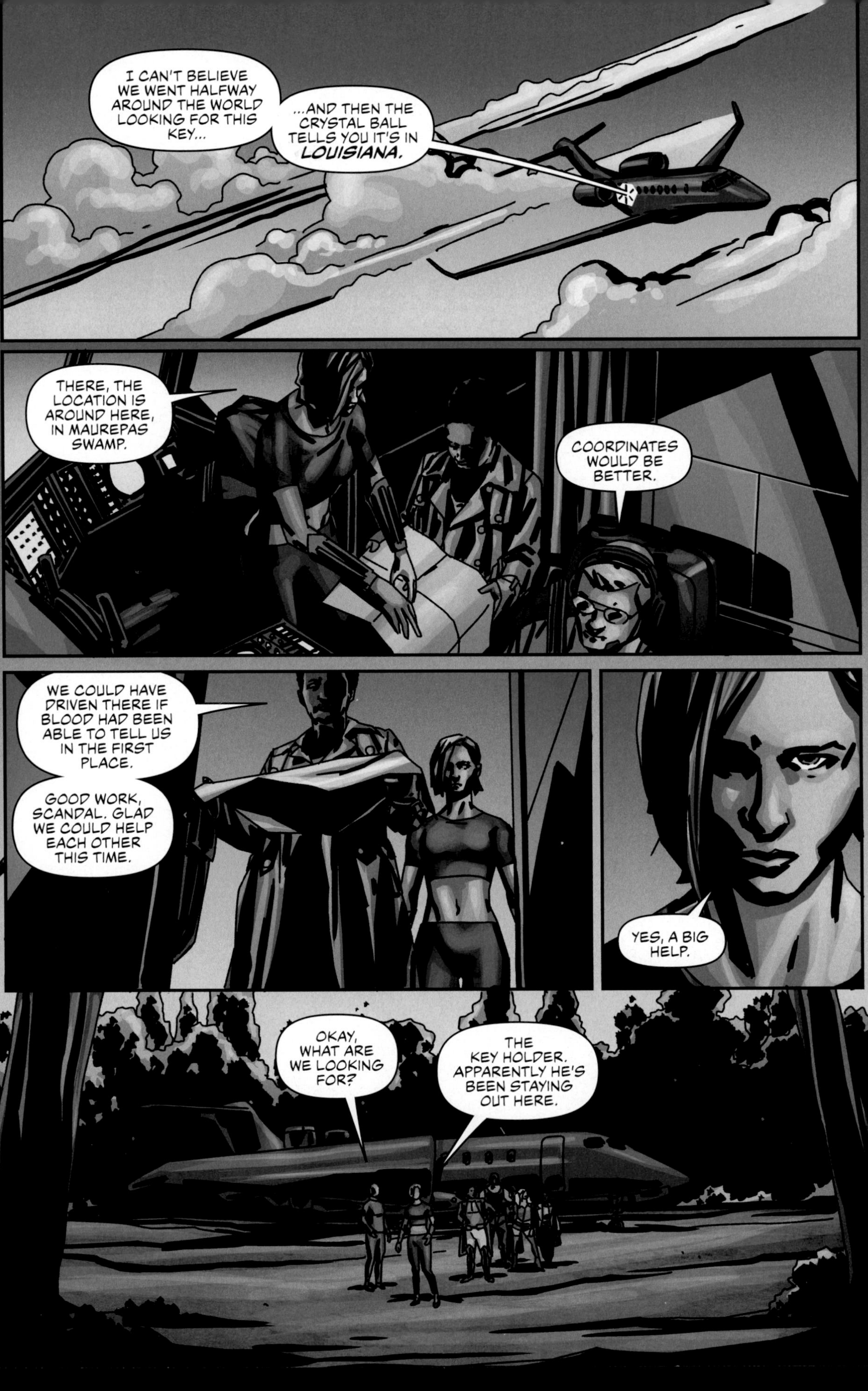
I CAN'T BELIEVE WE WENT HALFWAY AROUND THE WORLD LOOKING FOR THIS KEY...
...AND THEN THE CRYSTAL BALL TELLS YOU IT'S IN **LOUISIANA.**
THERE, THE LOCATION IS AROUND HERE, IN MAUREPAS SWAMP.
COORDINATES WOULD BE BETTER.
WE COULD HAVE DRIVEN THERE IF BLOOD HAD BEEN ABLE TO TELL US IN THE FIRST PLACE.
GOOD WORK, SCANDAL. GLAD WE COULD HELP EACH OTHER THIS TIME.
YES, A BIG HELP.
OKAY, WHAT ARE WE LOOKING FOR?
THE KEY HOLDER. APPARENTLY HE'S BEEN STAYING OUT HERE.

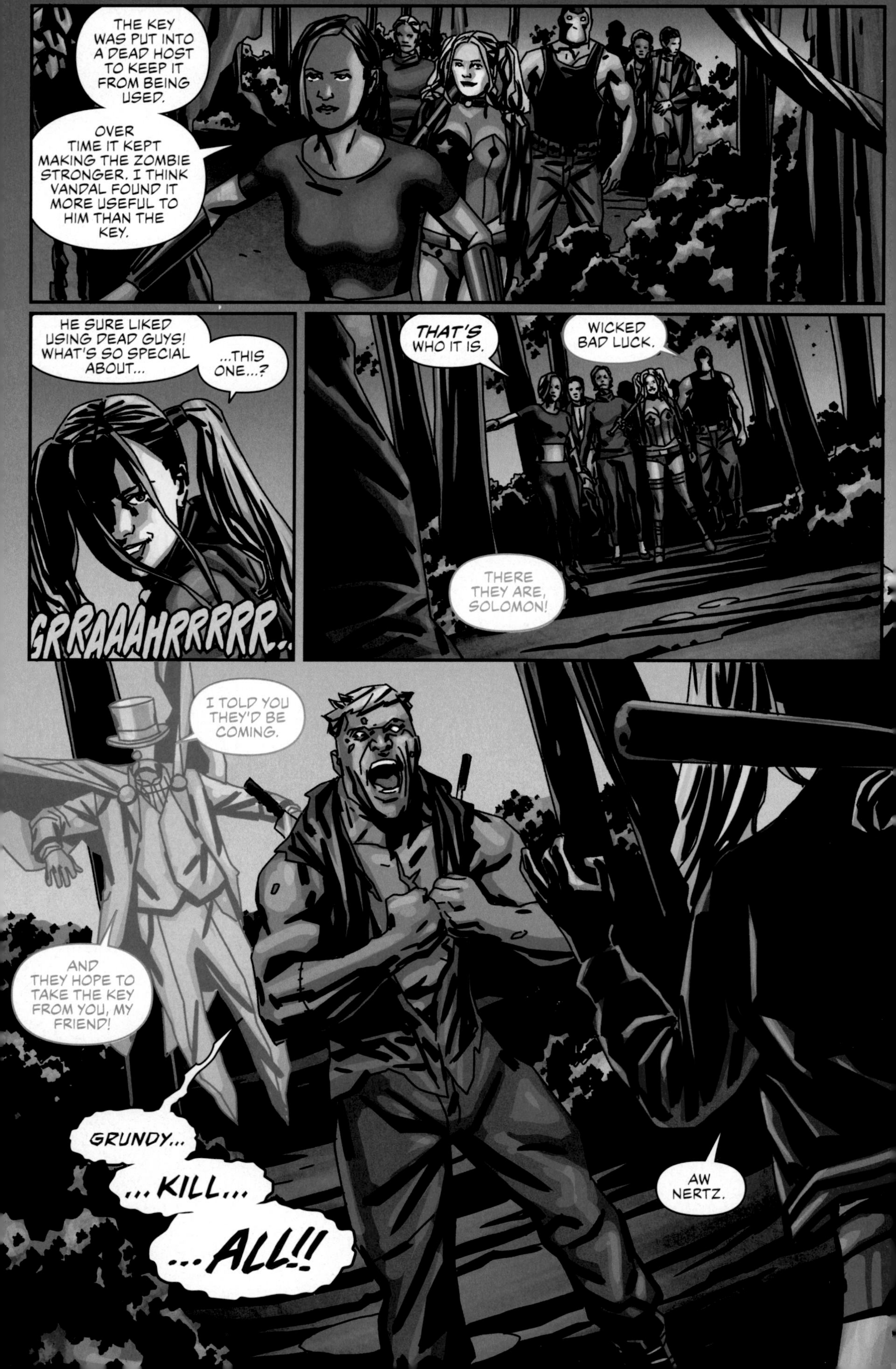
THE KEY WAS PUT INTO A DEAD HOST TO KEEP IT FROM BEING USED.
OVER TIME IT KEPT MAKING THE ZOMBIE STRONGER. I THINK VANDAL FOUND IT MORE USEFUL TO HIM THAN THE KEY.
HE SURE LIKED USING DEAD GUYS! WHAT'S SO SPECIAL ABOUT...
...THIS ONE...?
GRRAAAHRRRRR..
THAT'S WHO IT IS.
WICKED BAD LUCK.
THERE THEY ARE, SOLOMON!
I TOLD YOU THEY'D BE COMING.
AND THEY HOPE TO TAKE THE KEY FROM YOU, MY FRIEND!
GRUNDY...
...KILL...
...ALL!!
AW NERTZ.

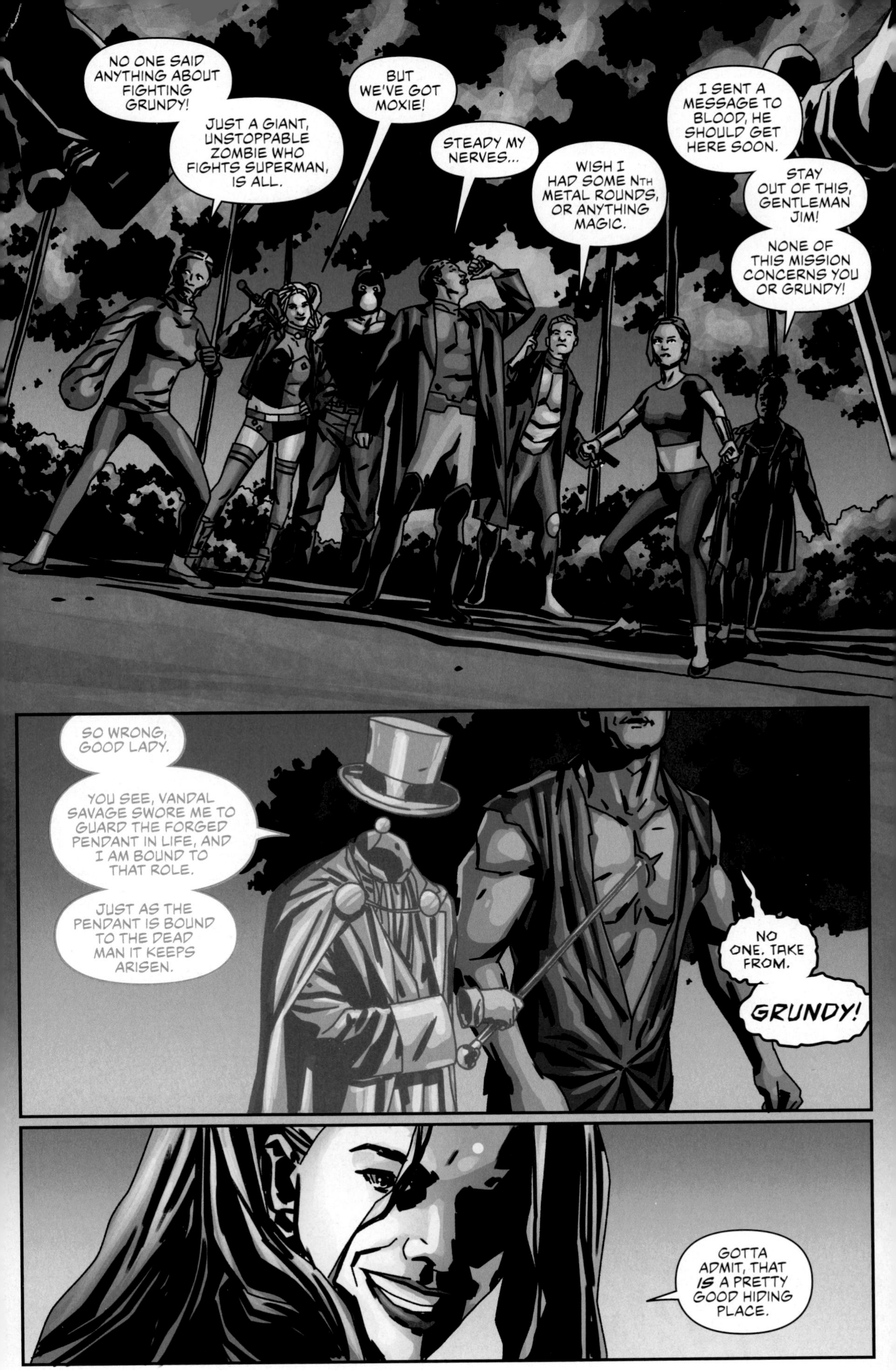
NO ONE SAID ANYTHING ABOUT FIGHTING GRUNDY!
JUST A GIANT, UNSTOPPABLE ZOMBIE WHO FIGHTS SUPERMAN, IS ALL.
BUT WE'VE GOT MOXIE!
STEADY MY NERVES...
WISH I HAD SOME NTH METAL ROUNDS, OR ANYTHING MAGIC.
I SENT A MESSAGE TO BLOOD, HE SHOULD GET HERE SOON.
STAY OUT OF THIS, GENTLEMAN JIM!
NONE OF THIS MISSION CONCERNS YOU OR GRUNDY!
SO WRONG, GOOD LADY.
YOU SEE, VANDAL SAVAGE SWORE ME TO GUARD THE FORGED PENDANT IN LIFE, AND I AM BOUND TO THAT ROLE.
JUST AS THE PENDANT IS BOUND TO THE DEAD MAN IT KEEPS ARISEN.
NO ONE. TAKE FROM.
GRUNDY!
GOTTA ADMIT, THAT *IS* A PRETTY GOOD HIDING PLACE.

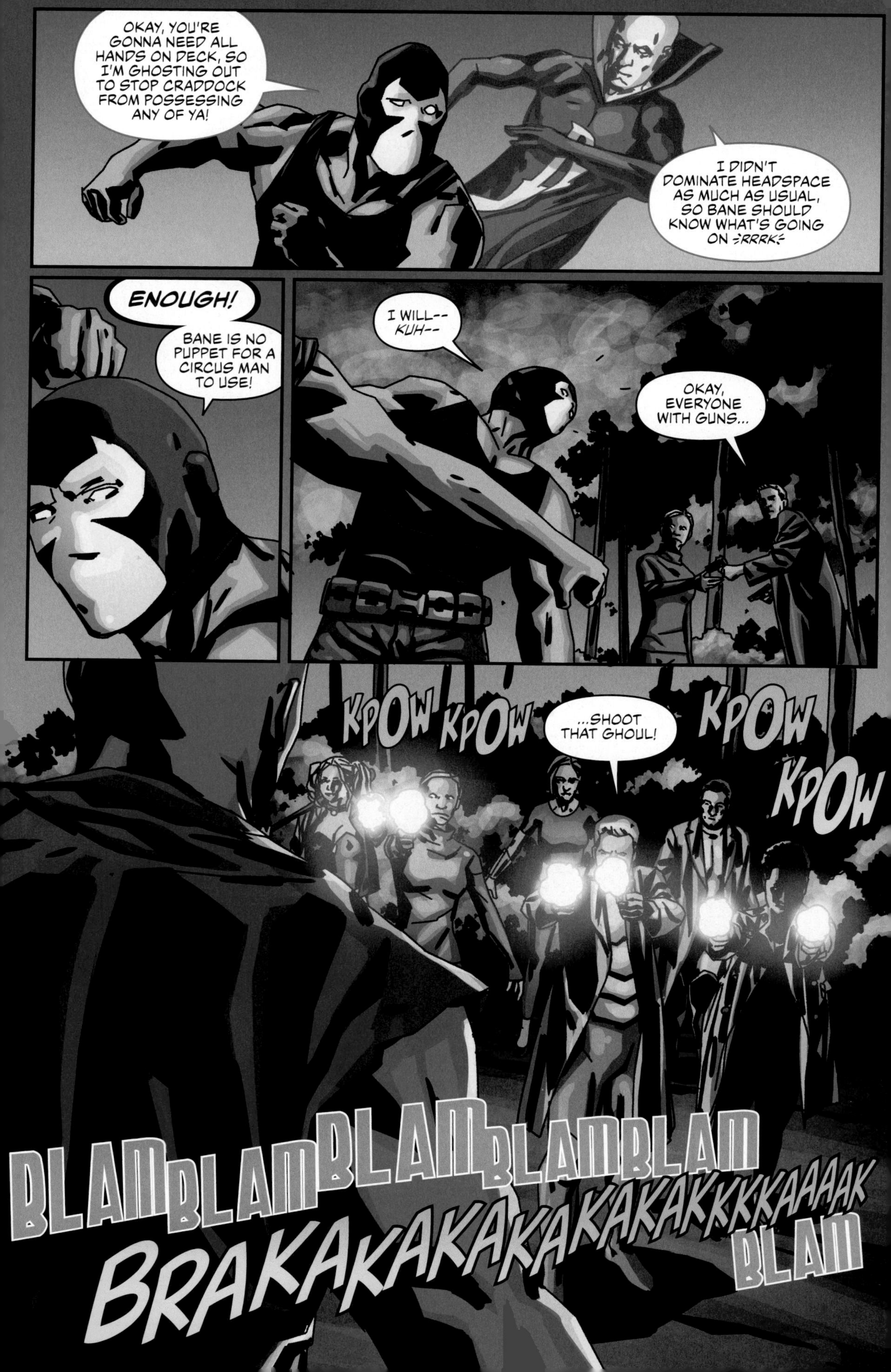
OKAY, YOU'RE GONNA NEED ALL HANDS ON DECK, SO I'M GHOSTING OUT TO STOP CRADDOCK FROM POSSESSING ANY OF YA!
I DIDN'T DOMINATE HEADSPACE AS MUCH AS USUAL, SO BANE SHOULD KNOW WHAT'S GOING ON =RRRK=
ENOUGH!
BANE IS NO PUPPET FOR A CIRCUS MAN TO USE!
I WILL-- KUH--
OKAY, EVERYONE WITH GUNS...
KPOW KPOW
...SHOOT THAT GHOUL!
KPOW
KPOW
BLAMBLAMBLAMBLAMBLAM
BRAKAKAKAKAKAKAKKKKAAAAK
BLAM

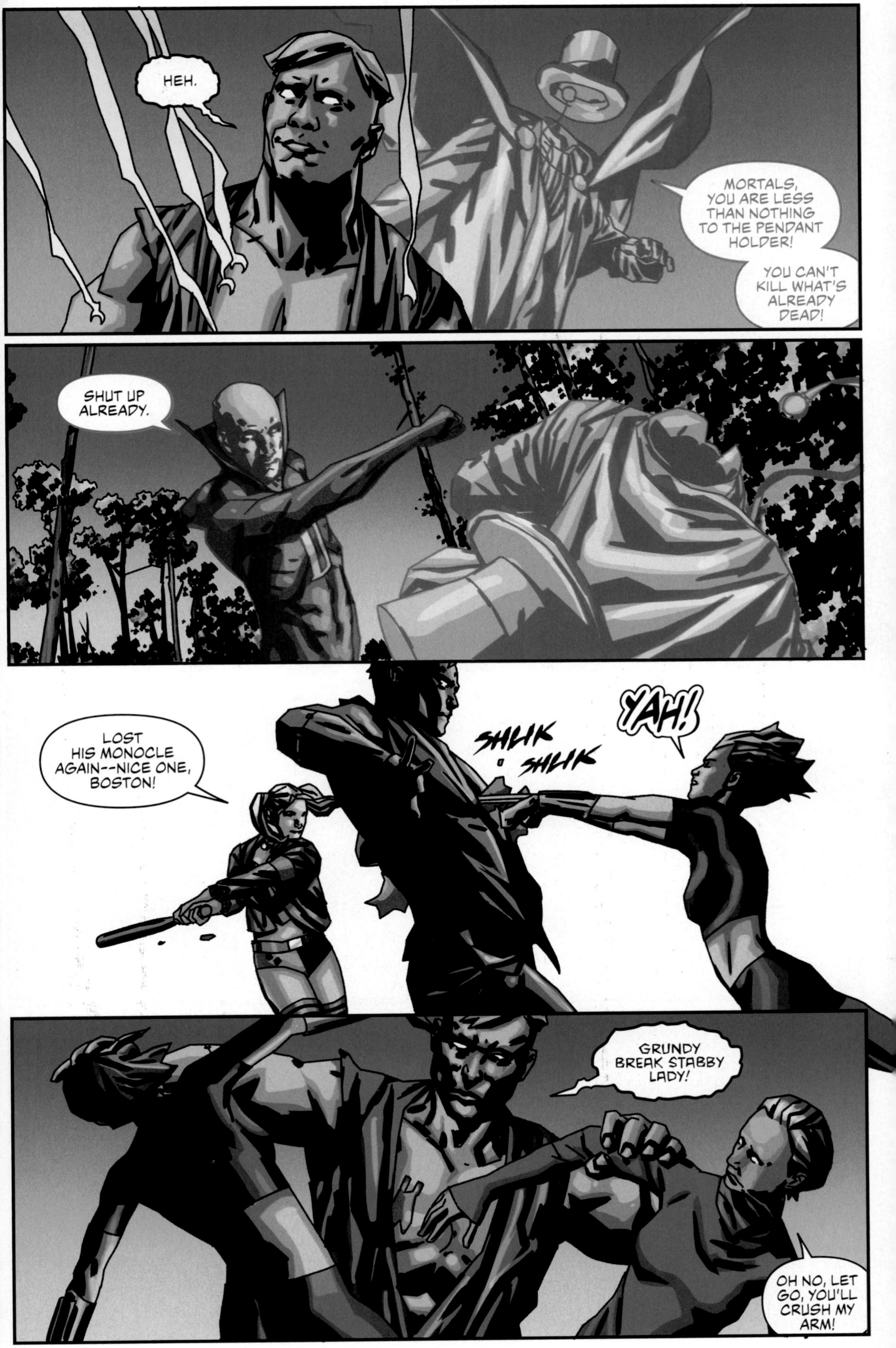
HEH.
MORTALS, YOU ARE LESS THAN NOTHING TO THE PENDANT HOLDER!
YOU CAN'T KILL WHAT'S ALREADY DEAD!
SHUT UP ALREADY.
LOST HIS MONOCLE AGAIN--NICE ONE, BOSTON!
SHLIK
SHLIK
YAH!
GRUNDY BREAK STABBY LADY!
OH NO, LET GO, YOU'LL CRUSH MY ARM!

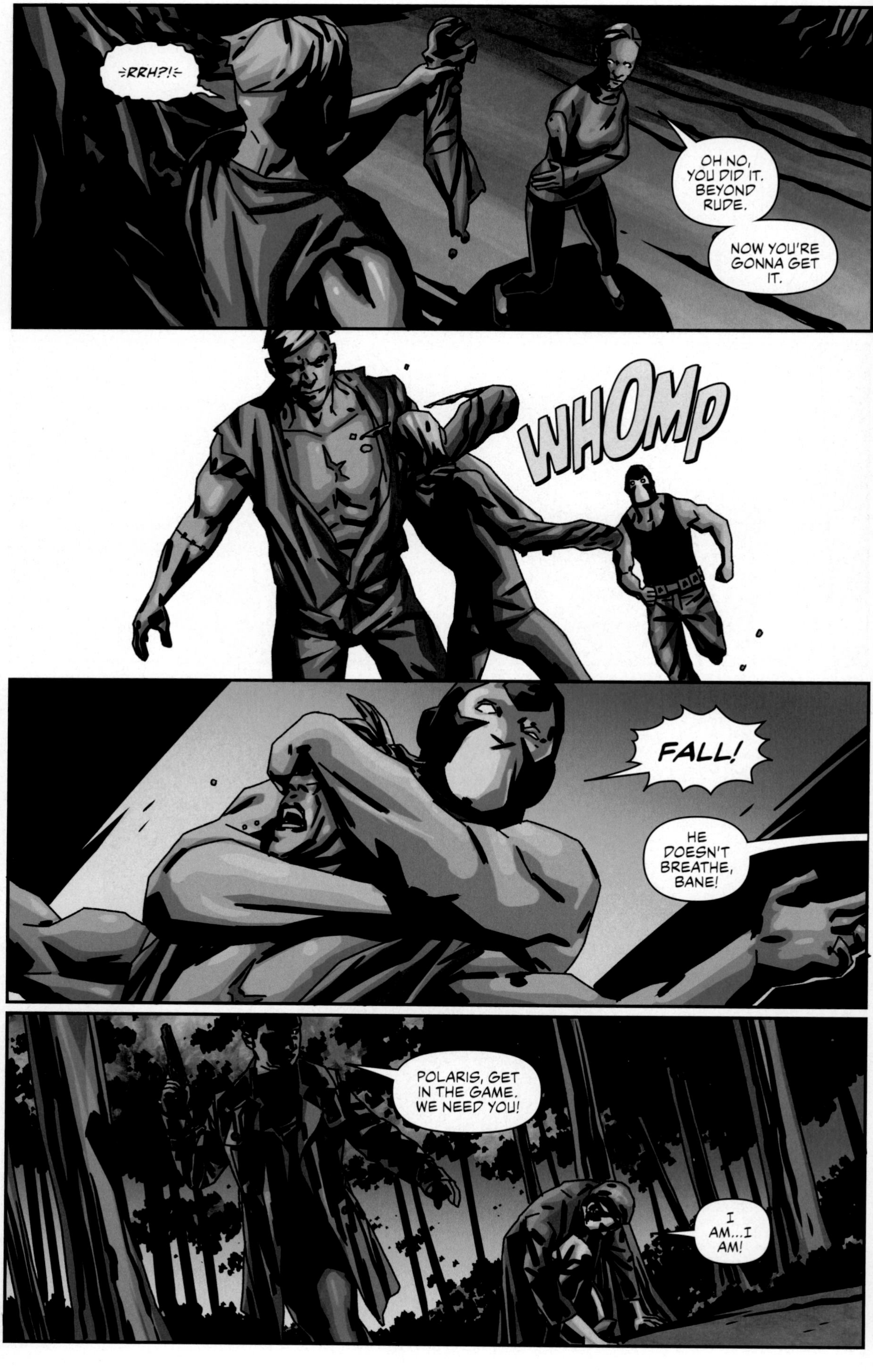
RRH?!
OH NO, YOU DID IT. BEYOND RUDE.
NOW YOU'RE GONNA GET IT.
WHOMP
FALL!
HE DOESN'T BREATHE, BANE!
POLARIS, GET IN THE GAME. WE NEED YOU!
I AM...I AM!

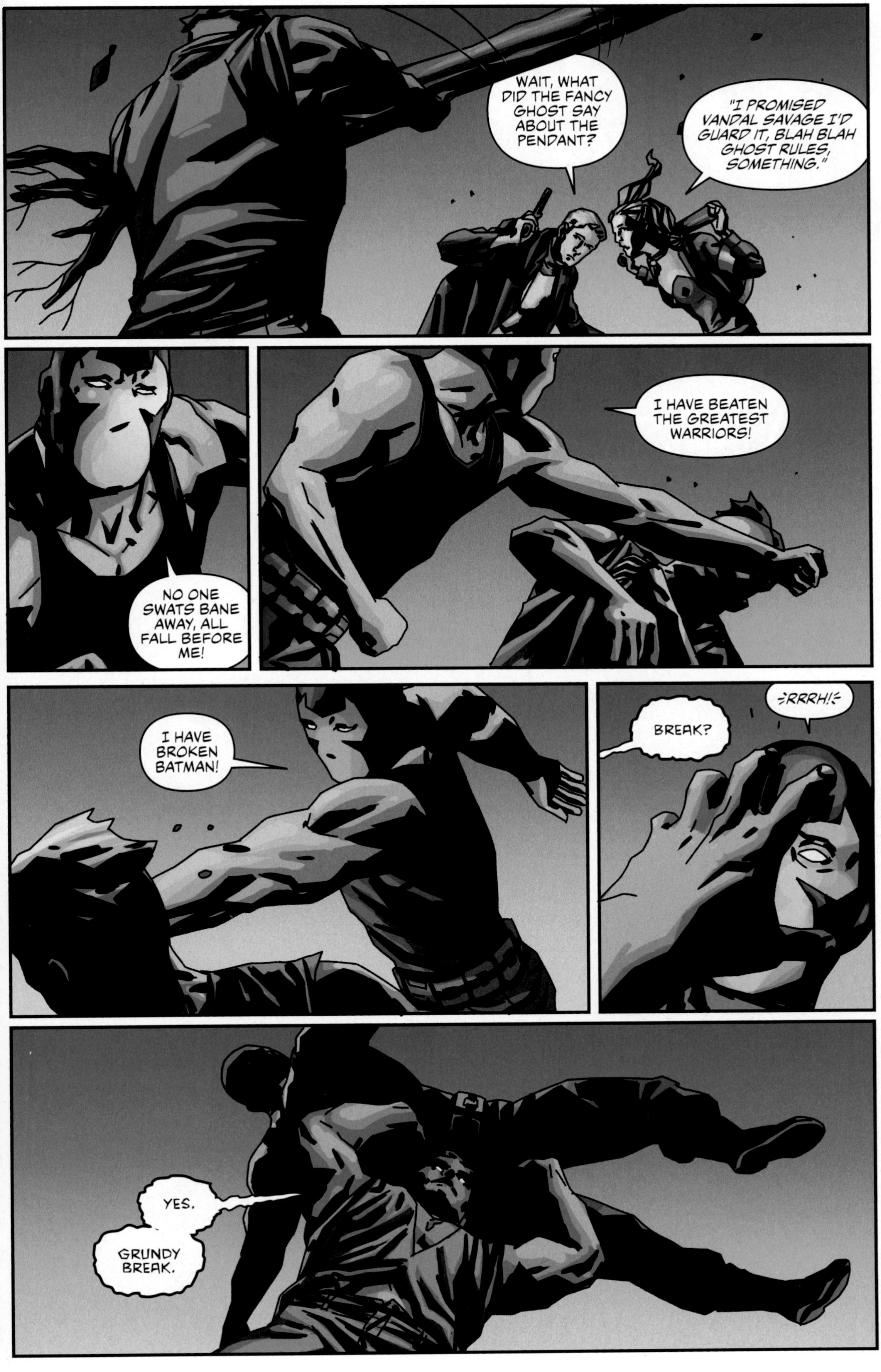
WAIT, WHAT DID THE FANCY GHOST SAY ABOUT THE PENDANT?
"I PROMISED VANDAL SAVAGE I'D GUARD IT, BLAH BLAH GHOST RULES, SOMETHING."
NO ONE SWATS BANE AWAY, ALL FALL BEFORE ME!
I HAVE BEATEN THE GREATEST WARRIORS!
I HAVE BROKEN BATMAN!
BREAK?
RRRH!
YES.
GRUNDY BREAK.

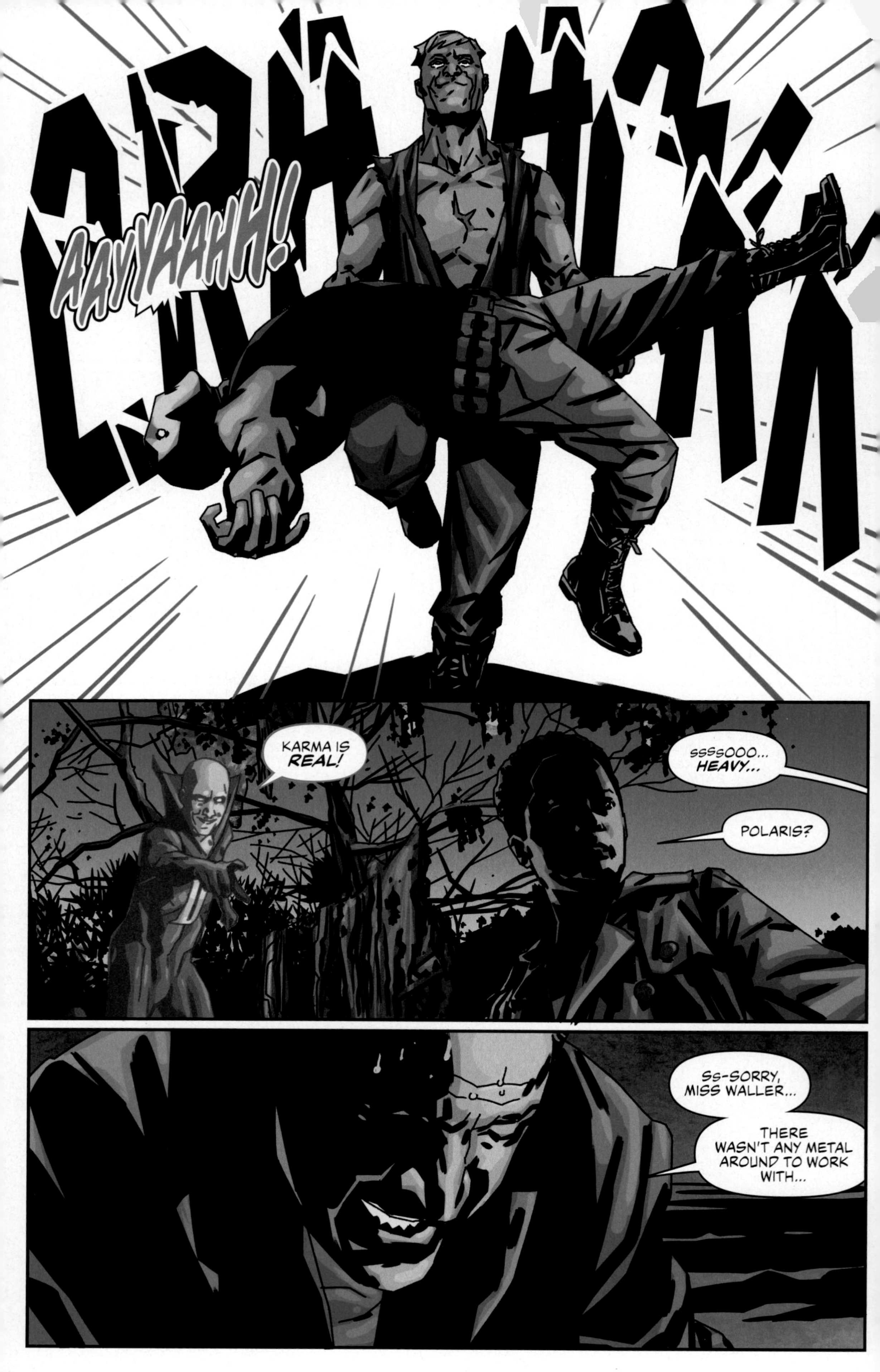
AAYYAAHH!
KARMA IS REAL!
SSSSOOO... HEAVY...
POLARIS?
Ss-SORRY, MISS WALLER...
THERE WASN'T ANY METAL AROUND TO WORK WITH...

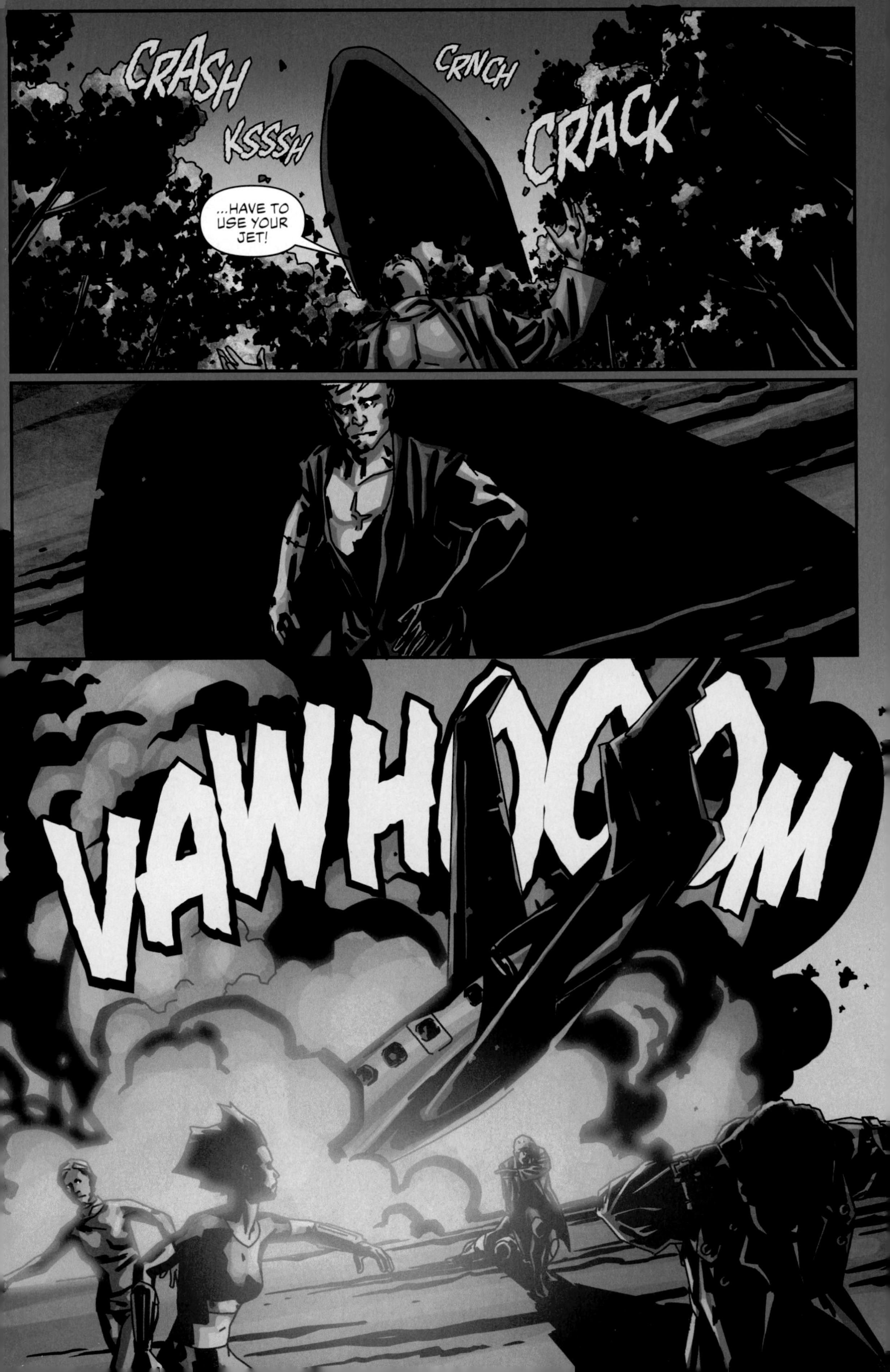
CRASH
KSSSH
CRNCH
CRACK
...HAVE TO USE YOUR JET!
VAWHOOOM

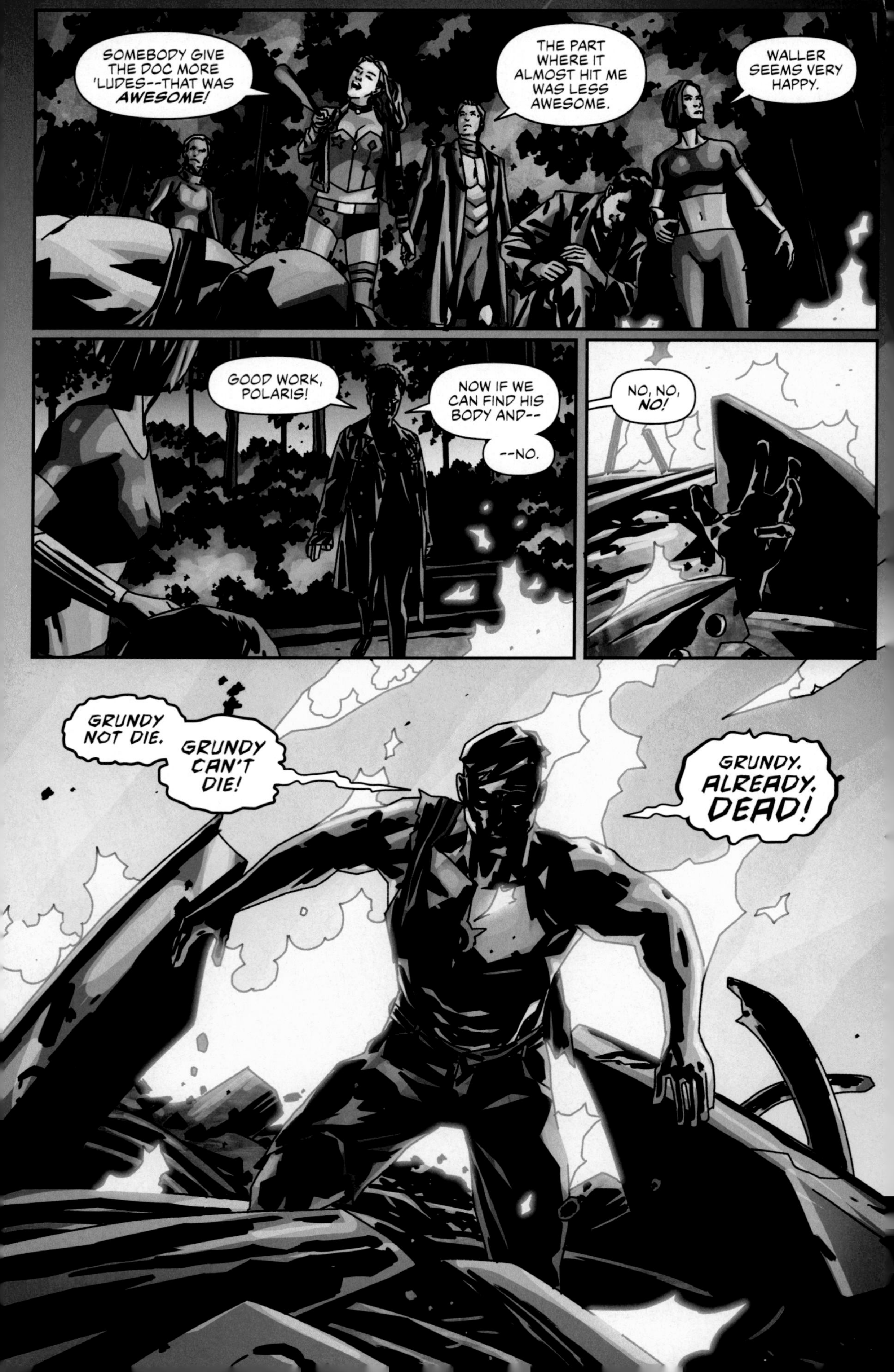
SOMEBODY GIVE THE DOC MORE 'LUDES--THAT WAS AWESOME!
THE PART WHERE IT ALMOST HIT ME WAS LESS AWESOME.
WALLER SEEMS VERY HAPPY.
GOOD WORK, POLARIS!
NOW IF WE CAN FIND HIS BODY AND--
--NO.
NO, NO, NO!
GRUNDY NOT DIE.
GRUNDY CAN'T DIE!
GRUNDY. ALREADY. DEAD!

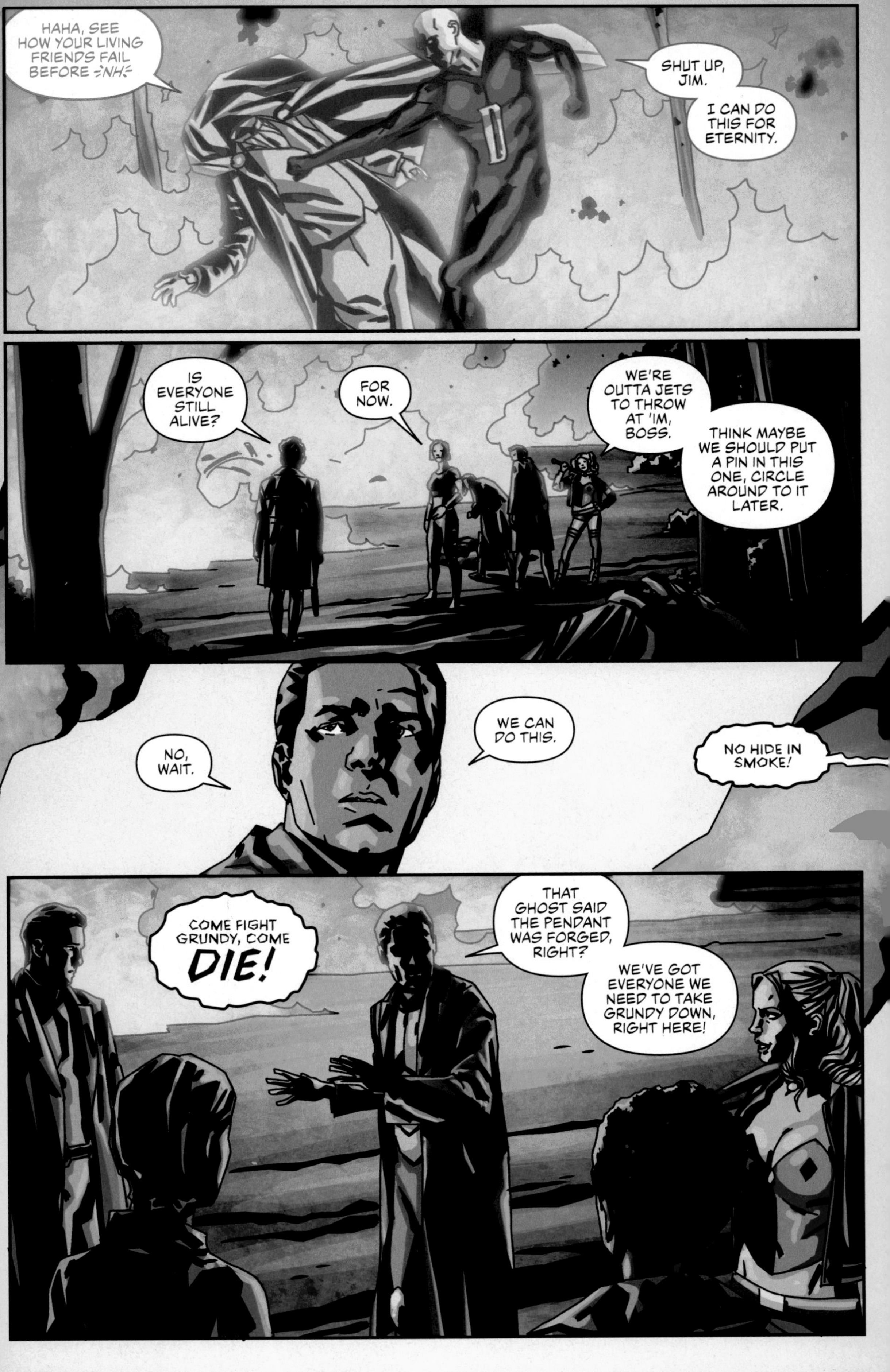
HAHA, SEE HOW YOUR LIVING FRIENDS FAIL BEFORE =NH=
SHUT UP, JIM.
I CAN DO THIS FOR ETERNITY.
IS EVERYONE STILL ALIVE?
FOR NOW.
WE'RE OUTTA JETS TO THROW AT 'IM, BOSS.
THINK MAYBE WE SHOULD PUT A PIN IN THIS ONE, CIRCLE AROUND TO IT LATER.
NO, WAIT.
WE CAN DO THIS.
NO HIDE IN SMOKE!
COME FIGHT GRUNDY, COME DIE!
THAT GHOST SAID THE PENDANT WAS FORGED, RIGHT?
WE'VE GOT EVERYONE WE NEED TO TAKE GRUNDY DOWN, RIGHT HERE!

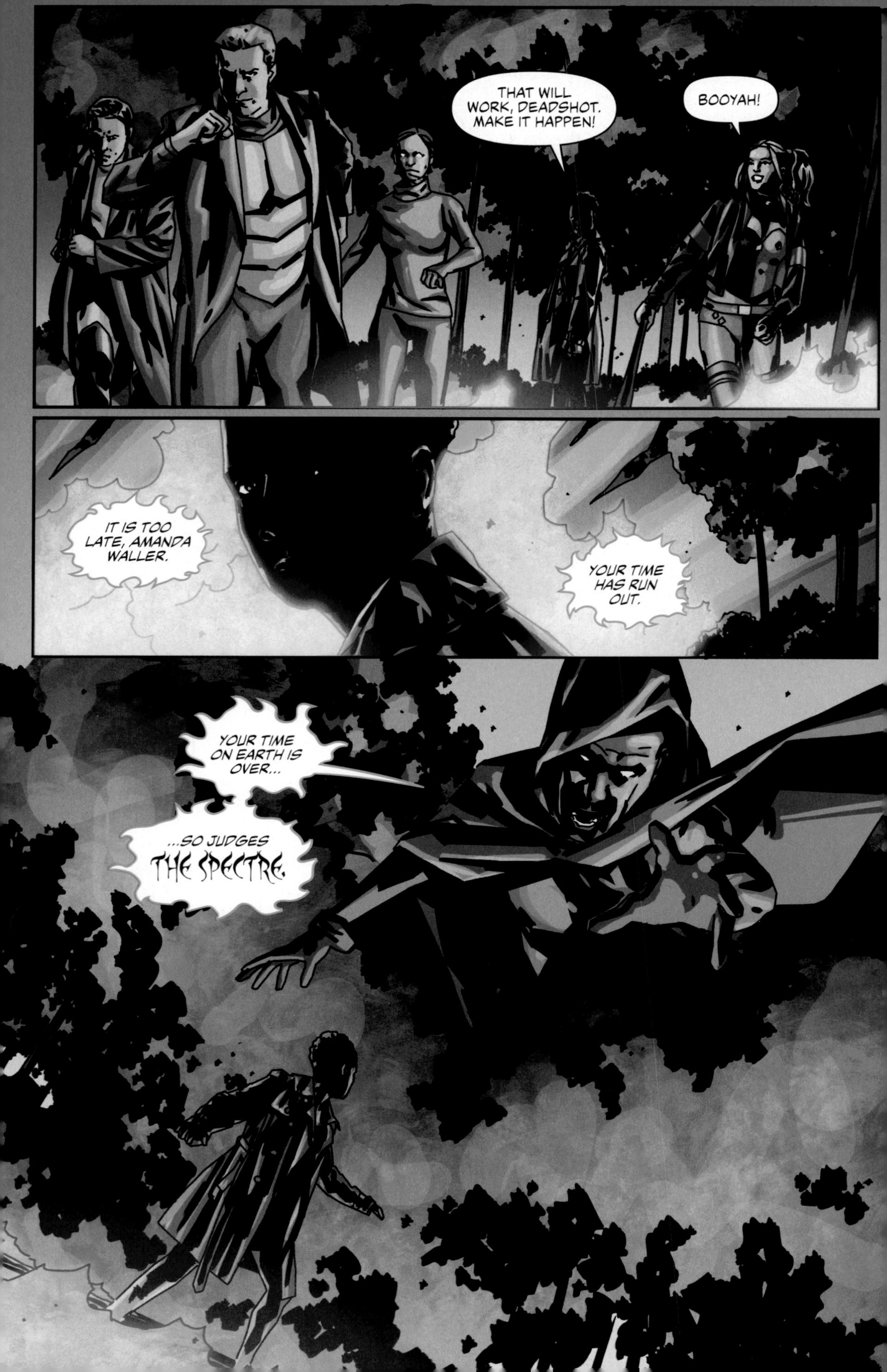
THAT WILL WORK, DEADSHOT. MAKE IT HAPPEN!
BOOYAH!
IT IS TOO LATE, AMANDA WALLER.
YOUR TIME HAS RUN OUT.
YOUR TIME ON EARTH IS OVER...
...SO JUDGES THE SPECTRE.

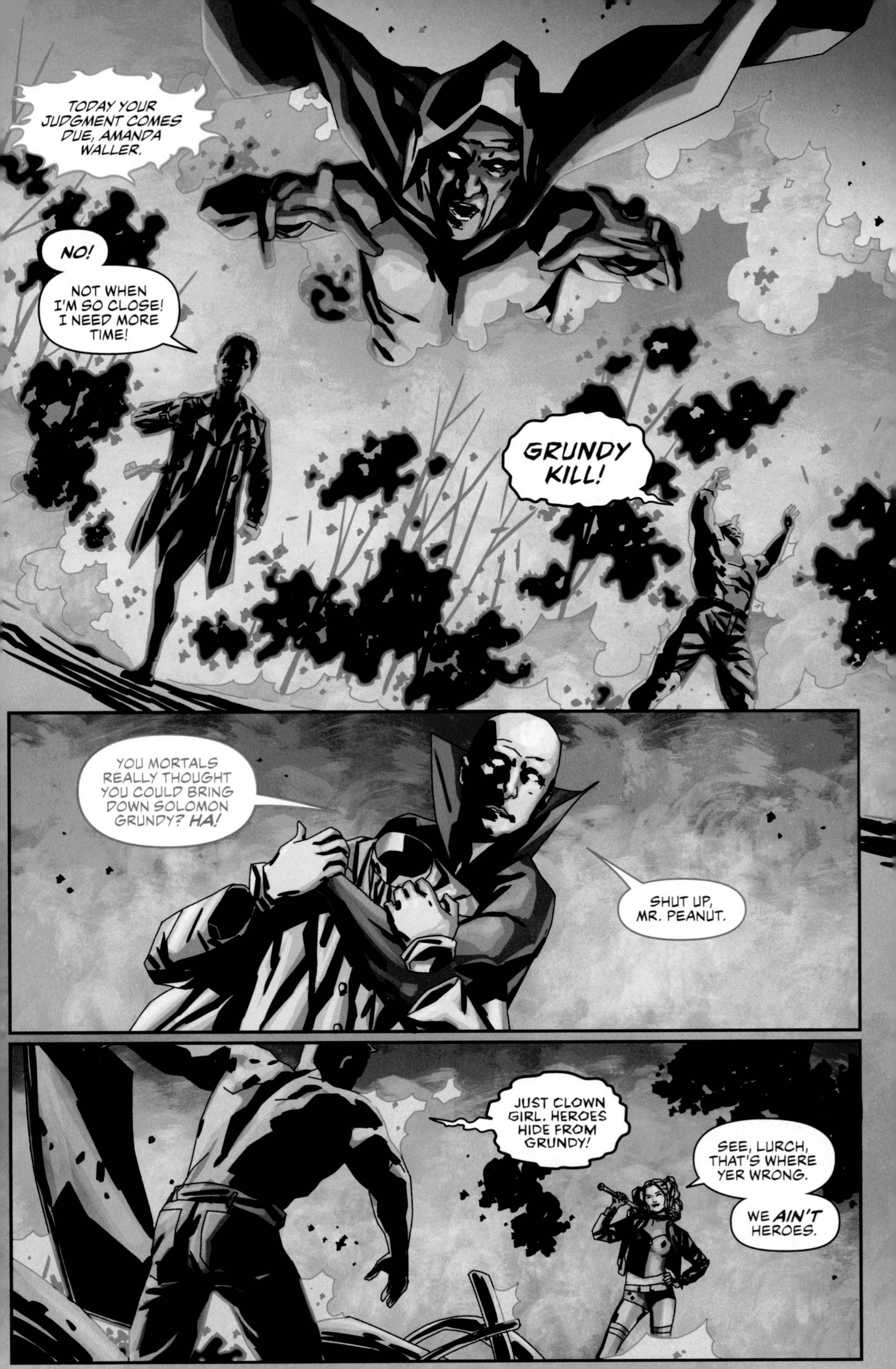
TODAY YOUR JUDGMENT COMES DUE, AMANDA WALLER.
NO!
NOT WHEN I'M SO CLOSE! I NEED MORE TIME!
GRUNDY KILL!
YOU MORTALS REALLY THOUGHT YOU COULD BRING DOWN SOLOMON GRUNDY? HA!
SHUT UP, MR. PEANUT.
JUST CLOWN GIRL. HEROES HIDE FROM GRUNDY!
SEE, LURCH, THAT'S WHERE YER WRONG.
WE AIN'T HEROES.

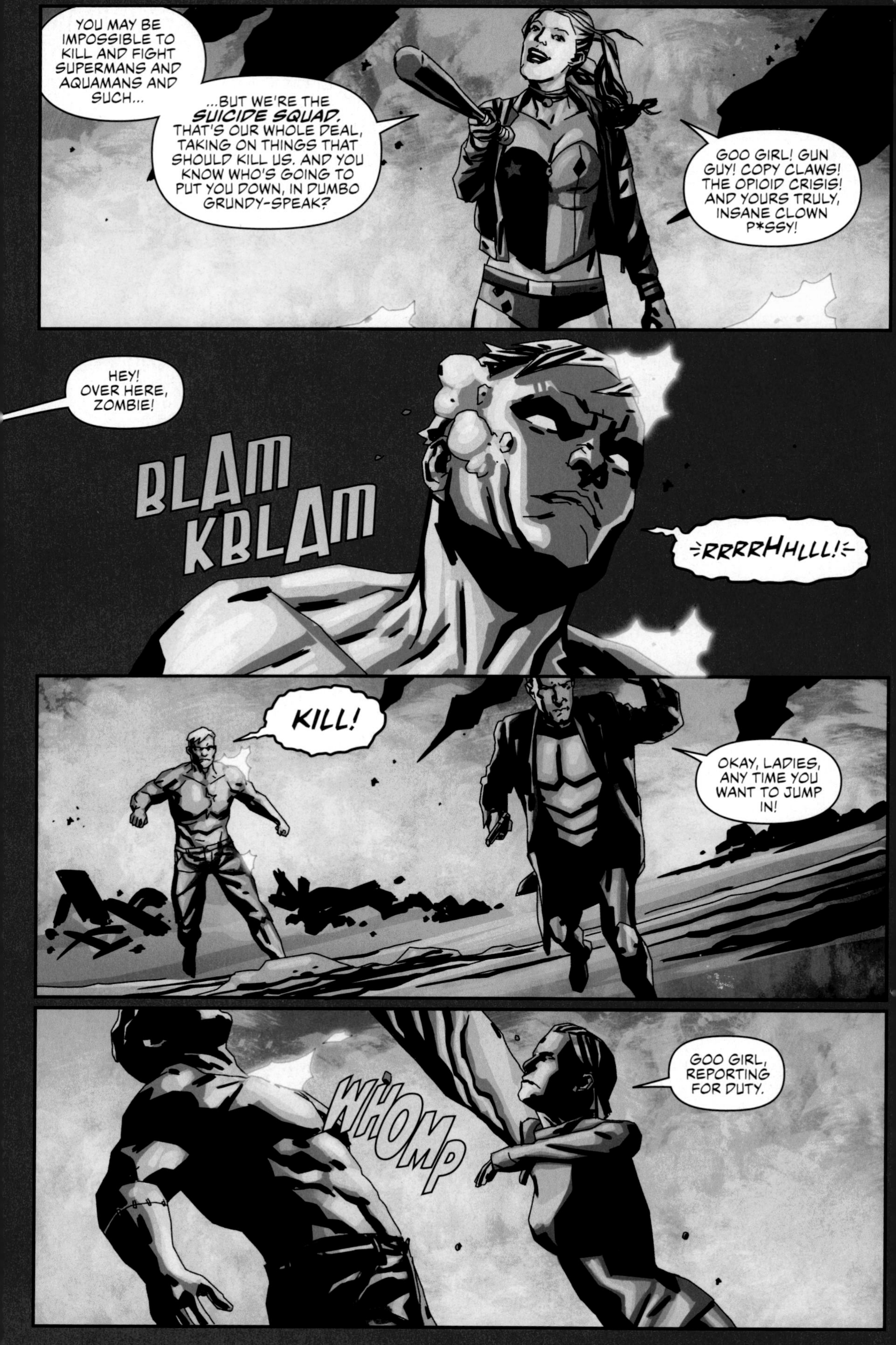
YOU MAY BE IMPOSSIBLE TO KILL AND FIGHT SUPERMANS AND AQUAMANS AND SUCH...
...BUT WE'RE THE ***SUICIDE SQUAD.*** THAT'S OUR WHOLE DEAL, TAKING ON THINGS THAT SHOULD KILL US. AND YOU KNOW WHO'S GOING TO PUT YOU DOWN, IN DUMBO GRUNDY-SPEAK?
GOO GIRL! GUN GUY! COPY CLAWS! THE OPIOID CRISIS! AND YOURS TRULY, INSANE CLOWN P*SSY!
HEY! OVER HERE, ZOMBIE!
BLAM KBLAM
RRRRHHLLL!
KILL!
OKAY, LADIES, ANY TIME YOU WANT TO JUMP IN!
GOO GIRL, REPORTING FOR DUTY.
WHOMP

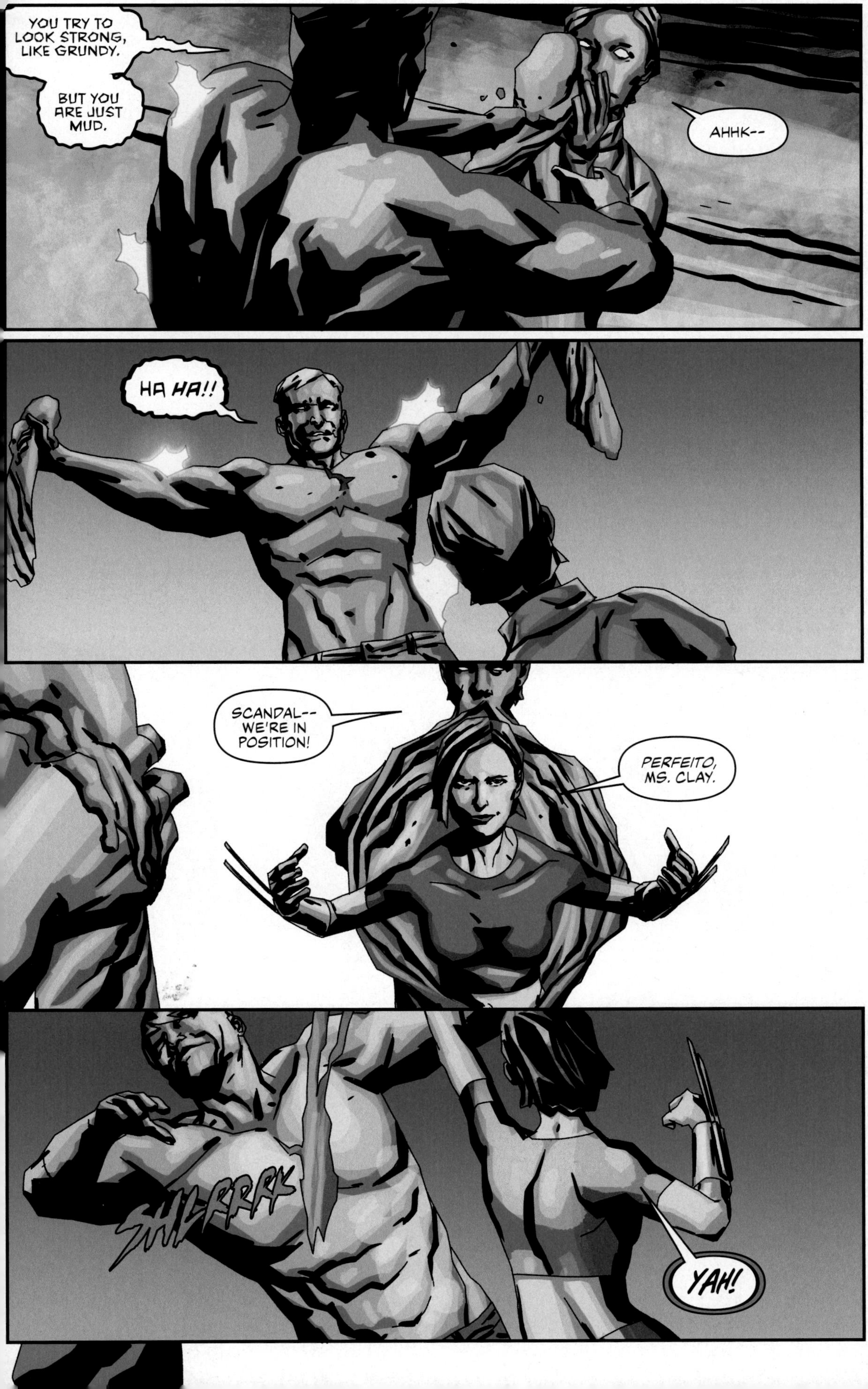
YOU TRY TO LOOK STRONG, LIKE GRUNDY.
BUT YOU ARE JUST MUD.
AHHK--
HA HA!!
SCANDAL-- WE'RE IN POSITION!
PERFEITO, MS. CLAY.
SHLRRRK
YAH!

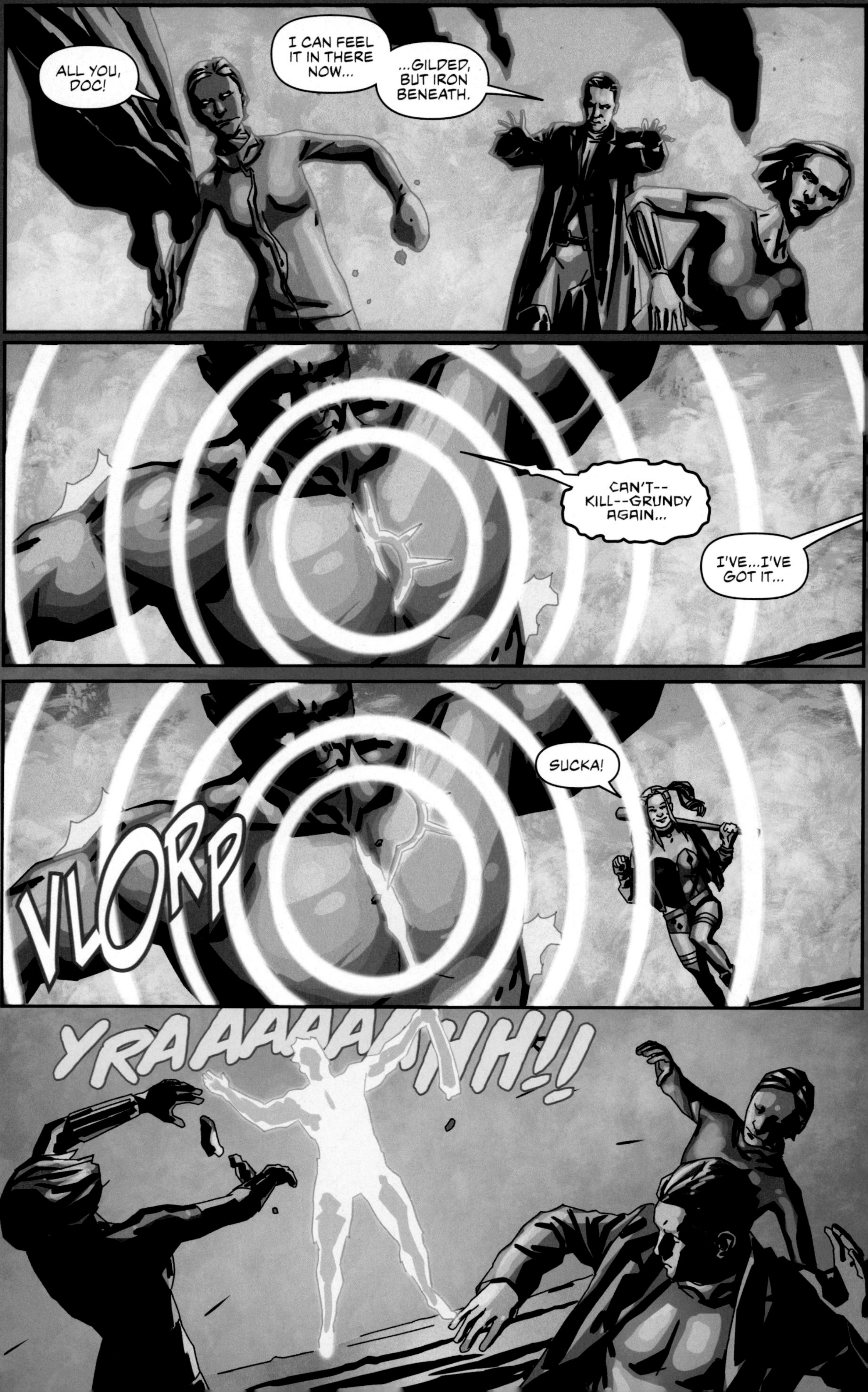
ALL YOU, DOC!
I CAN FEEL IT IN THERE NOW...
...GILDED, BUT IRON BENEATH.
CAN'T-- KILL--GRUNDY AGAIN...
I'VE...I'VE GOT IT...
SUCKA!
VLORP
YRAAAAAAHH!!

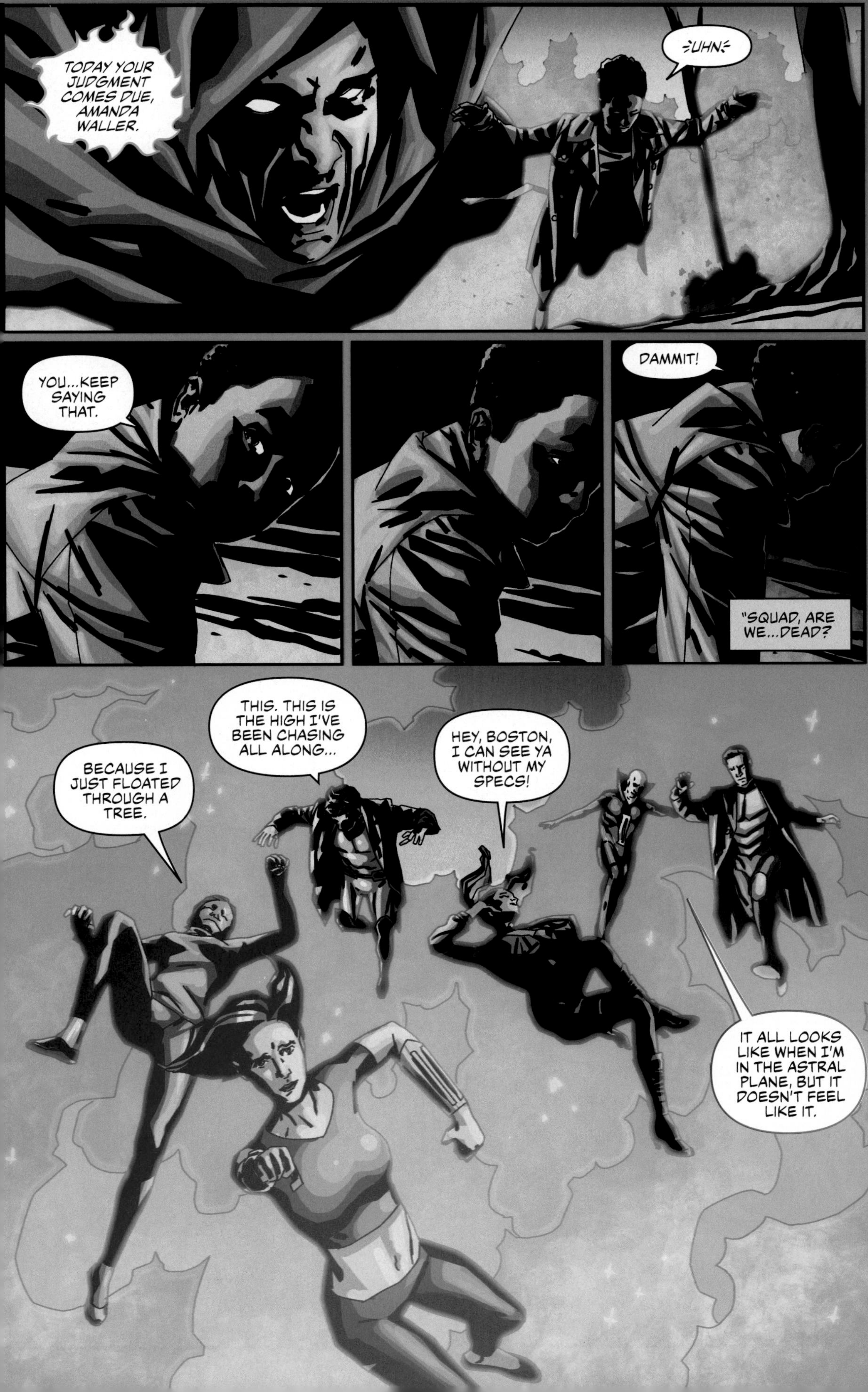
TODAY YOUR JUDGMENT COMES DUE, AMANDA WALLER.
UHN
YOU...KEEP SAYING THAT.
DAMMIT!
"SQUAD, ARE WE...DEAD?
BECAUSE I JUST FLOATED THROUGH A TREE.
THIS. THIS IS THE HIGH I'VE BEEN CHASING ALL ALONG...
HEY, BOSTON, I CAN SEE YA WITHOUT MY SPECS!
IT ALL LOOKS LIKE WHEN I'M IN THE ASTRAL PLANE, BUT IT DOESN'T FEEL LIKE IT.

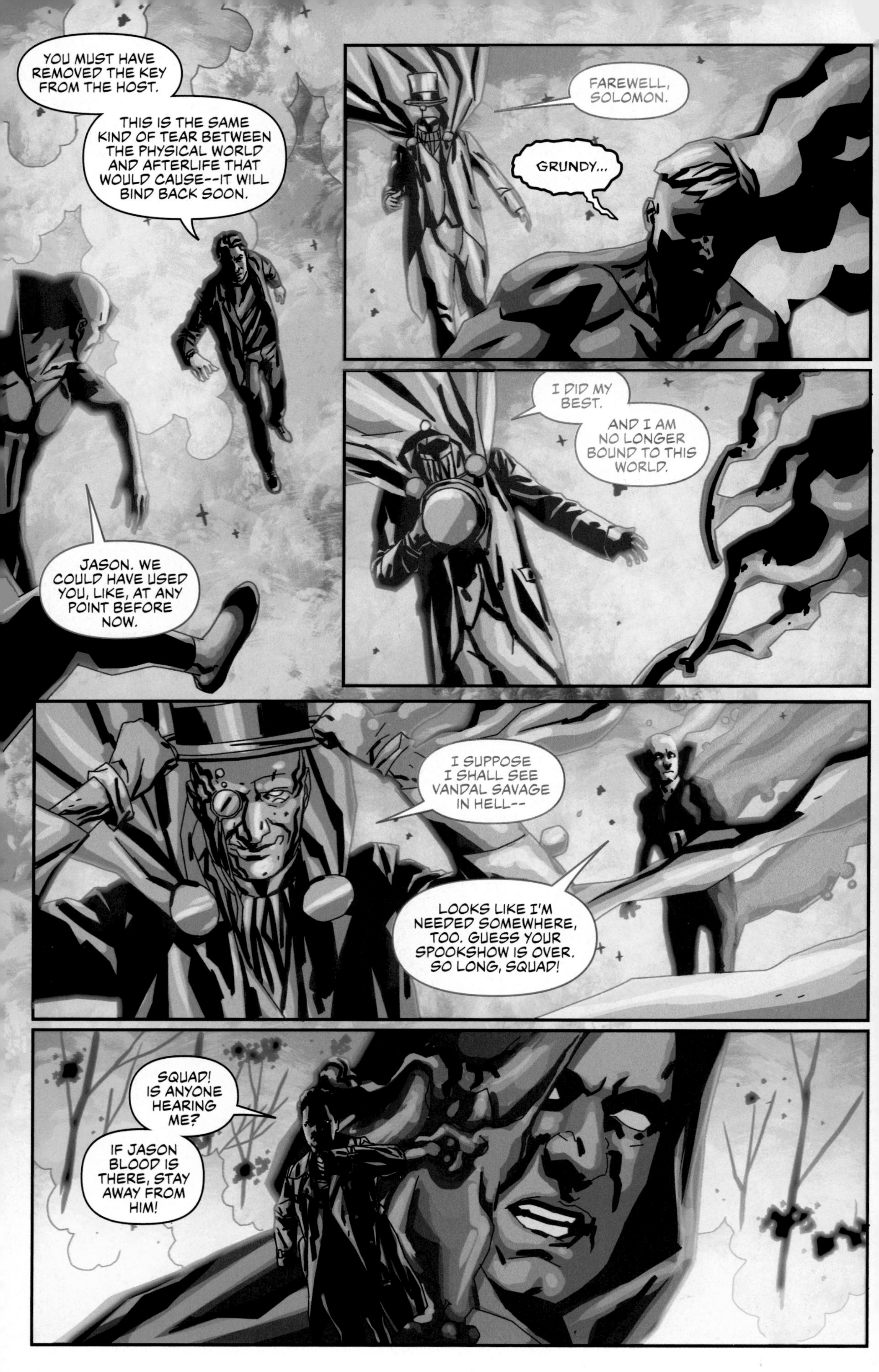
YOU MUST HAVE REMOVED THE KEY FROM THE HOST.
THIS IS THE SAME KIND OF TEAR BETWEEN THE PHYSICAL WORLD AND AFTERLIFE THAT WOULD CAUSE--IT WILL BIND BACK SOON.
FAREWELL, SOLOMON.
GRUNDY...
JASON. WE COULD HAVE USED YOU, LIKE, AT ANY POINT BEFORE NOW.
I DID MY BEST.
AND I AM NO LONGER BOUND TO THIS WORLD.
I SUPPOSE I SHALL SEE VANDAL SAVAGE IN HELL--
LOOKS LIKE I'M NEEDED SOMEWHERE, TOO. GUESS YOUR SPOOKSHOW IS OVER. SO LONG, SQUAD!
SQUAD! IS ANYONE HEARING ME?
IF JASON BLOOD IS THERE, STAY AWAY FROM HIM!

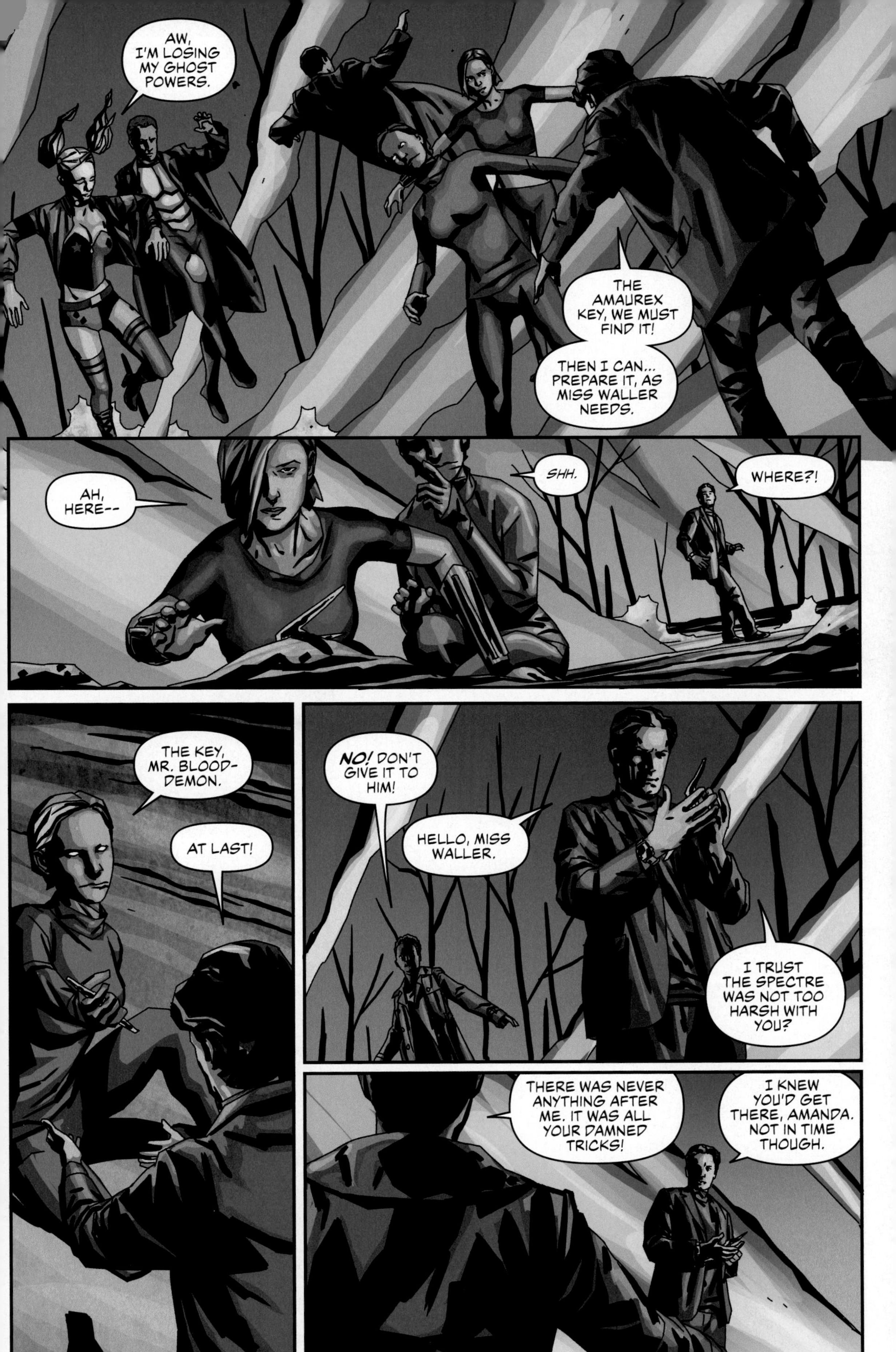
AW, I'M LOSING MY GHOST POWERS.
THE AMAUREX KEY, WE MUST FIND IT!
THEN I CAN... PREPARE IT, AS MISS WALLER NEEDS.
AH, HERE--
SHH.
WHERE?!
THE KEY, MR. BLOOD-DEMON.
AT LAST!
NO! DON'T GIVE IT TO HIM!
HELLO, MISS WALLER.
I TRUST THE SPECTRE WAS NOT TOO HARSH WITH YOU?
THERE WAS NEVER ANYTHING AFTER ME. IT WAS ALL YOUR DAMNED TRICKS!
I KNEW YOU'D GET THERE, AMANDA. NOT IN TIME THOUGH.

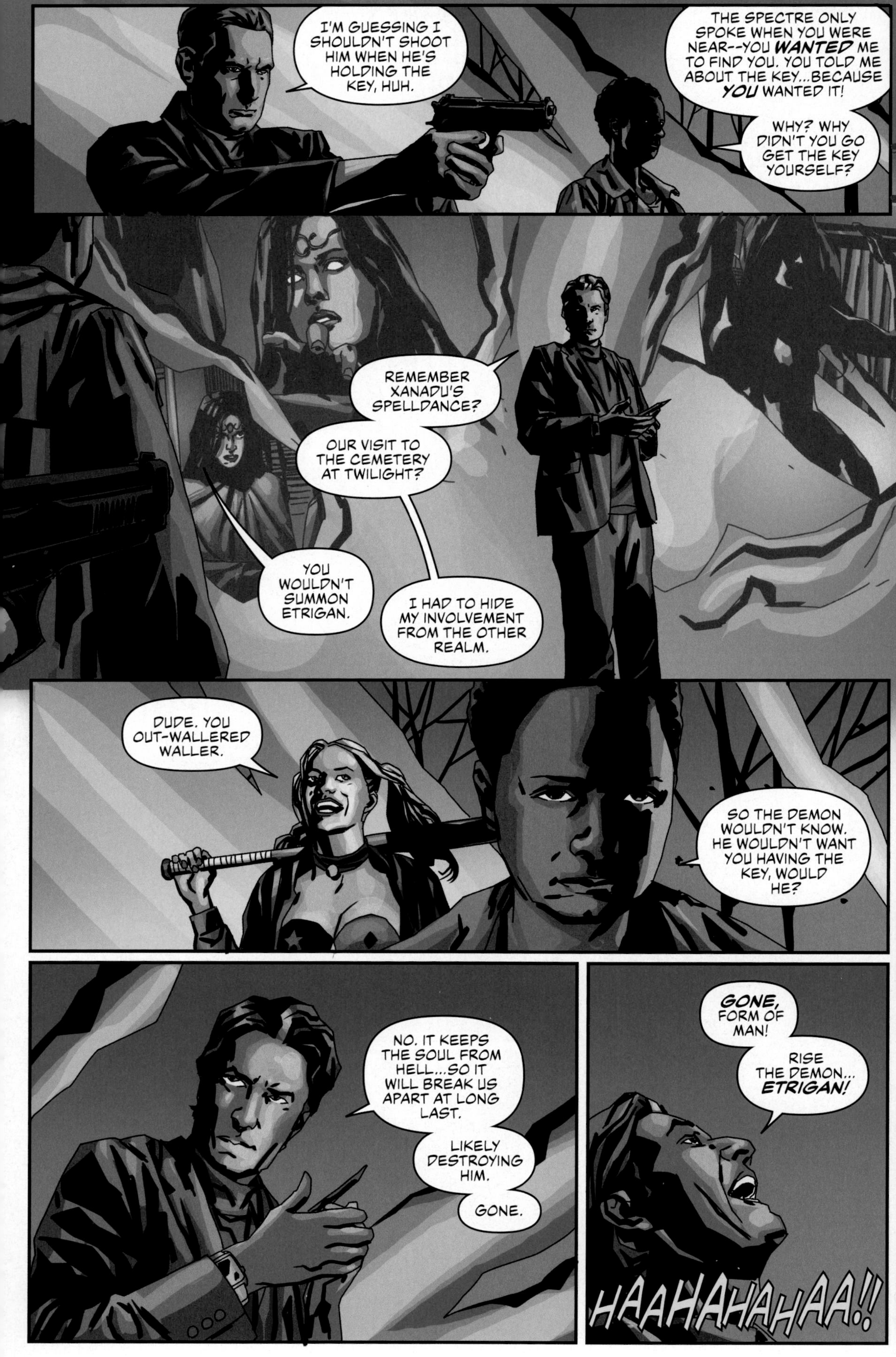
I'M GUESSING I SHOULDN'T SHOOT HIM WHEN HE'S HOLDING THE KEY, HUH.
THE SPECTRE ONLY SPOKE WHEN YOU WERE NEAR--YOU **WANTED** ME TO FIND YOU. YOU TOLD ME ABOUT THE KEY...BECAUSE **YOU** WANTED IT!
WHY? WHY DIDN'T YOU GO GET THE KEY YOURSELF?
REMEMBER XANADU'S SPELLDANCE?
OUR VISIT TO THE CEMETERY AT TWILIGHT?
YOU WOULDN'T SUMMON ETRIGAN.
I HAD TO HIDE MY INVOLVEMENT FROM THE OTHER REALM.
DUDE. YOU OUT-WALLERED WALLER.
SO THE DEMON WOULDN'T KNOW. HE WOULDN'T WANT YOU HAVING THE KEY, WOULD HE?
NO. IT KEEPS THE SOUL FROM HELL...SO IT WILL BREAK US APART AT LONG LAST.
LIKELY DESTROYING HIM.
GONE.
GONE, FORM OF MAN!
RISE THE DEMON... **ETRIGAN!**
HAAHAHAHAA!!

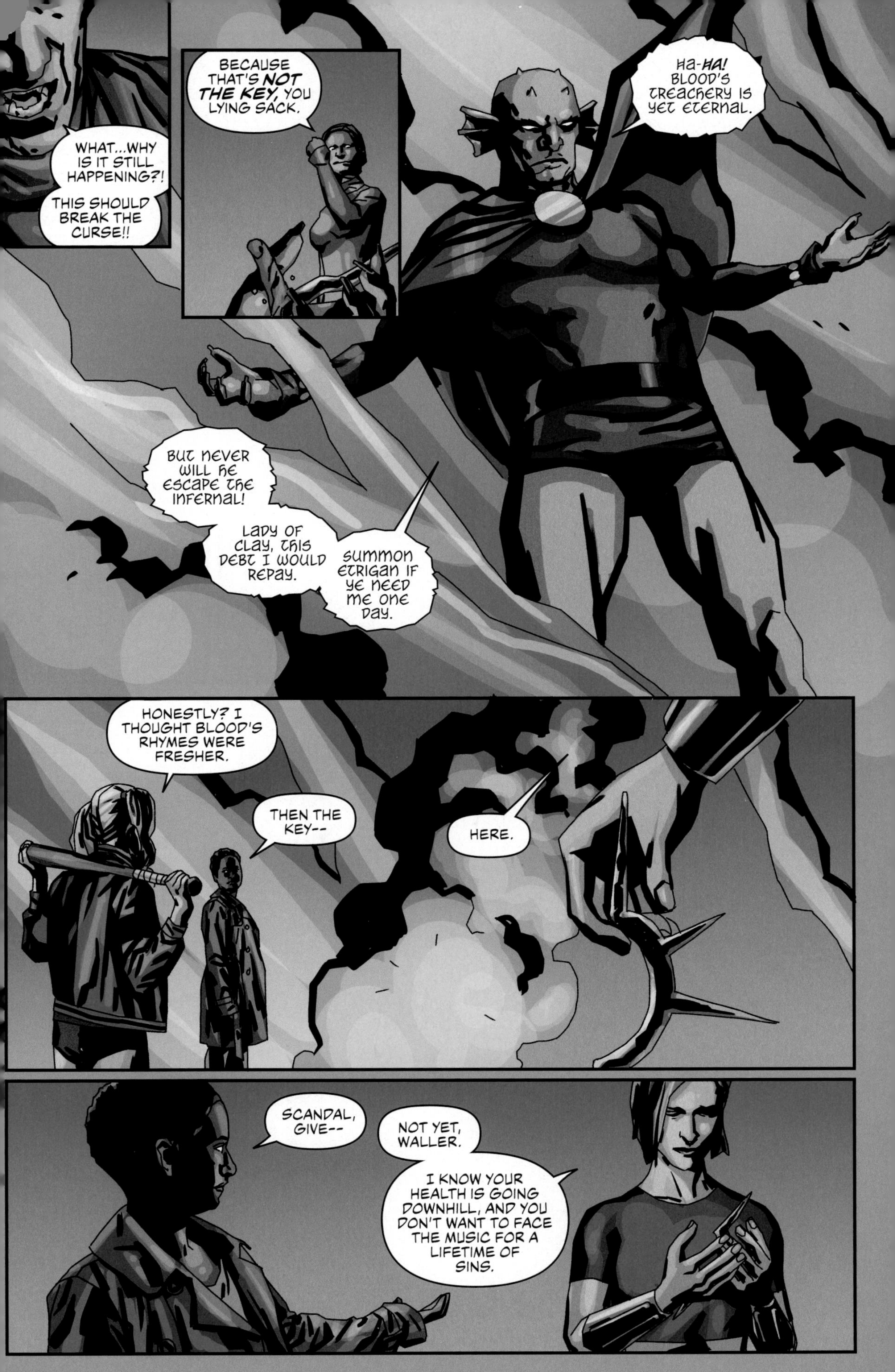
WHAT...WHY IS IT STILL HAPPENING?!
THIS SHOULD BREAK THE CURSE!!
BECAUSE THAT'S **NOT THE KEY,** YOU LYING SACK.
HA-*HA!* BLOOD'S TREACHERY IS YET ETERNAL.
BUT NEVER WILL HE ESCAPE THE INFERNAL!
LADY OF CLAY, THIS DEBT I WOULD REPAY.
SUMMON ETRIGAN IF YE NEED ME ONE DAY.
HONESTLY? I THOUGHT BLOOD'S RHYMES WERE FRESHER.
THEN THE KEY--
HERE.
SCANDAL, GIVE--
NOT YET, WALLER.
I KNOW YOUR HEALTH IS GOING DOWNHILL, AND YOU DON'T WANT TO FACE THE MUSIC FOR A LIFETIME OF SINS.

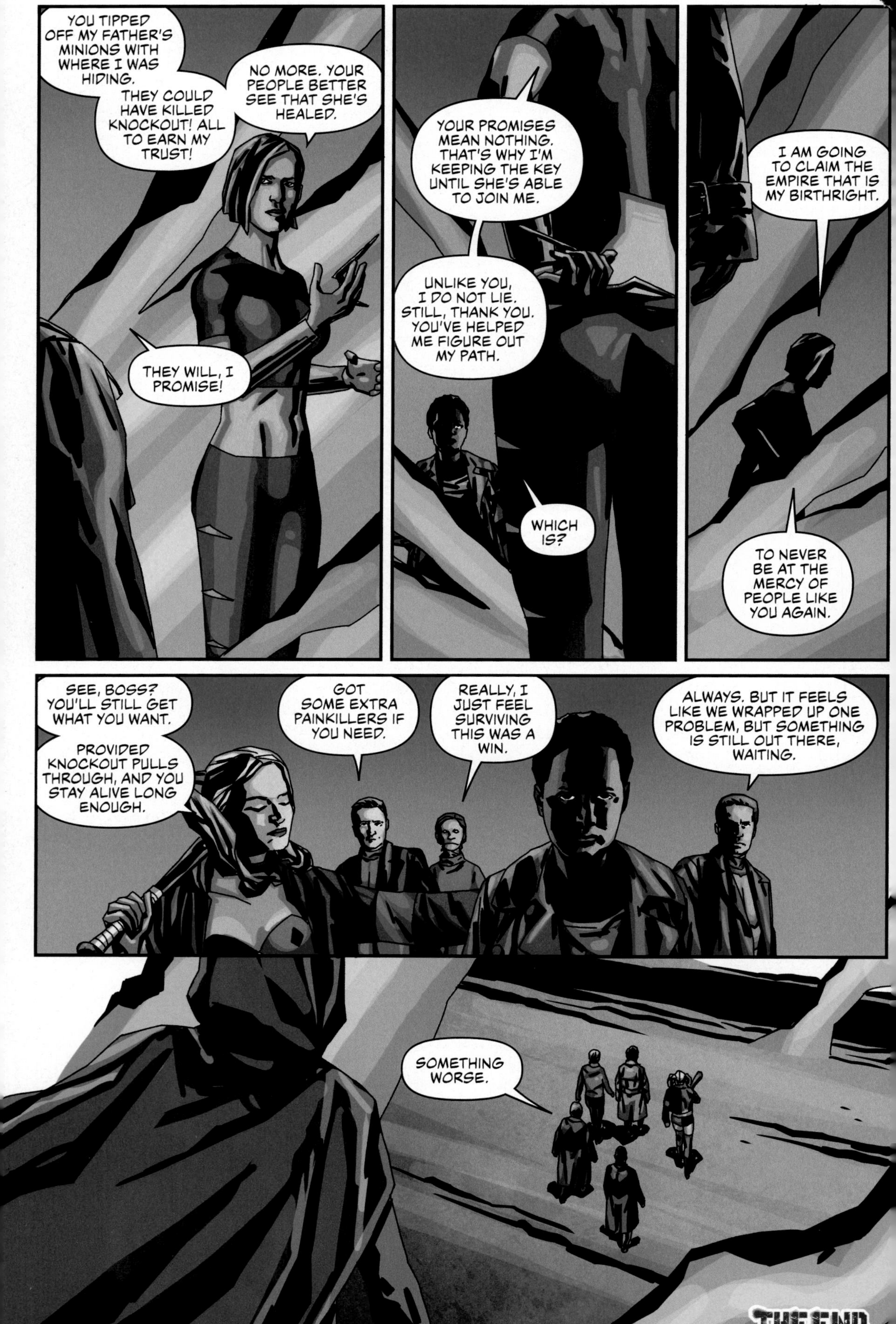
YOU TIPPED OFF MY FATHER'S MINIONS WITH WHERE I WAS HIDING.
THEY COULD HAVE KILLED KNOCKOUT! ALL TO EARN MY TRUST!
NO MORE. YOUR PEOPLE BETTER SEE THAT SHE'S HEALED.
THEY WILL, I PROMISE!
YOUR PROMISES MEAN NOTHING. THAT'S WHY I'M KEEPING THE KEY UNTIL SHE'S ABLE TO JOIN ME.
UNLIKE YOU, I DO NOT LIE. STILL, THANK YOU. YOU'VE HELPED ME FIGURE OUT MY PATH.
WHICH IS?
I AM GOING TO CLAIM THE EMPIRE THAT IS MY BIRTHRIGHT.
TO NEVER BE AT THE MERCY OF PEOPLE LIKE YOU AGAIN.
SEE, BOSS? YOU'LL STILL GET WHAT YOU WANT.
PROVIDED KNOCKOUT PULLS THROUGH, AND YOU STAY ALIVE LONG ENOUGH.
GOT SOME EXTRA PAINKILLERS IF YOU NEED.
REALLY, I JUST FEEL SURVIVING THIS WAS A WIN.
ALWAYS. BUT IT FEELS LIKE WE WRAPPED UP ONE PROBLEM, BUT SOMETHING IS STILL OUT THERE, WAITING.
SOMETHING WORSE.
THE END

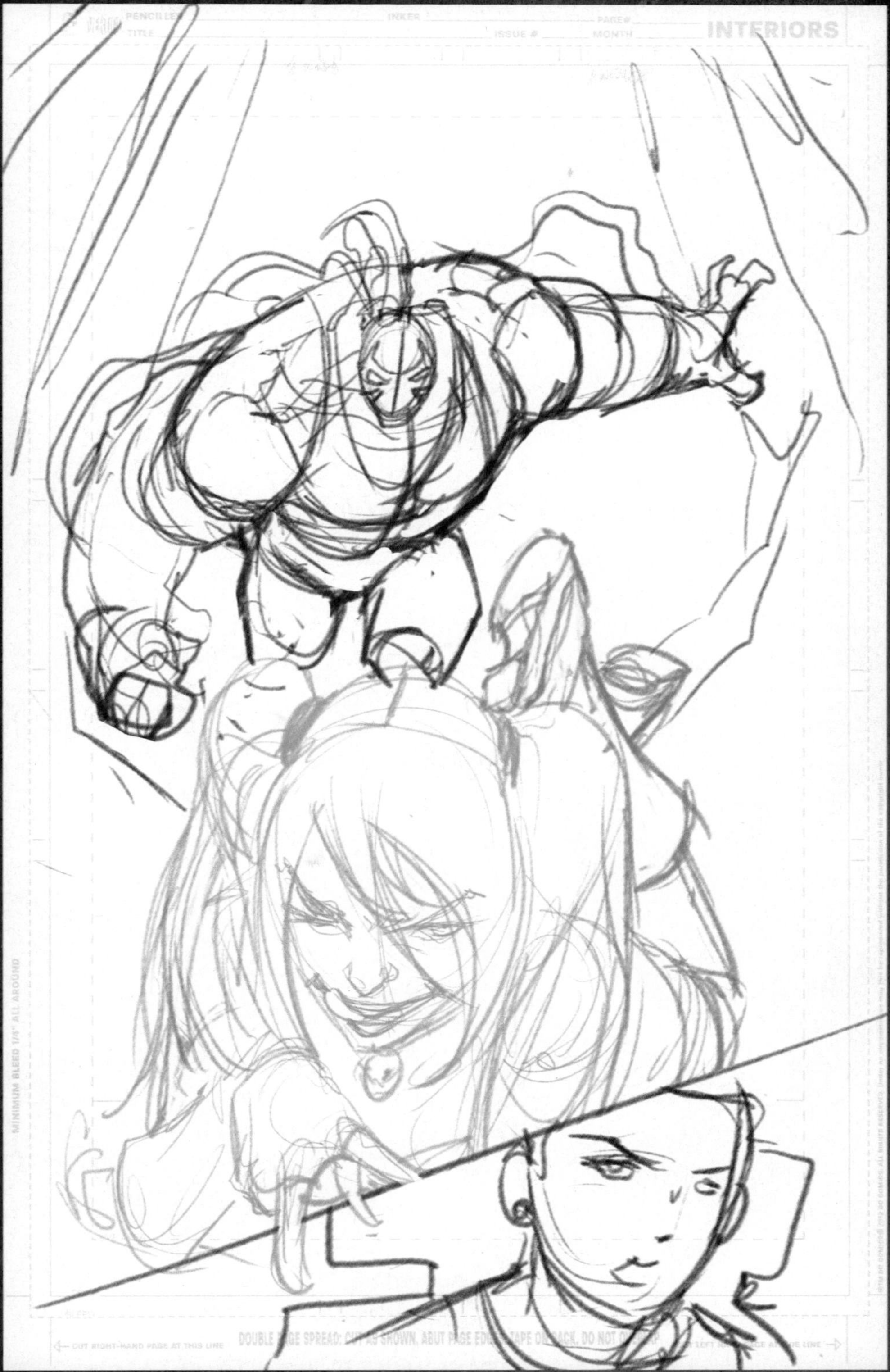
PENCILLER
INKER
PAGE#
TITLE
ISSUE #
MONTH
INTERIORS
MINIMUM BLEED 1/4" ALL AROUND

Collection cover sketch #1 by RYAN BENJAMIN

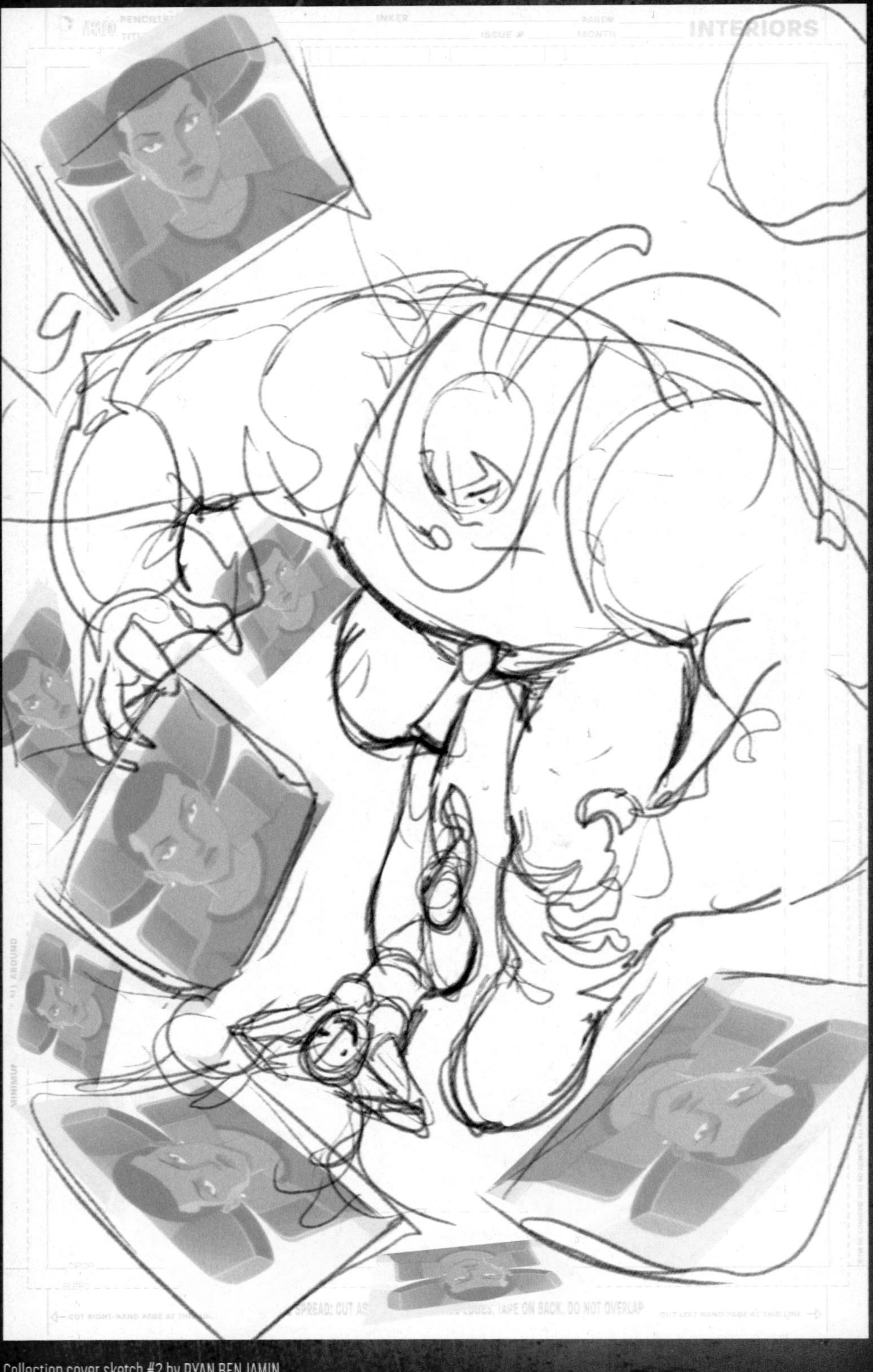
INKER
ISSUE #
MONTH
INTERIORS

Collection cover sketch #2 by RYAN BENJAMIN

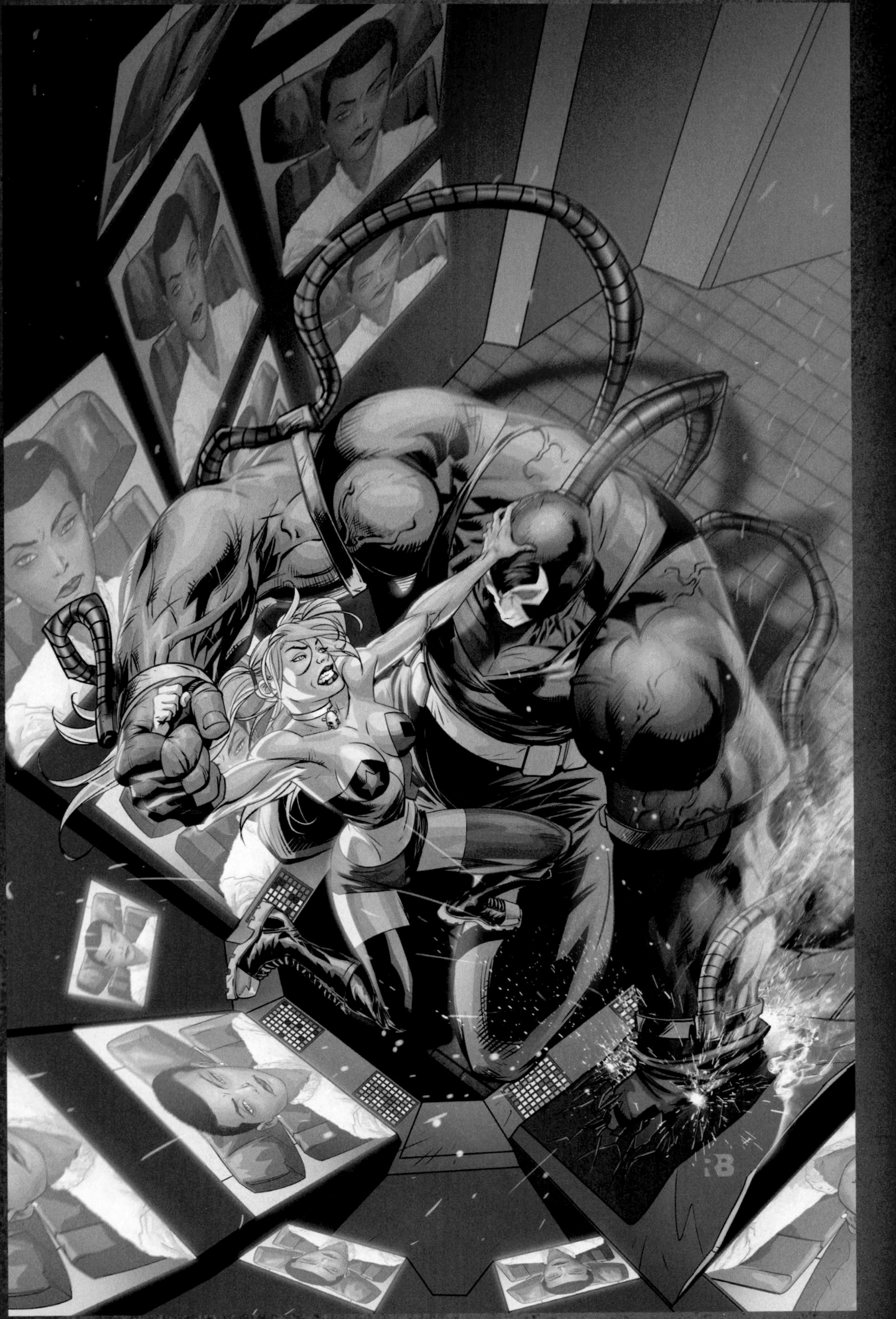
RB
Collection cover final by RYAN BENJAMIN

SUICIDE SQUAD

VOL. 1: KICKED IN THE TEETH

ADAM GLASS with
FEDERICO DALLOCCHIO

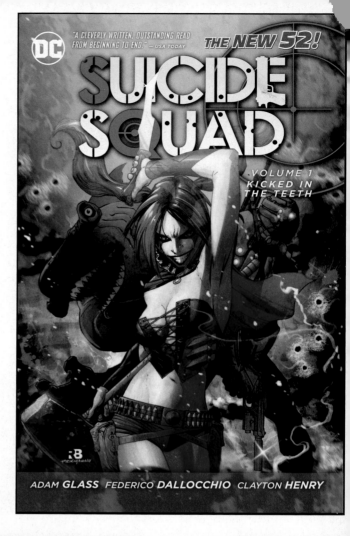

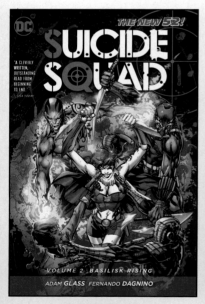

SUICIDE SQUAD
VOL. 2: BASILISK RISING

SUICIDE SQUAD
VOL. 3: DEATH IS FOR SUCKERS

READ THE ENTIRE EPIC!

SUICIDE SQUAD VOL. 4:
DISCIPLINE AND PUNISH

SUICIDE SQUAD VOL. 5:
WALLED IN

Get more DC graphic novels wherever comics and books are sold!